Police Interrogation, Language, and the Law

Recent calls for justice reform have put a spotlight on how the police enforce the law in the United States. How a person's constitutional rights may be legally thwarted during police interrogation, however, has not been part of any meaningful discussion on police reform. This novel book examines the intersections of the law and policing discourse through the detailed analysis of a large corpus of United States federal court rulings, starting with *Miranda* v. *Arizona* (1966). It covers a wide range of topics, including the history of police interrogation in the United States, the role of federal law in handicapping a person's ability to invoke their right to counsel, and the invocation game of police interrogation that may lead a variety of suspects to change their discursive preferences. It highlights the need for American police interrogation reform, exploring the paths taken by other jurisdictions outside of the United States.

This title is part of the Flip it Open programme and may also be available open access. Check our website, Cambridge Core, for details.

MARIANNE MASON is Associate Professor at James Madison University. Her notable publications include *The Discourse of Police Interviews* (coedited, 2020) and *Courtroom Interpreting* (2008). In 2018, she received an American Council of Learned Societies Fellowship.

Police Interrogation, Language, and the Law

The Invocation Game

Marianne Mason

James Madison University, VA, USA

CAMBRIDGE
UNIVERSITY PRESS

CAMBRIDGE
UNIVERSITY PRESS

Shaftesbury Road, Cambridge CB2 8EA, United Kingdom

One Liberty Plaza, 20th Floor, New York, NY 10006, USA

477 Williamstown Road, Port Melbourne, VIC 3207, Australia

314–321, 3rd Floor, Plot 3, Splendor Forum, Jasola District Centre, New Delhi – 110025, India

103 Penang Road, #05–06/07, Visioncrest Commercial, Singapore 238467

Cambridge University Press is part of Cambridge University Press & Assessment, a department of the University of Cambridge.

We share the University's mission to contribute to society through the pursuit of education, learning and research at the highest international levels of excellence.

www.cambridge.org
Information on this title: www.cambridge.org/9781009055017

DOI: 10.1017/9781009052047

First published 2024
First paperback edition 2025

A catalogue record for this publication is available from the British Library

ISBN 978-1-316-51152-7 Hardback
ISBN 978-1-009-05501-7 Paperback

Contents

Figures

Tables

Acknowledgments

This book would have not been possible without the support of the American Council of Learned Societies (ACLS) Fellowship. The ACLS fellowship provided me with the opportunity to devote myself to research, which was essential and invaluable for the completion of this book.

This book would have not been possible either without the initial spark that took me down the path of examining invocations for counsel and the discourse of police interrogations and interviews. I am incredibly grateful for the opportunity to have worked, as a forensic linguistic consultant, with attorney Kim Cornwell. Since the first case, I have not stopped researching and analyzing the discourse of police interrogations.

I also wish to thank Lauren Sudeall (Director) and Darcy M. Meals (Deputy Director) of the Center for Access to Justice, College of Law, Georgia State University, for providing me the opportunity to be a visiting researcher at the Center. Without the resources available at the College of Law I would not have been able to access such a rich corpus of federal criminal cases and research on *Miranda* case law and police interrogations.

I thank Anupama Rao (Director) and Sarah Monks (Assistant Director) at the Institute for Comparative Literature and Society, Columbia University, and Eileen Gillooly (Director) at the Society of Fellows and Heyman Center for the Humanities, Columbia University, where I was a visiting ACLS scholar. I also thank Anna Westerstahl-Stenport (former Director) and Sebnem Ozkan (former Associate Director) at the Atlanta Global Studies Center (AGSC), Georgia Institute of Technology, for providing me with the opportunity to be a visiting scholar and continue my research for the book.

I would also like to thank my colleagues at James Madison University and in particular Giuliana Fazzion who, as chair of the department of Foreign Languages, Literatures, and Cultures, encouraged and supported my research endeavors.

Also, I thank colleagues who at different stages of the journey to complete this research provided invaluable assistance and support. Thanks to William A. Kretzschmar, Gary David, Kyoko Masuda, and Aneta Pavlenko for supporting this research.

Special thanks to the three outside reviewers of the book for their insightful comments and recommendations and to Luis M. Negron-Portillo for his commentary regarding the legal portions of the book. Also, I am very grateful for the expertise of Rebecca Taylor, editor at Cambridge University Press, who helped me navigate the process of preparing the book for publication: from review to publishing stages. Thanks also to Isabel Collins at Cambridge University Press for handling the production stage of the book and for her helpful suggestions during this stage of the publication.

Finally, I would like to thank my family for their constant and unwavering support. My husband Robert, with whom I discussed many aspects of this book, in particular game theory and statistics, thank you. Our discussions were priceless.

1 Introduction

Legal rules are addressed to audiences. If the rules are vague, the audiences suffer. The audiences for the involuntary confession rule are police officers who interrogate and obtain confessions, lawyers who try criminal cases, and judges who decide them. Of these three audiences, the lawyers suffer least. They have the advantage of being advocates . . . The police and judges, on the other hand, are in a different situation. The police have to decide during the course of an interrogation what tactics to use and how far to go with them. Judges have to decide whether the police went too far. If the law governing these decision-making processes is vague, and it is, these processes will suffer.

(Herman, 1987)

From the moment a suspect is taken into custody,[1] police interrogation may begin. What happens once a suspect is detained may differ between suspects and jurisdictions, but there are several steps that are attendant to custody in the United States. Many of these steps, and what they involve, are not readily known to the general public: a problem that permeates most contexts mediated by the law and which often makes lay persons dependent on an attorney (Dunlap, 2014). Some of these steps include how long a person may be held in custody and when a person may be able to make a phone call. Unlike what is portrayed in popular culture, the "automatic phone call" is closer to a myth than to reality.

The lack of knowledge of what transpires in custodial settings contributes significantly to the asymmetry of knowledge between law enforcement and suspects. This extends to the Miranda warning, per *Miranda* v. *Arizona* (1966). The law states that suspects must be Mirandized and they must waive their rights prior to the start of custodial interrogation. The Miranda rights are a prophylactic measure aimed at curtailing undue coercion in custodial settings. An example of the Miranda warning is illustrated in Excerpt 1.1.

[1] An individual must be legally "in custody" to receive the benefits of Miranda. The Miranda warnings are only required for statements made during custodial interrogation. Of note, persons who are in custody may, or may not, be under arrest. Being lawfully detained is sufficient to meet the custody requirement of Miranda. Hence, herein the term suspect will be used to refer to someone in custody who has been read their Miranda rights prior to the start of custodial interrogation.

Excerpt 1.1

1 Det. B. Toms: All right, you know this by heart, but I'm going to go ahead and read it to you anyway . . .. You have the right to remain silent. Anything you say can be used against you in court. You have the right to an attorney before and during questioning. If you cannot afford an attorney, one will be appointed for you, by the court, free of charge, before questioning. Do you understand the rights I've just explained to you?

2 Petitioner: Yes I do.

(*Woosley* v. *McEwen*, 2014)

During the reading of the Miranda rights, suspects are also often asked to initial (after each right) and sign a waiver form that acknowledges having been Mirandized.

Post-Miranda rulings reframed the invocation of rights stage of a custodial interrogation, by way of exceptions and/or added limitations to the invocation of rights. Exceptions to *Miranda* include: booking phase (*Rhode Island* v. *Innis*, 1980), jailhouse informant (*Illinois* v. *Perkins*, 1990), and public safety exceptions (*New York* v. *Quarles*, 1984). The booking phase, for example, is relevant to invocations for counsel that occur prior to (or in the process of) the reading of Miranda rights. During this stage, suspects may complete a pre-waiver invocation and depending on the legal interpretation, it may not prevent officers from conducting an interrogation, with the possible exception, for example, that the interrogation was imminent (see Skelton & Connell, 2004). In *Davis* v. *United States* (1994), the Court created a new standard requiring invocations for counsel to be unequivocal/unambiguous (albeit undefined) to cease an interrogation, as determined by law enforcement (see Chapter 2 for a comprehensive discussion). Adding to the limitations and exceptions noted above, the evidentiary uses of a confession may also be Miranda-exempt. The Supreme Court of the United States ruled in *Harris* v. *New York* (1971) that a confession obtained in violation of the Miranda standards may nonetheless be used for purposes of impeaching the defendant's testimony; that is, if the defendant takes the stand at trial and the prosecution wishes to introduce the defendant's statements to attack the defendant's credibility.

The variety of factors that may affect suspects invoking counsel or their invocation having legal standing are key to understanding the role of the law in police officers' investigation of a crime. In police interrogations, where the goal is often to obtain a suspect's statements, the law may facilitate this process. Hence, the book explores the legal moorings of the Miranda rights, focusing on the invocation for counsel stage of police interrogation. The analysis is rich, taking a legal, discursive, and strategic approach to the examination of exercising Miranda rights in a custodial setting in the United States. The discussions range from qualitative to statistical, to game theoretic. The corpus for the study is large and includes federal criminal court cases, ranging from 1966 to 2021, that run the gamut of the federal court system.

1.1 The Legal Foundation of the Corpus: The Federal Court System and *Miranda* Case Law

The book examines 301 criminal federal court cases, including case law and (some) unpublished[2] opinions, that have ruled on the legal standing of defendants/petitioners' Miranda invocations for counsel. The corpus provides a window into the rationale behind these federal court rulings, while not dismissing possible unknowns that may not be captured by the corpus, such as (the number of) cases addressing potential *Miranda* violations that do not make it to the appeals level. Although this may be a consideration, the focus of the analysis is on the connection between the courts' historical interpretation of the legal standing of a suspect's invocation for counsel and the strategies interrogators use to conduct an interrogation. Hence to contextualize the corpus, this section starts with a brief overview of the federal court system that reviewed the cases. This examination will provide insights into the inner workings of the federal courts and the role of the judges in the federal court system. The section also provides a brief overview of the common grounds for appeals in cases reviewing potential Miranda violations, as well as definitions for the terminology often referred to in the chapters. A comprehensive analysis of the variables that comprise the corpus, including the statistical treatment of the corpus, will be provided in Chapter 5.

1.1.1 The Federal Courts

Federal courts are courts of limited jurisdiction, meaning they can only hear cases authorized by the United States Constitution or federal statutes. Federal Courts can decide any case that considers federal law, including constitutional law, federal crimes, some military law, and so on. Federal trial courts have also been established for a few subject-specific areas (e.g., bankruptcy, taxation, claims against the federal government, and international trade). The corpus includes federal courts at all levels of the federal court system and in a multitude of regions in the United States.

[2] Unpublished opinions, unlike published ones, are decisions of the court that are not available for citation as precedent. The court deems these types of opinions to have insufficient precedential value. For the purposes of the research, this distinction is irrelevant. Both types of opinions are adjudicated, appealable, and have a direct impact on a defendant's case.

The federal district court is the starting point for any case arising under federal statutes, the Constitution, or treaties. The federal district courts are the trial courts in the federal court system. In these courts, there are district and magistrate court judges. District court judges are nominated by the President of the United States and confirmed by the United States Senate for a life term, per Article III of the Constitution. District courts handle both civil and criminal trials within the federal court system. Magistrate judges can oversee a variety of actions in both criminal and civil cases. In criminal cases, they can oversee certain motions, such as motions to suppress evidence. Unlike United States district judges, who are nominated by the President and confirmed by the United States Senate for lifetime tenure, magistrate judges are appointed for a specified period by a majority vote of the federal district judges of a particular district.

Once a case has been adjudicated at the federal district court level, the case can be appealed to a United States court of appeal. The ninety-four district courts are organized into twelve circuits, or regions. Each circuit has its own Court of Appeals that reviews cases decided in United States District Courts within the circuit. The United States Court of Appeals for the Federal Circuit raises the federal appellate courts to thirteen.[3] Each circuit court has multiple judges. Circuit court judges are appointed for life by the President of the United States and confirmed by the United States Senate. Any case may be appealed to the circuit court once the district court has finalized a decision (some issues can be appealed before a final decision by making an "interlocutory appeal"). Appeals to circuit courts are first heard by a panel, consisting of three circuit court judges. Parties file "briefs" to the court, arguing why the trial court's decision should be "affirmed" or "reversed." After the briefs are filed, the court may schedule "oral argument" in which the attorneys come before the court to make their arguments and answer the judges' questions. The entire circuit court may consider certain appeals in a process called an *en banc* hearing: a case heard before all the judges of a court. *En banc* opinions tend to carry more weight and are usually decided only after a panel has first heard the case. Once a panel has ruled on an issue and "published" the opinion, no future panel can overrule the previous decision. The panel can, however, suggest that the circuit take up the case *en banc* to reconsider the first panel's decision.

Outside the Federal Circuit, a few courts have been established to deal with appeals on specific subjects, including military matters (United States Court of Appeals for the Armed Forces). In military courts, judges are commissioned officers of the armed forces who are members of the bar of a Federal court, or a member of the bar of the highest court of a State, and who are certified to be

[3] See www.uscourts.gov/.

qualified for duty under section 826 article 26 of the Uniform Code of Military Justice.

The book's corpus includes some cases heard by military courts, such as the United States Army Court of Military Review and the United States Air Force Court of Military Review. This part of the corpus is small, yet worth noting given the defendants were read their Miranda rights and subjected to interrogation. The United States Court of Appeals for the Armed Forces, which was previously named the Unites States Army Court of Military Review, is also part of the corpus. The United States Court of Appeals for the Armed Forces exercises worldwide appellate jurisdiction over members of the armed forces on active duty and other persons subject to the Uniform Code of Military Justice. The court is composed of five judges appointed by the President and confirmed by the Senate for fifteen-year terms. Cases on the court's docket address a broad range of legal issues, including constitutional law, criminal law, evidence, criminal procedure, ethics, administrative law, and national security law. Decisions by the court are subject to direct review by the Supreme Court of the United States.

The Supreme Court of the United States (herein the Court) is the highest court in the United States judicial system. Article III of the United States Constitution created the Court and authorized Congress to pass laws establishing a system of lower courts. The Court has the power to decide appeals on all cases brought in federal court or those brought in state court but dealing with federal law. The members of the Court are referred to as "justices" and they are appointed by the President and confirmed by the Senate for a life term. There are nine justices on the Court – eight associate justices and one chief justice. The chief justice acts as the administrator of the court and is chosen by the President and approved by Congress. Rulings at the Court level are done by vote and include, among others, majority opinion, dissenting opinion, concurring opinion, and *per curiam* (an opinion issued by the Court rather than by specific justices).

The corpus includes an array of opinions and rulings that provide insights into the judges' and justices' view of *Miranda* and its constitutional standing. The rationale of the judges' and justices' opinions, herein collectively judges, through time, also reveals the divide in the federal courts regarding *Miranda* and whether that divide has evolved in the course of over five decades and/or is mediated by factors, such as presidential appointment, case law post-*Miranda*, level and/or region of the court, among other factors. These will be explored further in Chapters 2 and 5.

1.1.2 Grounds for Criminal Appeals in Federal Courts

In the United States, after a district court has convicted and sentenced a criminal defendant, the defendant may file an appeal to a higher court, asking it to review the lower court's decision for legal errors that may have affected the outcome of the case. The appellate[4] court may reverse the lower court's decision in whole or in part. If the appellate court denies the appeal, the lower court's decision stands.

Possible grounds for appeal in a criminal case include legal error, juror misconduct, and ineffective assistance of counsel. Legal errors may result from improperly admitted evidence, incorrect jury instructions, or lack of sufficient evidence to support a guilty verdict. They may also include an error in the judge's interpretation of constitutional law, such as a violation of Miranda. If the errors would not have changed the outcome, they are considered harmless, and the conviction will stand. Of note, an appeal is not a retrial or a new trial of the case. The appeals courts do not consider new witnesses or new evidence.[5] Appeals in either civil or criminal cases are usually based on arguments that there were errors in the trial procedure or errors in the judge's interpretation of the law.

In the corpus, numerous cases petitioned the court for a writ of *habeas corpus*. This is a writ of inquiry, issued to test the reasons or grounds for restraint and detention. The law of *habeas corpus* is deeply rooted in Anglo-American jurisprudence and adopted in the United States:

> In 1833 Justice Story noted that the "whole structure, of our present jurisprudence stands upon the original foundations of the common law." . . . More specifically, Chief Justice Marshall wrote that "for the meaning of the term habeas corpus, resort may unquestionably be had to the common law." . . . Habeas corpus, as an integral part of that common law tradition, occupied an important place in the developing legal system of the American nation. (McFeeley, 2016, p. 590)

The writ of *habeas corpus* stands as a safeguard against imprisonment of those held in violation of the law, by ordering the responsible enforcement authorities to provide valid reasons for the detention. The writ, hence, is designed to obtain immediate relief from unlawful imprisonment. It may be used as a post-conviction remedy for state, federal, and military prisoners who challenge the legality of their detention. The purpose of the writ is not to determine the guilt or innocence of a prisoner, but to test the legality of a prisoner's current detention.

There are many elements to *habeas corpus* cases with the book focusing on Miranda violations. Another element that is also part of the legal rulings that comprise the corpus is failure to move to suppress. In the United States, a motion to suppress is a request made by a criminal defendant in advance of a criminal trial asking the court to exclude certain evidence from the trial, such

[4] Federal appellate courts may also hear cases that originate in state courts and that involve claims that a state or local law/action violates rights guaranteed under the Constitution.

[5] www.uscourts.gov/about-federal-courts/court-role-and-structure/about-us-courts-appeals#:~:text=How%20Appellate%20Courts%20are%20Different,do%20not%20hear%20witnesses%20testify.

as statements made during a custodial interrogation. Failure to read Miranda rights and suspects not voluntarily waiving rights, such as the right to counsel and/or the right to silence, are also grounds for statements to be suppressed.

Successful appeals, however, are not common. As noted previously, appellate courts give the trial court great latitude in conducting trials and often will only overturn verdicts that contain clear, serious errors of law. Hence, defendants/petitioners carry a heavy burden in proving that errors of law, such as admitting unlawfully obtained statements, were serious and not harmless. If an appellate court can find any reasonable argument that the error would not have changed the verdict, and hence was harmless, it will most probably not reverse the ruling. This outcome is observed often in the corpus with motions to suppress evidence. Even in cases in which the judge ruled that the defendant/petitioner invoked counsel unequivocally and the statements were obtained illegally, the introduction of such statements at trial was often considered harmless error. These cases, in particular, show the importance of addressing the shortcomings in the law, regarding what constitutes an unequivocal/unambiguous invocation for counsel and the role of law enforcement (and their training) in making this determination. Relying on the appeals process to reverse an error in the application of the law, as this book will show, will not resolve the legal quandary of invoking rights, specifically the right to counsel, and will fall short in addressing significant limitations in the protection of Miranda rights.

1.2 The Law and Police Interrogation in the United States

Questioning suspects provides officers with a unique opportunity to obtain what is generally held by the judicial system as one of the most important pieces of evidence in a criminal case: a first-person account of the events in question. As Heydon (2012) describes: "The investigative interview is a 'central and significant aspect of the investigative and criminal justice process … '. The significance of what is a relatively short interaction is matched by its singularity: opportunity, in the form of an evidentiary interview, rarely knocks twice" (pp. 101–102). Snook et al. (2010) further highlight the importance of police interviewing in an investigation by noting that: "Police interviewing is arguably the most fundamental aspect of any criminal investigation because it elicits the information from witnesses, victims, and suspects that is required to successfully resolve cases" (p. 204).

In the United States, custodial police-suspect exchanges occur in the context of an interrogation where often the main objective of the talk is to obtain a statement rather than gather information (Mason, 2020). Behavioral analysis approaches, such as the Reid technique (Inbau et al., 2005), have been widely used in United States policing since the 1960s. This technique places a premium on obtaining statements from suspects, albeit not through physical force but through psychological trickery, deception, and pressure. All of which, to an extent, are legally acceptable in the United States. Chapter 3 discusses this method, as well as other interviewing techniques, such as those highlighted in the High-Value Detainee Interrogation Group (HIG) report (2016), that are used by some law enforcement agencies (e.g., FBI) in the United States. These techniques, albeit they may differ in their approaches and goals, are all guided by what the law allows.

One of the main obstacles to obtaining a statement from suspects, irrespective of technique, is the Miranda rights. By law, police officers must recognize suspects' right to silence and right to counsel. Yet, during police interrogation the recognition of a valid invocation for counsel, such as an unequivocal/unambiguous one, often lies solely with the police interrogator, particularly since the *Davis* v. *United States* (1994) ruling (see Ainsworth, 1993, 2008, 2012, 2020; Leo, 2001; Mason, 2013, 2016, 2020; Mosteller, 2007; Weisselberg, 2008). As Chapter 2 discusses extensively, from the judges' perspective, when police officers have to decide whether a suspect "in fact wants a lawyer" (*Davis* v. *United States*, 1994) the decision either affects the important work of police investigators or places an undue burden on suspects who invoke their constitutional rights. The judiciary's historical interpretation of custodial suspects' invocation of rights, although often framed as a balancing act between protecting personal rights and police's ability to investigate crime, inevitably fails to satisfy these competing interests. Through time the "balance" seems to have tipped toward facilitating the custodial interrogation of suspects.

Of note, the right to silence and the right to counsel are part of the Miranda rights, yet this book will focus solely on the right to counsel. The choice to focus the analysis on invocations for counsel, excluding the other Miranda warning, is twofold. First, there are linguistic considerations. An invocation for counsel, unlike an invocation for silence, has a perlocutionary effect embedded in the invocation. That is, the suspect has an expectation that the addressee will recognize the speech act as a request for counsel or, at the least, as a desire to move the conversation forward. In contrast, invoking the right to silence often does not exhibit the varied linguistic functions or formulations observed in invocations for counsel.

Second, there are legal considerations. Once a person invokes counsel, at any point in the interrogation, all questioning must cease, unless the person waives counsel or initiates conversation with the police. A person's invocation for silence, however, does not automatically require the police to stop questioning under *Miranda*: "To invoke the right to remain silent, one must make a 'clear, consistent expression of a desire to remain silent'" (*United States* v. *Thompson*, 1989). The key statement in this portion of the ruling is "clear, consistent expression." That is, the person interrogated cannot invoke silence for some questions and answer others. The legal standard for this type of invocation, hence, requires a distinct analysis, which will be the object of future research.

1.3 The Strategic Linguistic Game of Police Interrogation: Invoking Counsel in Custodial Settings

The process of obtaining information from a suspect during police interrogation relies on strategic action. Chapter 4 will examine the discursive features of suspects' invocations for counsel during custodial interrogation, as well as the sequences of talk that follow the suspects' invocations. The research presented in this chapter challenges the law's current, and common, interpretation of indirect invocations as equivocal ones. The judiciary's view of language use, coupled with current police interrogation training, has provided a space in which police officers do not have to share a mutuality of understanding or common ground with suspects in order to move the conversation forward. In police interrogations, there only needs to be a semblance of understanding that keeps the conversation "going," but in actuality blocks one speaker (the suspect) from moving their discursive agenda (i.e., invoke counsel).

For this part of the analysis, Chapter 4 looks at how sequences of talk during the invocation of rights stage of custodial interrogation represent a type of invocation game (term coined and modeled by Mason & Mason, 2021), or hypergame (Bennett, 1980), where one player (suspect) is strategizing in a manner consistent with how speakers attempt to reach mutuality of understanding in conversation, whereas the other player (the interrogator) is simply responding, based on their training, in a manner that appears to address the other players' turns of talk while invalidating the common knowledge assumption (Varsos et al., 2021). This type of discursive strategy benefits from the application of game theory, specifically hypergame theory. In a hypergame of manipulation, if at least one player is aware of the inconsistency of beliefs of the opponent player's preferences, they can take advantage of this discrepancy of information and attempt to deceive their opponents into changing their preferences (Gharesifard & Cortés, 2010, 2012).

Modeling a high stakes discursive event, such as a police interrogation, as a type of game is a novel approach that has not been applied prior to this research to institutional discourse, or other types of discursive events, where one of the parties, unbeknownst to the other, is not observing common ground purposely to push a discursive agenda. In this strategic, discursive game suspects may invoke counsel in a manner that is ineffective in ending a police interrogation. This creates opportunities for police interrogators to play an invocation game based on manipulation (a type of discursive passive-aggression) aimed at altering the behavior and preferences of the suspect who is (rationally) not recognizing the game as formed. Hypergame theory will provide a model to examine the police interrogators' and suspects' linguistic moves.

Chapter 5 will part from the invocation game of police interrogation to examine the effect of multiple variables in the judicial rulings, including invocation for counsel (types), linguistic formulation of invocations for counsel, and the presidential appointments of the ruling judges, among other variables. The statistical analysis will provide further insights into the possible effect changes to the law, from *Miranda* to *Davis*, have had in the treatment of invocations for counsel in custodial interrogation, and by extension in the establishment of the invocation game played across police stations and other custodial settings in the United States.

1.4 Moving Forward: Tackling Police Interrogation and Legal Reforms in the United States

Addressing the connection between the law, interviewing techniques, and language use in custodial settings requires a next move – one that does not facilitate an invocation game, but rather facilitates the investigative functions of police interviewing while protecting constitutional rights. To accomplish this task, three areas need to be addressed: (1) police interrogation reform, (2) treatment of vulnerable populations, such as juveniles and nonnative (L2) speakers of English, and (3) changes to *Miranda* case law, in particular to the *Davis* ruling.

Chapter 6 discusses how countries in Europe, such as the United Kingdom and Norway, and other jurisdictions outside of Europe and the United States, such as Australia and Canada, have approached, with varying degrees of success, police interrogation reform. In the UK, for example, the Police and Criminal Evidence Act of 1984 (PACE) was introduced as a response to a growing perception that the public had lost confidence in the English criminal justice system, largely due to cases that highlighted unacceptable police behavior. PACE has been a pivotal point for police reform, and by extension police interrogation reform (e.g., PEACE method), in the United Kingdom and other countries who opted to adopt this model and adapt it to their legal systems.

The United States has also had its share of police scandals and calls for justice reform. These calls often have not taken enough traction, despite their popularity with the public. Of note, unlike the PACE legislation in the UK, none of these calls for justice reform in the United States have included or, more importantly, led to substantive, nationwide, reforms in the interviewing of custodial suspects, including juveniles and other vulnerable populations. Behavior Analysis techniques still appear to be commonly used in police stations across the United States (see Chapter 3). The treatment of L2 custodial suspects has also seen limited change. As Chapter 6 discusses, this is highly problematic since interrogators may assess without proper training a suspect's proficiency in the institutional language (e.g., English) and/or linguistically mediate a police interrogation (see Pavlenko, 2008).

In addition to changes in police interrogation techniques and treatment of vulnerable populations, Chapter 6 also examines the need for legal reforms. The *Davis* ruling changed the landscape of the law in the United States. *Miranda* did not define it, but *Davis* put the police in charge of making the determination of what constitutes an unequivocal invocation for counsel without considering the connection between the goal of police interrogation (i.e., obtain a custodial suspect's statements) and the law. Chapter 6 will examine some of the recommendations that have been presented in the literature, including (1) police requiring clarification of "equivocal" invocations for counsel, per the *Davis* concurring decision, (2) requiring the presence of counsel at the onset of a custodial interrogation, and (3) putting in place additional measures that test the voluntariness of a statement, such as a pretrial assessment of the reliability of confession evidence, and securing corroborating evidence for a confession.

Chapter 6 also discusses the Court revisiting the *Davis* ruling and/or the possible role of legislation aimed at protecting custodial suspects' rights from being violated, such as requiring the presence of counsel during police interrogation. These measures, in particular those initiated by the Court, seem unlikely in light of the recent Court ruling, *Vega* v. *Tekoh* (2022), which, albeit a civil case, highlights the justices' past and present disparate view of what constitutes a constitutional right. To provide some background, in *Tekoh*, the plaintiff (Tekoh) claimed that his constitutional rights were violated when the police interrogated him without reading him his Miranda rights and his statements were admitted against him at trial. Tekoh, who was found not guilty by a trial jury, proceeded to sue the police officer, Vega, and seek damages under 42 U.S. C. §1983 for alleged violations of his constitutional rights. Section 1983 "provides a cause of action against any person acting under color of state law who 'subjects' a person 'to the deprivation of any rights, privileges, or immunities secured by the Constitution and laws'" (*Vega* v. *Tekoh*, 2022). Although the Ninth Circuit ruled that the use of an un-Mirandized statement against a defendant in a criminal proceeding violates the Fifth Amendment and may support a §1983 claim against the officer who obtained the statement, the Court disagreed. Justice Alito, who delivered the majority opinion for the Court, argued that: "Because a violation of Miranda is not itself a violation of the Fifth Amendment, and because we see no justification for expanding Miranda to confer a right to sue under §1983, the judgment of the Court of Appeals is reversed, and the case is remanded for further proceedings consistent with this opinion."

This view that a violation of Miranda is not in itself a violation of the Fifth Amendment raised questions among the dissenting justices. Justice Kagan, who delivered the dissenting opinion, argued at page 2108 that:

> The Court's decision in Miranda v. Arizona, ... affords well-known protections to suspects who are interrogated by police while in custody. Those protections derive from the Constitution: Dickerson v. United States tells us in no uncertain terms that Miranda is a "constitutional rule," ... And that rule grants a corresponding right: If police fail to provide the Miranda warnings to a suspect before interrogating him, then he is generally entitled to have any resulting confession excluded from his trial. ... From those facts, only one conclusion can follow – that Miranda's protections are a "right []" "secured by the Constitution" under the federal civil rights statute. ... Yet the Court today says otherwise. It holds that Miranda is not a constitutional right enforceable through a §1983 suit. And so it prevents individuals from obtaining any redress when police violate their rights under Miranda.

The case noted in *Tekoh*'s dissenting opinion, *Dickerson* v. *United States* (2000), is particularly insightful, since the Court held that "Miranda and its progeny in this Court govern the admissibility of statements made during custodial interrogation in both state and federal courts."

The dissenting justices' perspective on the constitutionality of *Miranda*, coupled with concerns over the effectiveness of the suppression remedy raised by the majority in *Tekoh*, raises additional questions about a defendant's ability to "make right" a violation of Miranda procedures, as reflected in Justice Kagan's arguments:

> Today, the Court strips individuals of the ability to seek a remedy for violations of the right recognized in Miranda. The majority observes that defendants may still seek "the suppression at trial of statements obtained" in violation of Miranda's procedures ... But sometimes, such a statement will not be suppressed. And sometimes, as a result, a defendant will be wrongly convicted and spend years in prison. He may succeed, on appeal or in habeas, in getting the conviction reversed. But then, what remedy does he have for all the harm he has suffered? (*Vega* v. *Tekoh*, 2022, p. 2111).

The recent ruling in *Tekoh*, at its core, is a reflection of the conflicting stance of the Court regarding the constitutionality of *Miranda*. This conflicting view gave us the dissenting opinion in *Miranda* and the majority opinion of post-*Miranda* rulings, such as *Davis*, that limited the invocation of the right to counsel and as such enabled the invocation game of police interrogation observed in the corpus. As the book argues, at present there is no legal incentive for law enforcement to honor a custodial suspect's invocation of the right to counsel, particularly one that is deemed equivocal/ambiguous. Furthermore, the current legal perspective on police interrogation in the United States seems inconsistent with the general sentiment of *Miranda* and by extension limits the possibility of enacting much needed police interrogation reforms in the United States. The latter will require the Court revisiting the *Davis* ruling and/or legislative reforms that lead to comprehensive police interrogation reform that addresses the needs of a variety of custodial suspects. This is yet to be accomplished, but this book aims to show a new perspective to undertake much needed changes to the law and subsequently to the manner in which suspects' invocations for counsel are treated in custodial settings in the United States.

2 In the Judges' Own Words: The Law and Custodial Interrogation in the United States

> *Whether a suspect unequivocally invoked his right to counsel is a mixed question of law and fact. What the suspect said and the circumstances under which he said it are questions of fact. Whether what he said constituted an unequivocal request for counsel under the circumstances is a question of law.* (Judge Tuchi, *Newell* v. *Ryan*, 2019)

Law enforcement officers engage discursively with suspects and other lay persons, because of the potential to obtain meaningful information that will assist them in the investigation of a crime. The interrogators' ability to question suspects, however, is limited by the law. Judicial rulings regarding suspects' rights during custodial interrogation, such as the right to counsel, provide a window into how the United States federal court system, led by the main court of the land, the Supreme Court of the United States, views suspects' constitutional rights, on the one hand, and the societal benefit of police officers being able to conduct criminal investigations, on the other.

This chapter discusses the evolution of the right to counsel in the federal courts, since the seminal *Miranda* v. *Arizona* (1966) ruling, and the insights this history provides in framing the law as a facilitator or, alternatively, a deterrent to suspects invoking their Miranda protected rights, specifically the right to counsel, during custodial interrogation. This analysis of opinions from the Court, circuit courts, district courts, and a few military courts, that make up the corpus, will shed light on how judges have viewed the role of police in society through time, and whether some in the judiciary consider the *Miranda* ruling as overreaching in its "intended" constitutional protections: that is, constitutional law versus the Court's law.

2.1 Pre-*Miranda*: The Fifth and Sixth Amendments and Police Interrogation

The Fifth and Sixth Amendments provide protections to those who will undergo custodial interrogation. While sometimes overlapping, there are several differences between these rights. The Sixth Amendment right to counsel attaches once criminal proceedings against an individual, such as an arraignment, indictment, and post-indictment interrogation, begin. The Fifth Amendment protects persons against self-incrimination. Under Fifth Amendment protections a person does not have to answer official questions in any proceeding, civil or criminal, formal or informal, in which the statements might incriminate the person. The right to silence as a protection against self-incrimination is part of the Fifth Amendment. Now, the right to silence in custodial settings, as the right to counsel, were recognized as part of the Court's ruling in *Miranda* v. *Arizona* (1966). The Court instituted the prophylactic provision of the Miranda warnings to protect persons from the pressures of custodial interrogation.

Prior to the institution of the Miranda warnings confessions needed only be voluntary on the part of the suspect. Historically, and at present, the Court has often ruled on the involuntariness of a statement if there is "genuinely outrageous conduct by the government" (Marcus, 1993, p. 98), such as beatings and deprivation of food or water, as well as other egregious inhumane behavior. Other less obvious forms of coercion that may render a suspect unable to provide a voluntary statement during custodial interrogation are less defined. Hence, the law requires that confessions be voluntary, yet "answering the voluntariness question requires making assumptions that transform the decision maker into as much psychoanalyst as fact finder" (Sundby, 2020, p. 125). As Sundby notes, justices have historically framed the matter of voluntariness with two (divided) characterizations of a suspect being interrogated: the "rugged individual" and the "susceptible individual." The former "will be able to withstand the pressures inherent to interrogation, and any confession will be presumed voluntary absent either extreme techniques or particular individual vulnerabilities" (p. 136). The latter, on the other hand, "is someone who when faced with the inherent authority of the police in an interrogation atmosphere is likely to be vulnerable to either threats or promises of hope – even if innocent" (p. 141). This characterization at its peak gave us the landmark *Miranda* decision, which, through time, has been mostly replaced by the "rugged individual" perspective.

As with the notion of voluntariness, the application of *Miranda* and its effectiveness in protecting suspects' right to counsel, in practice, is still debated in the courts. The lack of clarity as to what constitutes an unequivocal, voluntary, invocation for counsel in *Miranda* set the stage for a longstanding legal debate on the concept of unequivocalness and the voluntariness of a suspect's confession. This debate split between incorporating human nature (*Miranda*) and placing the onus on the "rugged individual." The *Miranda* ruling, which some justices refer to as "our decision" rather than a "Constitutional command," shows the division of the Court on the need for suspects to be protected against coercive interrogation practices, on the one hand, and police interrogators' ability to investigate crime, on the other. The justices' views, some concurring and others dissenting, have shaped lower court rulings and, in many regards, gave us the current and established "*Miranda* divide" in the federal court system.

2.2 *Miranda* v. *Arizona* (1966): A Prophylactic Rule Riddled with Dissent

In *Miranda*, the defendant (Ernesto Miranda) was arrested by the Phoenix Police Department, on kidnapping and rape charges of an eighteen-year-old woman. Police officers interrogated Miranda for two hours. Afterward, he signed a confession to the rape charge. Prior to the start of the interrogation, Miranda was not informed of his right to counsel. At trial, when prosecutors offered Miranda's written confession as evidence, his court-appointed lawyer objected on the grounds that the confession was not voluntary and should be suppressed. Based on his confession and other corroborating evidence, Miranda was convicted of rape and kidnapping. Miranda appealed to the Arizona Supreme Court. The Arizona Supreme Court affirmed the lower court's decision to admit the confession. The case was subsequently appealed and, ultimately, reviewed by the Court. The basis of the case is "the admissibility of statements obtained from an individual who is subjected to custodial police interrogation and the necessity for procedures which assure that the individual is accorded his privilege under the Fifth Amendment to the Constitution not to be compelled to incriminate himself" (*Miranda* v. *Arizona*, 1966, p. 440).

Miranda set a precedent for protecting persons' rights during police questioning and defining what constitutes custodial interrogation. Chief Justice Warren, who delivered the majority opinion of the Court, addressed both key matters in his ruling:

> Our holding will be spelled out with some specificity in the pages which follow but briefly stated it is this: the prosecution may not use statements, whether exculpatory or inculpatory, stemming from custodial interrogation of the defendant unless it demonstrates the use of procedural safeguards effective to secure the privilege against self-incrimination. By custodial interrogation, we mean questioning initiated by law enforcement officers after a person has been taken into custody or otherwise deprived of his freedom of action in any significant way. As for the procedural safeguards to be employed, unless other fully effective means are devised to inform accused persons of their right of silence and to assure a continuous opportunity to exercise it, the following measures are required. Prior to any questioning, the person must be warned that he has a right to remain silent, that any statement he does make may be used as evidence against him, and that he has a right to the presence of an attorney, either retained or appointed. The defendant may waive effectuation of these rights, provided the waiver is made voluntarily, knowingly and intelligently. If, however, he indicates in any manner and at any stage of the process that he wishes to consult with an attorney before speaking there can be no questioning. Likewise, if the individual is alone and indicates in any manner

that he does not wish to be interrogated, the police may not question him. The mere fact that he may have answered some questions or volunteered some statements on his own does not deprive him of the right to refrain from answering any further inquiries until he has consulted with an attorney and thereafter consents to be questioned. (*Miranda* v. *Arizona*, 1966, p. 445)

The ruling emphasizes the risks inherent in a police-dominated atmosphere and the need for individuals to be informed of their right to silence and be advised by counsel.

The Court also made a point to address the recurrent argument that the need for interrogation outweighs the privilege. The Court points to the way law enforcement agencies, such as the Federal Bureau of Investigation (FBI), who conducted interrogations in this case, advise any suspect or person under arrest: "A letter received from the Solicitor General in response to a question from the Bench makes it clear that the present pattern of warnings and respect for the rights of the individual followed as a practice by the FBI is consistent with the procedure which we delineate today" (*Miranda* v. *Arizona*, 1966, p. 484). The responses provided in the letter indicate that the "warning may be given to a person arrested as soon as practicable after the arrest, . . . but in any event it must precede the interview with the person for a confession or admission of his own guilt" (p. 485). These guidelines are per the passage of the Criminal Justice Act of 1964, which provides free counsel for federal defendants who are unable to pay. The responses also include the statement that if a person indicates that they wish to speak to counsel prior to providing statements, the interview is terminated unless the person is indecisive in their request for counsel. The Court argues that the practice of the FBI can readily be followed by state and local law enforcement agencies. Of note, it is important to highlight that the undefined, indecisive requests for counsel noted in the "letter" are in contrast with Justice Warren's majority opinion about invoking counsel which emphasizes that an individual who indicates in any manner that they wish to consult with counsel cannot be questioned by police. This issue is not clarified or overtly addressed in the ruling.

Another consistent theme in the Court's *Miranda* opinion is the need to protect persons from law enforcement's potentially deceptive practices that may lead them to waive their rights. To this end, Justice Warren provided extensive background of past and present interrogation techniques. He discussed the Reid technique, which he refers to as the "manuals," and the police officers' responses when suspects express a wish to speak to a relative or an attorney. He states:

If the request is for an attorney, the interrogator may suggest that the subject save himself or his family the expense of any such professional service, particularly if he is innocent of the offense under investigation. The interrogator may also add, "Joe, I'm only looking for the truth, and if you're telling the truth, that's it. You can handle this by yourself." (*Miranda* v. *Arizona*, 1966, p. 454)

Justice Warren's opinion reflects his view of the constitutional foundation underlying the privilege: "To maintain a 'fair state-individual balance,' to require the government to shoulder the entire load" (*Miranda* v. *Arizona*, 1966, p. 460). For the Court, the warnings provide suspects who are subject to custodial interrogation a protection that takes speculation out of the interrogation room:

> Assessments of the knowledge the defendant possessed, based on information as to his age, education, intelligence, or prior contact with authorities, can never be more than speculation; a warning is a clearcut fact. More important, whatever the background of the person interrogated, a warning at the time of the interrogation is indispensable to overcome its pressures and to ensure that the individual knows he is free to exercise the privilege at that point in time. (*Miranda* v. *Arizona*, 1966, p. 469)

The Court specified that the right to counsel "does not mean, as some have suggested, that each police station must have a 'station house lawyer' present at all times to advise prisoners" (*Miranda* v. *Arizona*, 1966, p. 474). The warnings, however, place a heavy burden on the government to demonstrate suspects have knowingly and voluntarily waived their rights to self-incrimination and to counsel.

The dissenting opinions on the Court's majority ruling include applying the equal protection rule of the Fifth Amendment and the due process "voluntariness" test under the Fourteenth Amendment (Justice Clark), rather than "extending the Fifth Amendment's privilege against self-incrimination to the police station" (Justice Harlan joined by Justice Stewart and Justice White). For the dissenting justices, extending the Fifth Amendment to include the right to counsel provision to the police station is a "dubious" application of constitutional law. They note that coercion in the traditional due process sense is not at question in the case, but solely a lack of counsel or lack of reading of the warnings. Justice Clark opined that he was unable to join the majority:

> Custodial interrogation has long been recognized as "undoubtedly an essential tool in effective law enforcement." . . . Recognition of this fact should put us on guard against the promulgation of doctrinaire rules. Indeed, even in Escobedo the Court never hinted that an affirmative "waiver" was a prerequisite to questioning; that the burden of proof as to waiver was on the prosecution; that the presence of counsel – absent a waiver – during interrogation was required; that a waiver can be withdrawn at the will of the accused; that counsel must be furnished during an accusatory stage to those unable to pay; nor that admissions and exculpatory statements are "confessions." To require all those things at one gulp should cause the Court to choke over more cases . . . which it expressly overrules today. (*Miranda* v. *Arizona*, 1966, p. 502)

Justices Harlan, Stewart, and White also chimed in noting that the majority's opinion was "poor constitutional law" (*Miranda* v. *Arizona*, 1966, p. 504) and the creation of new constitutional law. They, as Justice Clark, also argued that "the Court has given ample recognition to society's interest in suspect questioning as an instrument of law enforcement" (p. 509). The justices opine that reminding suspects of their right to silence and that their confession may be used in court are "minor obstructions" (p. 516). But to require "an express waiver by the suspect and an end to questioning whenever he demurs must heavily handicap questioning. And to suggest or provide counsel for the suspect simply invites the end of the interrogation" (p. 517). These statements reflect the justices' differing views on how much, and which type of, constitutional oversight police questioning requires. As the justices' opinions in *Miranda* show, the Court has been consistently divided on this issue. Subsequent rulings reflect the Court's stance on this longstanding "fight" (see *Oregon* v. *Elstad*, 1985, which stresses *Miranda*'s prophylactic purpose and its origin in the Court rather than in the Constitution).

Since the *Miranda* decision, the Court has narrowed the scope of Miranda guarantees. This is partly due to the ruling being "riddled with exceptions and strapped with limitations" (Marcus, 1993, p. 94). The ambiguities in *Miranda*, rather than the sentiment of the majority opinion of the Court, opened the door for continued debate as to what constitutes an unequivocal invocation for counsel. A debate that, predominantly, has two sides: one that places a higher burden on the suspect to invoke counsel and the other that places a higher burden on police investigators to observe individual rights. The next sections will explore post-*Miranda* rulings that have shaped the invocation for counsel discussion. These rulings will be divided into three key (legal) periods in the invocation for counsel debate: post-*Miranda* and *Edwards*, post-*Edwards* and *Davis*, and post-*Davis* to present-day law.

2.3 1966–1981: Post-*Miranda* and *Edwards*

The discussion on Miranda guarantees, such as the right to counsel, unequivocalness of an invocation for counsel, voluntariness, and what constitutes custodial interrogation are at the center of four defining post-*Miranda* rulings (1979–81): *Fare* v. *Michael C.* (1979), *Nash* v. *Estelle* (1979), *Rhode Island* v. *Innis* (1980), and *Edwards* v. *Arizona* (1981).

In *Fare* v. *Michael C.* (1979), the Court reviewed *en banc* whether the California Supreme Court erred in finding that the respondent's request for his probation officer was a per se invocation of his Fifth Amendment rights under *Miranda* and whether the statements obtained during the defendant's subsequent interrogation after he requested to see his probation officer were admissible. The Court also addressed whether the defendant voluntarily and

Excerpt 2.1

1 Q. Do you want to give up your right to have an attorney present here while we talk about it?
2 A. Can I have my probation officer here?
3 Q. Well I can't get a hold of your probation officer right now. You have the right to an attorney.
4 A. How I know you guys won't pull no police officer in and tell me he's an attorney?

(*Fare* v. *Michael C.*, 1979, p. 710)

knowingly waived his rights and consented to continued interrogation after denial of request to consult with his probation officer.

The interrogation occurred after the respondent, Michael C., who was a juvenile at the time (sixteen and a half years of age) and implicated in a murder, was read his Miranda rights at the police station. The question regarding the right to counsel prompted the following exchange, as shown in Excerpt 2.1.

The exchange continued for a short period with the police officer providing responses consistent with redirecting the respondent to respond specifically as to whether he wanted to talk to them (the police) without an attorney present and waive his rights or not say anything. The respondent chose to talk to the police: "A. Yeah I want to talk to you."

The Supreme Court of California ruled that the respondent's request to see his probation officer at the onset of the interrogation indicated his unwillingness to discuss his case with the police and, thus, he invoked his Fifth Amendment privilege. The court opined that a minor's request for a probation officer was akin to requesting to see a parent during interrogation, and thus, under the *Burton* rule, constituted an invocation of the minor's Fifth Amendment rights. On appeal, the Court disagreed. The Court's ruling states that the California court "significantly has extended this rule by providing that a request by a juvenile for his probation officer has the same effect as a request for an attorney" (*Fare* v. *Michael C.*, 1979, p. 719). The Court opined that the Supreme Court of California erred in ruling that the police needed to cease interrogating the respondent, after he asked to speak with a probation officer, and that the statements he made during interrogation should have been suppressed.

Two points are particularly salient in the Court's ruling. First, the Court discusses the notion of the Miranda per se rule, which the Court argues lies with an attorney and should not be extended to other persons: "we decline to find that the request for the probation officer is tantamount to the request for an attorney" (*Fare* v. *Michael C.*, 1979, p. 724). Of note, the Court does not address what constitutes an unequivocal invocation for counsel within the Miranda per se rule. This matter will continue to be argued and debated by the courts. Second, the Court's analysis on the voluntariness of a juvenile's statements and the role of the police in the interrogation provides insights into how the Court and, in its application, the federal court system, assesses juveniles, persons who commit crimes, and police conduct during an interrogation (i.e., the context discussion). In this case, the Court argues that "the interrogation reveals that the police officers conducting the interrogation took care to ensure that respondent understood his rights" (*Fare* v. *Michael C.*, 1979, p. 726). The Court adds that the respondent, despite his age and the circumstances that may disadvantage minors, voluntarily waived his rights and continued the interrogation:

> no special factors indicate that respondent was unable to understand the nature of his actions. He was a 16 1/2-year-old juvenile with considerable experience with the police. He had a record of several arrests. He had served time in a youth camp, and he had been on probation for several years. He was under the full-time supervision of probation authorities. There is no indication that he was of insufficient intelligence to understand the rights he was waiving, or what the consequences of that waiver would be. He was not worn down by improper interrogation tactics or lengthy questioning or by trickery or deceit. (*Fare* v. *Michael C.*, 1979, pp. 726–727)

The notion that a person's criminal record adds to their sophistication when navigating police interrogation and the criminal justice system is a common theme among federal court rulings in the corpus. In these rulings, the judiciary considers experience with the criminal justice system as being directly correlated with suspects' ability to engage in a police interrogation and knowingly and voluntarily waiving their rights. In *Fare*, the fact that the suspect's background knowledge and experience was mostly in institutional settings supervised by probation authorities, however, is not considered a significant factor in the suspect's thought process when invoking counsel during custodial interrogation.

In *Nash* v. *Estelle* (1979), the Fifth Circuit argued further on the Miranda per se rule. The court's analysis specifically raised the question of equivocalness when invoking counsel. In *Nash*, the defendant who was arrested for murder, was brought before a magistrate judge and informed of his Miranda rights. The dispute lies on whether the district attorney (Files) violated Nash's right to the presence of counsel during the course of their initial June 2 conversation. The dialogue is lengthy. The interrogation includes the reading of the rights, obtaining oral acknowledgment of the rights as read, and the signing of the Miranda waiver form. Excerpt 2.2 shows where Nash's, at question, invocation for counsel occurs:

Excerpt 2.2

1 Nash: If I want a lawyer present, I just put down I want him present?
2 Files: Please just tell us about it. Any time we are talking and you decide that you need somebody else here, you just tell me about it and we will get somebody up here.
3 Nash: Well, I don't have the money to hire one, but I would like, you know, to have one appointed.
4 Files: You want one to be appointed for you?
5 Nash: Yes, sir.
6 Files: Okay. I had hoped that we might talk about this, but if you want a lawyer appointed, then we are going to have to stop right now.
7 Nash: But, uh, I kinda, you know, wanted, you know, to talk about it, you know, to kinda, you know, try to get it straightened out.
8 Files: Well, I can talk about it with you and I would like to, but if you want a lawyer, well, I am going to have to hold off, I can't talk to you. It's your life.
9 Nash: I would like to have a lawyer, but I'd rather talk to you.
10 Files: Well, what that says there is, it doesn't say that you don't ever want to have a lawyer, it says that you don't want to have a lawyer here, now. You got the right now, and I want you to know that. But if you want to have a lawyer here, well, I am not going to talk to you about it.
11 Nash: No, I would rather talk to you.
12 Files: You would rather talk to me? You do not want to have a lawyer here right now?
13 Nash: No, sir.
14 Files: You are absolutely certain of that?
15 Nash: Yes, sir.
16 Files: Go ahead and sign that thing.

(*Nash* v. *Estelle*, 1979, p. 517)

The district court held that Files had no doubt that Nash wanted an attorney and, without holding an evidentiary hearing, granted Nash's petition for a *writ of habeas corpus* on the grounds that a written confession introduced against Nash had been obtained in violation of his Miranda rights. The majority opinion of the circuit court disagreed with this ruling.

The court cites one of its own rulings, *United States* v. *Priest* (1969), to address the question of whether Nash voluntarily waived his right to counsel. In *Priest*, the court ruled that if there is a request for an attorney prior to any questioning "a finding of knowing and intelligent waiver of the right to an attorney is impossible" (p. 493). Furthermore, if the request is not observed and statements are given these must not be construed as the result of a voluntary waiver. The *Nash* court notes: "We construe *Priest* to bar inquiry as to waiver when, prior to any questioning, the suspect makes an unequivocal request for an attorney's presence, as was done in *Priest*, and when the request is disregarded and the questioning proceeds" (p. 517). The court argues that unlike *Priest* the defendant did not invoke counsel unequivocally. On the contrary, Nash was informed of his rights and responded with both a desire for counsel and a desire to continue talking with police without the presence of counsel: "Where the suspect's desires are expressed in such an equivocal fashion, it is permissible for the questioning official to make further inquiry to clarify the suspect's wishes" (p. 517). The court argues that *Miranda* also contemplated a suspect's indecisiveness regarding the presence of an attorney: "If [a suspect] is indecisive in his request for counsel, there may be some question on whether he did or did not waive counsel. Situations of this kind must necessarily be left to the judgment of the interviewing Agent" (*Nash* v. *Estelle*, 1979, p. 517, citing *Miranda* v. *Arizona*, 1969, p. 485). In *Nash*, the court opines that although a suspect has the right to terminate an interrogation, some suspects may want to confess their crimes and others may want to assess their options. Citing *Michigan* v. *Mosley* (1975): "[A] blanket prohibition against the taking of voluntary statements or a permanent immunity from further interrogation, regardless of the circumstances, would transform the Miranda safeguards into wholly irrational obstacles to legitimate police activity, and deprive suspects of an opportunity to make informed and intelligent assessments of their interests" (*Nash* v. *Estelle*, 1979, p. 517). In *Nash*, the per se precedent of *Priest* does not exclude police seeking clarification. Yet, the circuit court warns that police interrogators cannot use clarification as a guise to coerce or intimated the suspect.

The circuit court's conclusion in *Nash* is that the suspect never requested an attorney during questioning and merely sought assurances. The court disagreed with the inferences drawn by the district court and concluded that Nash never requested an attorney's presence during questioning, and Files' responses were not subtle attempts to dissuade Nash from invoking his right to counsel. The court adds that Nash's use of the word "lawyer" is not endowed with talismanic qualities, hence the questioning did not have to cease. This would have denied Nash his desire to continue questioning. The court concludes that "considering the actors and the setting, the exchange is not infected with a sinister undertone. Files did not violate any right accorded Nash by *Miranda* or *Priest*. The district court erred in granting the writ" (*Nash* v. *Estelle*, 1979, p. 520).

The majority opinion of the circuit court in *Nash* is not supported entirely by the court with some of the judges concurring in part and others dissenting in part. All the judges who dissented agreed that the majority ruling "creates precedents that endanger the right of those suspected of crimes to be free from coercive interrogations" (p. 521). One of the most significant points in the dissent is captured in the characterization and potential effect of the ruling on custodial suspects' rights:

> a grudging and strained opinion . . . that creates an exception to the *per se* rule, described as "equivocalness," rather than ambiguous, that has the potential for largely undermining the prophylactic effect of the rule and for transferring from accused to interrogator the control over the right to an attorney. (p. 521)

The latter is a powerful argument that expresses concern on the legal precedent that *Nash* creates, such as establishing an exception based on the equivocalness of the invocation, and the "motivations" of public officers that conduct interrogations:

> by applying the administrative presumption that a public officer performs his duties with regularity and in compliance with the Constitution, the majority opinion threatens the established body of law governing the right of suspects in custody to be free from the effects of even subtly coercive police interrogation techniques. (p. 521)

The dissenting judges also cast doubt on the need for clarification after Nash asked "If I want a lawyer present, I just put down here [on the waiver form] I want him present?" They argue that the alleged need for clarification arose from interrogation that continued after it should have ceased. The notion of "equivocalness" created by continued interrogation after an unambiguous, unequivocal request for the presence of counsel cannot serve as the basis for an exception to the Priest per se rule. The judges add that the creation of an equivocalness exception, which is susceptible to a clear definition, may create a context in which the officers are able to find or create "equivocalness where there is none and in so doing force the suspect constantly to reassert his right to counsel" (p. 526). When the interrogator gets to decide what the suspect truly intends a shift in control from accused to interrogator may occur. Removing the bright-line rule of stopping an interrogation when the suspect requests counsel may benefit the interrogator and facilitates postponing the supply of counsel after a request. For the dissenting (in part) judges there is no doubt that Files understood that Nash wanted an attorney and that the alleged equivocation occurred after continued questioning: "Attempts by interrogators to persuade the suspect that he does not need an attorney present are nothing more than attempts to get the suspect to accept the untruth that the interrogators are 'acting solely in [the suspect's] best interest'" (p. 524).

The judges' dissent in *Nash* also addresses Nash's alleged intellectual limitations and impaired cognitive skills:

> In sum, there is evidence tending to show Nash's sub-normal intelligence and education, a highly suggestible state of mind during the interview, confusion on Nash's part about

his constitutional rights, the possibility that Files' disapproval of his request for counsel triggered Nash's waiver of his rights, and the possibility that Nash's confession was the fruit of prior coercive interrogations. (p. 530)

The *Nash* ruling puts a spotlight on the possible pitfalls of creating an arbitrary standard of "equivocalness" and police interrogators using clarifications to resolve alleged equivocal/ambiguous requests for counsel. On the issue of invocation, *Nash* relies on a portion of the majority opinion in *Miranda* that deals with a suspect being indecisive (undefined) in a request for counsel. Reflecting on *Miranda*, this portion of the ruling does not represent the general spirit of the Court in protecting suspects from coercive police interrogation tactics, often requiring a broad interpretation of suspects' invocations for counsel. This aspect of *Miranda* is lost in *Nash*'s majority opinion but is consistent with the conflicting views of many in the judiciary on the issue of unequivocalness, voluntariness, and custodial interrogation. The legal standing of these matters is examined further in *Rhode Island* v. *Innis* (1980).

A suspect's invocation for counsel, per *Miranda*, attaches once a suspect is under custodial interrogation. In *Rhode Island* v. *Innis* (1980), the Court qualified the definition of *Miranda* as "any words or actions on the part of the police other than those normally attendant to arrest and custody that the police should know are reasonably likely to elicit an incriminating response from the suspect" (p. 292). The Court added that courts must consider the circumstances of each case when making a determination of custody. The Court ruled that questioning aimed at gathering background biographical data does not constitute interrogation. This created a booking exception to *Miranda*. In this sense, if a suspect is not under custodial interrogation, *Miranda* does not limit the use of a suspect's statements. This includes scenarios in which a suspect has requested counsel and provided statements during the booking phase of police interrogation (see Mason, 2013).

The Court's majority opinion was supported in concurring opinions by Justice Burger, who opined that the results of the ruling were not inconsistent with *Miranda*, and Justice White. The dissenting opinion of Justice Stevens, however, highlights the perspective of some justices that the term "interrogation" in *Miranda* should be interpreted broadly. Justice Stevens noted that the *Innis* ruling narrows the definition of interrogation in a manner inconsistent with the rights protected in *Miranda*:

In short, in order to give full protection to a suspect's right to be free from any interrogation at all, the definition of "interrogation" must include any police statement or conduct that has the same purpose or effect as a direct question. Statements that appear to call for a response from the suspect, as well as those that are designed to do so, should be considered interrogation. (p. 311)

To this statement, Justice Stevens adds:

> the Court's test creates an incentive for police to ignore a suspect's invocation of his rights in order to make continued attempts to extract information from him. If a suspect does not appear to be susceptible to a particular type of psychological pressure, . . . the police are apparently free to exert that pressure on him despite his request for counsel, so long as they are careful not to punctuate their statements with question marks. And if, contrary to all reasonable expectations, the suspect makes an incriminating statement, that statement can be used against him at trial. The Court thus turns Miranda's unequivocal rule against any interrogation at all into a trap in which unwary suspects may be caught by police deception. (pp. 313–314)

This opinion exemplifies the view of some Court justices of the need to broadly apply *Miranda* guarantees in order to ensure suspects' rights are observed during all stages of custodial interrogation, including the booking phase. This perspective is further captured in the Court's *Edwards* v. *Arizona* (1981) ruling. The Court's subsequent attempt at addressing Miranda protections almost two decades later.

In *Edwards*, the petitioner (Edwards) was arrested and taken to the police station where he was read his Miranda rights. He stated that he understood his rights and was willing to talk to the police. At some point in the interrogation, he is informed that another suspect in custody has implicated him in the crime. Edwards denied the accusation and tried to "make a deal." The detectives informed Edwards that they didn't have the authority to make a deal but wanted a statement from him. After, Edwards made a phone call to a county attorney, but hung up without talking to counsel. Edwards then said: "I want an attorney before making a deal." At that point, the detectives ceased the interrogation and Edwards was taken to the county jail. The next morning the detectives went to the jail and asked to talk to Edwards. Edwards told the detention officer that he did not wish to talk to them. The guard told him he "had" to talk to the officers and took him to see them. Edwards was re-Mirandized. After listening to the tapes in which another suspect implicates Edwards, he replied to the officers: "I'll tell you anything you want to know, but I don't want it on tape. He thereupon implicated himself in the crime" (p. 479).

The majority Court ruled: "We think it is clear that Edwards was subjected to custodial interrogation on January 20 within the meaning of *Rhode Island v. Innis* and that this occurred at the instance of the authorities. His statement made without having had access to counsel, did not amount to a valid waiver and hence was inadmissible" (p. 487). The justices ruled to reverse the judgment of the Arizona Supreme Court. The concurring judgments of Justices Burger, Powell, and Rehnquist, albeit are supportive of the reversal of the state court judgment, provide insights into another important aspect of case law: the concept of "initiation" after a suspect's invocation for counsel.

Justice Burger opines that although he concurs with the judgment, he does not agree with the notion that a "special rule" is needed for protecting a custodial suspect from being "free from interrogation" (p. 488). Justice Burger argues that: "The extraordinary protections afforded a person in custody suspected of criminal conduct are not without a valid basis, but, as with all 'good' things, they can be carried too far" (p. 488). He adds: "The notion that any 'prompting' of a person in custody is somehow evil per se has been rejected" (p. 488). For Justice Burger, the legal standard should be whether the resumption of an interrogation is the result of a knowing and voluntary waiver.

Justice Powell, with whom Justice Rehnquist joins, concurs with the ruling. However, they, as Burger, expressed concerns over the Court's emphasis on "initiation." Justice Powell argues that the ruling is unclear: "If read to create a new per se rule, requiring a threshold inquiry . . . as to precisely who opened any conversation between an accused and state officials, I cannot agree. I would not superimpose a new element of proof on the established doctrine of waiver of counsel" (p. 490). Justice Powell adds that police may inquire whether suspects have changed their minds about speaking to them without the assistance of counsel: "It is not unusual for a person in custody who previously has expressed an unwillingness to talk or a desire to have a lawyer to change his mind and even welcome an opportunity to talk. Nothing in the Constitution erects obstacles that preclude police from ascertaining whether a suspect has reconsidered his original decision" (p. 490). Justice Powell refers to this as a "paternalistic rule" consistently rejected by the Court protecting a suspect from making a knowing and voluntary waiver:

> In sum, once warnings have been given and the right to counsel has been invoked, the relevant inquiry – whether the suspect now desires to talk to police without counsel – is a question of fact to be determined in light of all of the circumstances. Who "initiated" a conversation may be relevant to the question of waiver, but it is not the sine qua non to the inquiry. The ultimate question is whether there was a free and knowing waiver of counsel before interrogation commenced. (p. 491)

Justice Powell concludes that he hesitated to join the opinion of the Court precisely due to the undefined emphasis on "initiation." The element of "initiation," coupled with the equivocalness standard, will challenge what some justices later refer to as the "bright-line" *Edwards*' rule.

2.4 Post-*Edwards* to *Davis*: 1981–1994

One of the first post-*Edwards*' rulings in the corpus that address the (un)equivocalness of an invocation for counsel is *United States* v. *Prestigiacomo* (1981). In *Prestigiacomo*, a ruling of the United States District Court, E. D. New York, the defendant (Prestigiacomo) was arrested on drug related charges. The defendant was a native speaker of Italian and required the aid of an interpreter. A senior customs inspector, Frank Giordano, was asked to serve as an interpreter. He would also conduct the interrogation. While in custody, Prestigiacomo was Mirandized, and Giordano informed the defendant that he was going to ask him some questions. In response, the defendant said the cans contained olive oil and had been given to him by somebody named Finazzo. After he mentioned the name of Finazzo the defendant said: "Maybe it would be good to have a lawyer." Giordano made no attempt to clarify the defendant's intent or get him a lawyer: "[i]t was up to him to request one" (p. 682). Giordano continued the interrogation after asking the defendant whether he was willing to continue answering questions, to which the defendant replied in the affirmative.

The defendant argued that his statement "Maybe it would be good to have a lawyer" constituted an unequivocal request for counsel, hence all questioning should have ceased until an attorney was present. In its review of the case, the court argues:

> Under the circumstances of this case defendant's statement "maybe it would be good to have a lawyer" was a sufficient request for counsel. The decision in the *Miranda* case does not require a suspect to adopt any particular wording to manifest his wishes. It is enough if the suspect "indicates in any manner" that he wishes to consult with an attorney. At that moment there can be no further questioning. (p. 683)

The court also notes that the defendant was not a native speaker of English and was unfamiliar with United States law – factors that should be considered. Furthermore, there was no significant amount of time between the defendant's statement "Maybe it would be good to have a lawyer," and Giordano's initiation of questioning. The court ruled that the defendant did not make an intelligent and voluntary waiver of his Miranda rights.

The *Prestigiacomo* case exemplifies how some lower district courts have applied legal precedence after *Edwards* in cases that deal with questions such as: (1) what constitutes an invocation for counsel *per* Miranda?; (2) is clarification needed or suggested after a potentially equivocal invocation for counsel?; (3) does the bright-line rule of Edwards apply to all suspect "initiations" (later addressed in the Court's *Shatzer's* (2010) ruling regarding the two-week Miranda break in custody)?; and (4) should the role of individual factors, such as a person's understanding of English, United States law, level of education, and intellectual/cognitive abilities be considered when examining a suspect's invocation for counsel and waiving of rights? Lower courts' interpretation of these queries must not contradict Court precedence, but as the cases in the corpus show an interpretation of undefined legal questions, such as what constitutes an unequivocal invocation for counsel, is often "left" to the lower courts to interpret without specific guidance from the Court.

Smith v. *Illinois* (1984), also cited as *Smith I*, is one of those seminal cases in which the Court takes on the question of unequivocalness, but without providing a definition for equivocal/unequivocal invocations for counsel. In *Smith I*, the petitioner (Smith), who was eighteen years old, was arrested and read his Miranda rights. When the police interrogator asked him whether he understood his right to consult an attorney, Smith responded "Uh, yeah. I'd like to do that" (p. 93). Prior to this, the defendant expressed concerns as to whether the police would "railroad" him. The police interrogation continued after his response to securing counsel and Smith provided incriminating statements.

To address Smith's invocation for counsel, the Court took an approach that departed from the per se standard and adopted instead the "threshold of inquiry." The latter approach is moored in the broad interpretation of Miranda guarantees. The Court argued that an accused's request for counsel may be ambiguous or equivocal: "As the majority and dissenting opinions below noted, courts have developed conflicting standards for determining the consequences of such ambiguities . . . We need not resolve this conflict in the instant case" (p. 96). For the Court, if an accused expresses the desire to have legal representation during custodial interrogation, and where there is nothing about the request for counsel to render it ambiguous, questioning must cease. The Court also made a clear distinction between invocation and waiver:

> As Justice Simon emphasized below, "[a] statement either is such an assertion [of the right to counsel] or it is not . . . ." Where nothing about the request for counsel or the circumstances leading up to the request would render it ambiguous, all questioning must cease. In these circumstances, an accused's subsequent statements are relevant only to the question whether the accused waived the right he had invoked. Invocation and waiver are entirely distinct inquiries, and the two must not be blurred by merging them together. (p. 98)

In a *per curiam* decision, the Court granted the appeal, reversed the judgment of the Illinois Supreme Court, and remanded the case for further proceedings. The dissenting opinion of Justice Rehnquist, joined by the Chief Justice and Justice Powell, however, shows a different perspective of the role police interrogators play in interpreting a suspect's invocation for counsel. The dissenting judges argue that the Court assumes that there is no equivocation in Smith's statement: "Uh, yeah. I'd like to do that." The justices remind the Court that: "As the Illinois Appellate Court observed, the officer reading petitioner his rights did not understand the statement as a clear request. After first reading petitioner the fourth Miranda right, he immediately sought clarification by asking petitioner pointedly, 'Do you wish to talk with me at this time without a lawyer being present?'" (p. 101). For the dissenting justices, the Court has erroneously concluded that Smith made a clear request for counsel and the police interrogators' subsequent behavior was coercive and aimed at badgering and tricking the petitioner into waiving his rights. In the justices' opinion, the police interrogators behaved within clearly established case law.

Smith I, and its dissenting opinion, raises some important points moving forward: (1) the interpretation of *Edwards*, specifically the effect of an absent Edward's bright-line rule when a suspect requests counsel; (2) the importance of assessing, through context, whether a request for counsel is ambiguous (albeit without defining it); (3) the Court's differing views on what constitutes a suspect being "badgered" to speak to police, (for some) absent a bright-line rule; and (4) the notion, and applicability, of "police overreaching." These concepts in practice and at the discursive level are often intertwined, adding to the complexity of the Court's perception of the role of police interrogators in interpreting and giving (or not) discursive relevance to a suspect's invocation for counsel. The police interrogators' use of follow-ups to "clarify" a suspect's equivocal/ambiguous invocation for counsel and/or to initiate talk after an invocation is also at the center of post-*Edwards* rulings.

In *United States* v. *Fouche* (1987), often cited as *Fouche II*, the Ninth Circuit reviewed Fouche's claim that interrogators did not clarify his equivocal request for counsel, which violated his Miranda rights and rendered his statements inadmissible. The exchange in question occurs shortly after the defendant was Mirandized. The defendant asked to call an attorney: "[he] might want to talk to a lawyer" (p. 1286). The agent left the room and the defendant called his wife instead. When the agent returned, he reread the defendant his Miranda rights. The defendant told the agent that he had not called an attorney but had called his wife and she had told him to do whatever he wished. He then asked the agent, "What should I do?" (p. 1290). The agent told him he wasn't an attorney, and he couldn't give him advice. The agent then asked him, "Do you want to make a statement?" (p. 1291) and the defendant said he did. The court held that the defendant had made an equivocal request for counsel, and his Fifth Amendment rights had not been violated. The court reasoned that the agent's failure to specifically ask the defendant if he wanted a lawyer was not error, in that the *Nash* decision does not require a "mechanical and talismanic repetition of the word lawyer when Miranda warnings have been given twice in great detail and the suspect has understood his rights" (p. 1289). The court ruled that the agent sufficiently clarified Fouche's equivocal request for counsel, the interrogation did not violate *Miranda*, and Fouche's confession was legally obtained. The court affirmed the decision of the lower court on these grounds. The court's opinion, however, is not unanimously shared.

The dissenting opinion in *Fouche II* offers a different perspective to Fouche's invocation for counsel that is more consistent with prior rulings anchored on the per se standard of *Miranda*. In Judge Ferguson's dissenting opinion, he argues that the exchanges that followed Fouche's first request for counsel "he might want to talk to a lawyer" did not serve to clarify and added to the uncertainty of the request. The judge argues that Fouche was requesting legal advice and the agent should have asked him whether he wanted an attorney, rather than respond that he was not a lawyer and could not advise him on legal matters. The judge adds that Fouche's second request for legal advice to the agent, "what should I do?," may constitute a second equivocal request for counsel following *Miranda*: "The Supreme Court stated in Miranda that a suspect invokes his right to counsel when he 'indicates in any manner and at any stage of the process that he wishes to consult an attorney'" (*United States* v. *Fouche*, 1987, p. 1290). The judge notes that although the Court has not defined what constitutes an unequivocal assertion of the right to counsel, other courts have found an equivocal assertion of counsel to be sufficient to invoke Miranda rights. Following this reasoning, Fouche's statements were inadmissible.

In *Connecticut* v. *Barrett* (1987), the question before the Court is whether a broad application of *Miranda* applies to a suspect in custody who indicates a willingness to respond to questions orally but refuses to make a written statement without an attorney present. This case shows the continuous unsettled debate in the courts, post-*Miranda*, regarding the validity of broad versus (more) narrow interpretations of Miranda invocations.

In *Barrett*, the respondent (Barrett) was read his Miranda rights three times and each time he stated that "he was willing to talk about [the incident] verbally but he did not want to put anything in writing until his attorney came" (p. 523). Barrett provided a confession after making these statements. The Supreme Court of Connecticut reversed the conviction and held that Barrett had invoked his right to counsel when he refused to make written statements without an attorney present. In the court's view, "Barrett's expressed desire for counsel before making a written statement served as an invocation of the right for all purposes" (p. 523). The lower court based its decision, in part, on the broad interpretation of Miranda invocations for counsel: "No particular form of words has ever been required to trigger an individual's fifth amendment protections; nor have requests for counsel been narrowly construed" (*Connecticut* v. *Barrett*, 1987, citing *State* v. *Barrett*, 1985, p. 527). The Court, which reviewed the case on appeal, disagreed.

Chief Justice Rehnquist, who delivered the majority opinion for the Court, argued that the lower court's judgment was erroneous, since Barrett made it clear to the police interrogators that he was willing to talk to them about the crime for which he was accused. As the trial court found, there was no evidence that the interrogators coerced or tricked the suspect into waiving his rights. Rehnquist adds that Barrett's statement that he will not put anything in writing without the presence of counsel is not an ambiguous interpretation that requires a broad interpretation, which the Chief Justice notes is a settled approach: "we do not denigrate, nor the distinction between written and oral statements which are irrelevant and do not interfere with the suspect's voluntariness" (*Connecticut* v. *Barrett*, 1987, citing *Michigan* v. *Jackson*, 1986, p. 530). Justice Stevens, with whom Justice Marshall joins, dissented. The justices raise two questions: "why did the Court decide to exercise its discretion to grant review in this case?" (p. 536) and "why was respondent's request for the assistance of counsel any less ambiguous than the request in *Edwards v. Arizona*?" (p. 537). For the justices, the Court's inconsistent treatment of *Barrett* and *Edwards* – making Barrett's request for counsel less than Edwards – "is not adequately explained in the Court's opinion" (p. 537).

In *Smith* v. *Endell* (1988), also cited as *Smith II*, the Ninth Circuit tackled the legal assessment of invocations for counsel that are (newly) deemed "conditional," an outcome of the more prevalent debate on the unequivocal–equivocal invocation for counsel continuum. The court also revisited the role of clarifications with invocations that fall short of being unequivocal/unambiguous. In *Smith II*, the defendant (Smith) who had been Mirandized and had waived his rights talked to the police interrogators. After an hour of interrogation, Smith made the following request for counsel: "Can I talk to a lawyer? At this point, I think maybe you're looking at me as a suspect, and I should talk to a lawyer. Are you looking at me as a suspect?" (p. 1529). The interrogators engaged Smith and did not cease the interrogation. Smith and the police interrogators continued their back and forth regarding Smith being considered a suspect. At one point the police reminded him of his rights, including the right to an attorney. Here, Smith's defense alleges he made his second attempt at requesting counsel: "I don't know if I need one or not. That's why I'm trying to make my mind up, if I need to go that route for myself, you know" (p. 1530). The Superior Court denied Smith's motion to suppress, on the grounds that Smith's two references to counsel: "was merely underscoring the fact that he has a right to counsel . . . He's undecided whether he needs one and elects to go forward" (p. 1530). The Alaska Court of Appeals affirmed the lower court's decision. The magistrate judge found Smith's first request for counsel, conditional, and the police interrogators' behavior, albeit fell short of asking for clarification, constitutional. The Ninth Circuit found the magistrate judge's analysis flawed. The court ruled that although Smith's request for counsel was conditional, it was not ambiguous and questioning should have stopped. The court adds that even if the request was ambiguous or equivocal the police interrogators should have limited their questions to clarification and to providing a direct response as to whether he was a suspect. Circuit Judge O'Scannlain's dissent provides another perspective.

Judge O'Scannlain argues that Smith never invoked counsel, was merely "thinking out loud," and the police clarified Smith's statements regarding counsel. For Judge O'Scannlain, Smith's alleged requests for counsel were ambiguous-equivocal:

> Until now, right to counsel jurisprudence recognized two categories of request with a bright line rule to deal with each: "unequivocal" (all interrogation ceases until accused initiates further communication: *Miranda-Edwards*) or "ambiguous-equivocal" (clarifying questions only: *Fouche I-Fouche II*). The majority sets up a new category of "conditional" somewhere between *Miranda* and *Fouche I*; I would place "conditional," if such a category were to exist at all, entirely within "ambiguous-equivocal." (*Smith* v. *Endell*, 1988, footnote 5, p 1536)

The dissenting opinion, as the majority ruling of the court, provides no clear definition for these categories of invoking counsel and, ostensibly, uses equivocal and ambiguous interchangeably.

The next case, *Owen* v. *Alabama* (1988), also addresses the issue of clarification raised in *Smith I* and *Fouche II*, but with the added caveat of "harmless error." For context, shortly after the *Miranda* ruling, the Court decided in *Michigan* v. *Tucker* (1974) that it was permissible to use against the defendant the testimony of a witness who was discovered because of statements obtained from the defendant in violation of Miranda. This also applies if a defendant's testimony is inconsistent with prior statements to police. The prior illegally obtained statements may also be admissible to show the inconsistency and impeach the defendant's testimony. Thus, a court may rule that the introduction of statements at trial is/was "harmless error," even if the statements were obtained in violation of *Miranda*. The legal definition of "harmless error" may have significant repercussions for a suspect who may have invoked counsel unequivocally, but due to the continuation of the police interrogation provided incriminating statements that were entered as evidence at trial.

In *Owen*, the defendant, a former police officer, while being read his Miranda rights interrupted the police interrogators and said: "I know my damn rights" (p. 537). Later at the police station, the police officers reread Owen his Miranda rights. When the police officers informed Owen that he had the right to an attorney, the defendant said: "I think I'll let ya'll [*sic.*] appoint me one" (p. 537). The police officers continued to read Owen his Miranda rights. He refused to sign the waiver of rights form. Owen was interrogated and he confessed to the crime of murder of which he was accused. The police interrogator testified that the defendant said something like "can I call my lawyer now" or "I want my lawyer now" (p. 538). At this point, questioning stopped. Owen argued that his confession should be suppressed, since it was obtained in violation of Miranda. The Eleventh Circuit affirmed the district court's ruling granting the *writ of habeas corpus*.

Judge Johnson, who delivered the opinion of the court, argued that the facts in *Owen* were very similar to those in *Smith I*. The judge states that: "The settled approach to questions of waiver requires courts 'to give a broad, rather than a narrow interpretation to a defendant's request for counsel'" (p. 539). The judge adds that even if Owen's statement was not unequivocal, it was at a minimum an equivocal request for counsel. In such situations: "This Court employs an equally 'rigid prophylactic rule.' When a defendant makes an equivocal request for an attorney during a custodial interrogation: the scope of that interrogation is immediately narrowed to one subject and one only. Further questioning thereafter must be limited to clarifying that request until it is clarified" (p. 539). Judge Johnson points that the fact that Owen was a former police officer should not cast doubt on his request for an attorney, because it was formulated equivocally. As the Court ruled in *Smith I*: "post request responses to further interrogation cannot be used to cast doubt on the clarity of the initial request" (cited in *Owen* v. *Alabama*, 1988, p. 538).

The subsequent, and noteworthy point, addressed in this case is whether the State's failure to suppress the defendant's confession constitutes harmless error: "The failure to suppress statements obtained in violation of Miranda can be harmless error" (p. 540), per *Cape* v. *Francis* (1984). To qualify as harmless error, the error in admitting a confession cannot contribute to the defendant's conviction. To determine this, the court must review the facts and the effect of unlawfully admitted evidence. In Owen's trial: "The Court must consider 'whether absent the so-determined unconstitutional effect, the evidence remains not only sufficient to support the verdict but so overwhelming as to establish the guilt of the accused beyond a reasonable doubt'" (p. 540). The circuit court ruled that Owen's confession constituted significant evidence. Hence, the introduction of Owen's confession at trial was not harmless error. Furthermore, the police did not seek clarification when Owen made, at a minimum, an equivocal request for counsel and continued the interrogation, in violation of the Eleventh Circuit's precedents. This opinion reiterated several key points: (1) the conflicting and varied interpretations of what constitutes an invocation for counsel (not yet defined); (2) the need for police to clarify equivocal invocations; and (3) the harm of not suppressing an illegally obtained confession in the outcome of a trial. As the chapter shows, judges have disparate views of the role of confessions in shaping the trajectory and outcome of a trial.

The next case, *Robinson* v. *Borg* (1990), a ruling of the Ninth Circuit, exposed the relationship between a suspect's invocation for counsel, police follow-ups, and making a knowing and voluntary waiver. Robinson claimed that he did not make a knowing and voluntary waiver and that prior to making incriminating statements he unequivocally invoked his right to counsel when he stated: "I have to get me a good lawyer, man. Can I make a phone call?"

(p. 1390). The circuit court agreed with Robinson and reversed and remanded the district court's denial of Robinson's petition for *habeas corpus* relief. Circuit Judge Reinhardt, who delivered the opinion of the court, argued that the rigid prophylactic rule of *Edwards* applied in this case. He stated, reiterating case law, that a suspect's requests for counsel are to be given broad effect, doubts need to be clarified, and post responses cannot be used "to cast retrospective doubt on the clarity of the initial request itself" (p. 1391). For Judge Reinhardt "the simple fact that defendant has requested an attorney indicates that he does not believe that he is sufficiently capable of dealing with his adversaries singlehandedly" (p. 1392). The judge noted that the State's contention that Robinson did not invoke counsel because he was not attempting to invoke at the moment he made the request is inconsistent with case law: "we take a defendant's words 'understood as ordinary people would understand them'" (see *Connecticut* v. *Barrett*, 1987). Furthermore, the Court does not impose a "magical formulation" when invoking rights. A suspect only needs to clearly express the desire to consult with counsel.

Circuit Judge Trott offered a dissenting opinion. Judge Trott's opinion raises several points regarding the treatment of ambiguous invocations for counsel. The judge argues that the suspect's statement: "I have to get me a good lawyer man. Can I make a phone call?" requires interpretation in context, due to its potential ambiguity. The judge notes that Robinson's statements were preceded by a waiver and continued interrogation where he expressed the desire to speak to police without the presence of counsel. For judge Trott, the court's ruling on Robinson may constitute overreaching: "the distinction between rights themselves, on the one hand, and suggested safeguards . . . not intended to 'create a constitutional straitjacket,' on the other . . . is one of considerable substance" (p. 1399). This view that *Miranda* is not a "Constitutional command" is noted in *Miranda*'s dissenting opinion, as well as post-*Miranda* main opinions, and persists until present, showing the divide among some in the judiciary about the interpretation (broad versus narrow) and application of Miranda guarantees.

The broad approach to interpreting Miranda warnings takes a different turn in *United States* v. *Lux* (1990). In this Tenth Circuit ruling, the court reviewed Lux's contention that her statements to police during custodial interrogation were not provided freely or voluntarily and she had requested an attorney. The court found no error with the trial court's decision. The court determined that Lux had been advised of her Miranda rights, she acknowledged the rights and voluntarily waived them, and her "request" for an attorney "by asking how long it would take if she wanted a lawyer and if she would have to stay in jail while she waited for a lawyer" (p. 1382) did not constitute a clear or even equivocal invocation for counsel. The court also finds that the police interrogators' behavior and alleged false promises/lies were neither egregious nor coercive to support Lux's claim that her free will had been overborne by the police interrogators' tactics. This ruling, unlike others discussed previously in this chapter, is limited in its application of case law. The court takes a more succinct interpretation that relies on examining the "facts" of the case, which support the court's assessment that the suspect did not invoke counsel, even equivocally. This ruling does not adopt a broad interpretation of Miranda invocations, as many prior rulings, and reiterated the notion that not all statements that include the word lawyer (the "talismanic" effect argument) are invocations for counsel. The court also stresses the lawful use of interrogation tactics that include lying to the suspect: a not uncommon practice in police interrogation and often considered legal if the suspect provides a voluntary waiver of rights.

Cannady v. *Dugger* (1991), a highly cited Eleventh Circuit ruling, considers invocations for counsel that include hedges, such as "think," and the discursive context in which this type of invocation occurs. In *Cannady,* the appellant (Cannady) made incriminating statements after he was read his Miranda rights and questioned on several occasions. At one of his initial interrogations, the police interrogator asked Cannady whether he killed the victim. Cannady responded at some point after the question: "I think I should call my lawyer" (p. 754). The interrogator continued questioning Cannady and asked him "if he wanted 'to talk about it'" (p. 754). At this point, Cannady broke down and provided a confession of the crime. Judge Dubina ruled that Cannady's statement to the police officer, "I think I should call my lawyer," was an unequivocal request for counsel, and the police officer violated Cannady's Miranda rights when he continued the interrogation by asking "would you like to talk about it?" and did not attempt to clarify the request for counsel (yet, "pushed the phone toward Cannady and waited for him to make the call"; p. 755). The court argues that the police interrogator's actions were in violation of *Edwards* and *Miranda*. The context and the police interrogator's verbal and nonverbal actions in response to the defendant's request for counsel were essential to the court's ruling and reversal of this case. Of note, it is unclear given the (yet) lack of definition of what constitutes an unequivocal invocation for counsel, whether Cannady's invocation for counsel would have been ruled unequivocal, if the police officer had behaved differently and had not pushed the phone toward the appellant.

The context and discursive exchange, particularly the police interrogators' use of clarifications, was also highlighted in *United States* v. *De La Jara* (1992). Here, the Ninth Circuit reviewed whether de la Jara's statement to the police interrogator should have been suppressed after he invoked the right to counsel: "debo yo llamar a mi abogado." The district court denied the court's motion on the grounds that de la Jara's invocation was "ambiguous and equivocal." Furthermore, the district court argued that the police interrogators attempted to clarify the "equivocal" request and de la Jara waived his right to counsel.

The *De La Jara* case raises an important question: How significant is context in determining the unequivocalness of a suspect's invocation for counsel? Although this case involves an L2 speaker of English – these types of cases will be discussed further in a separate section of the chapter – it is important to include *De La Jara* in this section due to the court's "common sense" approach at determining the most probable intent of the appellant's invocation for counsel.

In the review of the case, the Chief Judge of the Ninth Circuit, Judge Poole, notes that "de la Jara testified that he had requested to speak to his attorney several times, saying 'I should have my lawyer present.' He also testified that he had told his secretary, Rose Alvarez, to call his attorney, but that she said she was not able to do so" (p. 751). Alvarez corroborated the appellant's version of events at the suppression hearing. The police report on the day of de la Jara's arrest also provides context to de la Jara's claims of requesting counsel. One of the arresting police officers stated that he heard (through a door that was slightly ajar) de la Jara say in Spanish that he wanted to call his attorney. The officer informed another agent "that it sounded like de la Jara was invoking his rights because he just asked to call his attorney. The agent asked me if that's what I heard and I said 'yes'" (p. 751).

The circuit court's review also looked at de la Jara's request formulated in Spanish, noting the complications the Spanish language interpretation raises:

> At the hearing on the motion to suppress statements, the court interpreter noted that de la Jara's statement to the interrogating officer ("debo yo llamar a mi abogado") could be either a question or assertion depending on inflection, and that the meaning would depend to some extent on the context. The interpreter offered the following possible translations of the phrase: (1) "Can I call my attorney?", (2) "Should I call my attorney?", (3) "I should call my lawyer." (p. 750)

The judge notes that the different interpretations carry varying legal connotations, from a clear invocation for counsel ("Can I call my lawyer?" or "I should call my lawyer") to a question that may not rise to an equivocal invocation ("Should I call my lawyer?"). As with prior cases reviewed by the Ninth Circuit and the Court, the court opts for a "common sense" application (see *Barrett*), arguing that: "We conclude that de la Jara's words understood as ordinary people would understand them, and as Officer Perez did understand them, clearly invoked the right to counsel" (p. 752). The court argues that de la Jara's statements should have been suppressed, per *Miranda* and *Edwards*. The court also ruled that the introduction of de la Jara's statements at trial was not harmless error: "the appellant may not have been convicted of any of the counts absent the evidence" (p. 752). The court ruled to reverse his conviction.

In *United States* v. *March* (1993), the Tenth Circuit took a similar approach to *De La Jara*, but the outcome of the review was very different. Here, the court examined the matter of equivocalness, specifically emphasizing the difference between questions that (may) ask for counsel versus those that ask for information. The court also reviewed the importance of police officers requesting clarification and the harmlessness of introducing evidence that is the result of an equivocal–ambiguous request for counsel.

In *March*, the defendant (March) was read his Miranda rights and he signed the waiver of rights form. The interrogators (FBI agents) asked several background questions. The defendant was questioned for about twenty to thirty minutes, and he provided incriminating statements. Shortly after, he requested an attorney. One of the agents provided the following testimony, illustrated in Excerpt 2.3, regarding March's request for counsel:

Excerpt 2.3

1 Q: Okay. What happened after he went through details of all four bank robberies?
2 A: Well, Mr. March said – asked Agent Jobe and myself, "Do you think I need an attorney?" And I said, "Billy, you know, look, we advised you of your rights in the beginning. If you want an attorney, you know, we'll stop at any time. You have that right, you know, it's your call. We cannot advise you one way or the other." And Billy chose to continue talking.
3 Q: Okay. Did he make some expression that he was going to continue talking?
4 A: I said, "It's your choice. What do you want to do?["] He says, "Well, you know, go ahead ask me the questions."
5 Q: So he said, "Go ahead and ask me some questions"?
6 A: Yeah; he just led us – led us on, didn't say, "Stop, I want an attorney." You know. If he'd done that, we would have stopped.
7 Q: And what happened after – after he said, "Go ahead and ask me some questions"?
8 A: His words weren't, "Go ahead and ask me some questions." I said, you know, "Billy, what do you want to do here?"
9 Q: Okay.
10 A: "I mean, would you like to continue?" He – he said, "Go ahead."
11 Q: All right.
12 A: I said, "Okay, I mean, just so it's – so it's clear."
13 Q: All right.
14 A: We just continued. There wasn't much more. What I did was at that point got him to sign the back of the photographs.

The defendant argues that the question he asked the agents ("Do you think I need an attorney?") constituted a request for counsel. The circuit court, in reviewing the district court's denial of the defendant's suppression motion, opined:

> We must determine here whether defendant's question constituted an invocation of his right to counsel, an issue on which the Supreme Court has provided little guidance. In *Smith*, the Court explicitly refused to address it: "We do not decide the circumstances in which an accused's request for counsel may be characterized as ambiguous or equivocal as a result of events preceding the request or of nuances inherent in the request itself, nor do we decide the consequences of such ambiguity or equivocation." *Connecticut* v. *Barrett* (1987), is more helpful, stating that "[i]nterpretation is only required where the defendant's words, understood as ordinary people would understand them, are ambiguous." Most recently, the Court said that invoking the right to counsel "requires, at a minimum, some statement that can reasonably be construed to be expression of a desire for the assistance of an attorney in dealing with custodial interrogation by the police" *McNeil* v. *Wisconsin* (1991). (p. 460)

The circuit court's perspective on this case shows a departure from a common previously held view of understanding invocations for counsel (as "ordinary people would"), albeit with little guidance from the Court, to a narrower interpretation that attempts to establish a "minimum" standard for a suspect's expression of a desire for counsel. This is further argued in the court's assessment that the defendant's question "Do you think I need an attorney?" does not rise to the level of clarity that other past cases have argued, as for example *Cannady*, *Robinson*, and *Smith II*. The court, hence, makes a distinction between the defendant's question as an equivocal request seeking advice from the police officers and a request that clearly invokes counsel. Here the court states:

> The various cases making the distinction between equivocal requests and statements that are not considered requests have held that the proper focus is on whether a defendant's statement evinces a contemplation of exercising the right to have an attorney present, or merely seeks a clarification of what his or her rights are. (p. 461)

The arguments laid out in *March* are significant, because they put forth a change in the court's perspective as to how broadly invocations for counsel should be interpreted. Reminiscent of past rulings, however, the court hedges:

> whenever a suspect makes a statement or asks a question that appears to contemplate invocation of his right to counsel, as opposed to seeking a better understanding of what his rights are, that constitutes an equivocal invocation of the right to counsel.
>
> Such an invocation requires the interrogating officers to take appropriate action. We agree with our sister circuits that when confronted with an equivocal request for counsel, the interrogating officers must cease all substantive questioning and limit further inquiries to clarifying the subject's ambiguous statements. (p. 461)

In this case, the court rules that the police interrogators did their due diligence when the defendant asked an ambiguous request for counsel by ceasing the interrogation and asking clarification. The court ruled that the introduction of the defendant's confession was harmless error, a stance often taken in later rulings in our corpus, and the district court properly denied the defendant's motion to suppress his legally obtained confession.

The Fourth Circuit case, *Poyner* v. *Murray* (1992), is another example of the shift between broad interpretations of suspects' equivocal or ambiguous requests for counsel and the police interrogators' (seeming) "due diligence" in asking clarification when these types of requests are made. *Poyner* also reiterates the view of some in the judiciary that suspects who have been through the criminal justice system "know better" when it comes to knowingly and intelligently waiving counsel. The role of the police's mindset during custodial interrogation is also an important component of this ruling.

Poyner was read his Miranda rights prior to being questioned at the police station. Poyner indicated understanding of the rights. One of the police interrogators informed Poyner about the information they had about his involvement in the crime of which he was accused, to which Poyner responded: "Didn't you say I have a right to an attorney?" The police interrogator responded: "Yes, you do, that is correct." The police interrogators begin to rise from their seats after what they state was Poyner's intent to invoke counsel. As the police interrogators began to rise from their seats and cease the interrogation, Poyner said "Let me tell you about the car" (p. 1409). The interrogation proceeded and Poyner provided incriminating statements about the abduction and murder of which he was accused.

Poyner contends that his statement "Didn't you tell me I had the right to an attorney?" constituted a request for counsel per *Miranda* and *Edwards* and, hence, all interrogation should have ceased. In reviewing Poyner's case *de novo* (or "anew") and his claim that he invoked counsel, the circuit court argues: "It appears that neither the Supreme Court nor this court yet has had occasion to consider the effect of a suspect's statement that, like Poyner's, mentions the Miranda right to counsel without suggesting any desire to speak with an attorney at that moment" (p. 1411). The court points to *United States* v. *Jardina* (1984) where the court ruled that once a suspect makes an unequivocal request for counsel, interrogation must cease, except for clarifying questions regarding the desire for counsel, if needed. The court adds that in Poyner's case, as in *Jardina*, "the suspect's statement was not an equivocal request for an attorney; rather, it was not a request at all. Thus, continued interrogation did not violate the suspect's Miranda rights. In so holding the court stated that [t]he word 'attorney' has no talismanic qualities" (p. 1411). The court further opines that Poyner's statement was less asserting than Jardina's.

The court also addressed a final argument that Poyner contends is supportive of his request for counsel claim. Poyner stated that the fact that the officers rose from their seats is indicative that they wanted to terminate the interrogation. The court does not support Poyner's contention:

> we find no support in the post-Miranda cases for such a rule. To the contrary, in the closely-related context of determining when a suspect has effectively waived his Miranda rights, the Supreme Court has stated that "the state of mind of the police is irrelevant to the question of the intelligence and voluntariness of respondent's election to abandon his rights . . . ." Detectives Spinner and Browning in this case displayed an admirable degree of solicitude for Poyner's Miranda rights, and we decline the invitation to adopt an analysis that would penalize police officers for erring on the side of even excessive caution in observing the suspect's rights during custodial interrogation. (p. 1412)

The court added that Poyner's statement after his "nonrequest" for counsel does not violate *Edwards*, as Poyner argues. The court stated that Poyner reinitiated talk with the police officers and waived his rights freely and voluntarily. The court ruled that the lower, district, court did not err in denying Poyner's petition and affirmed the ruling.

Poyner's case puts forth an important notion that is carried over to future rulings. The notion that a police officer's response to a suspect's request for counsel, including the use of bodily actions (see Johnson, 2020), during custodial interrogation is irrelevant in the analysis of such invocation or, as in the *Poyner* case, merely erring on the side of excessive caution. This ruling, as previous ones, shows the gradual erosion of the bright-line rules of *Miranda* and *Edwards*, extending to the limitation of the broad interpretation of (undefined) equivocal–ambiguous invocations for counsel. *Poyner* also furthers the notion that some invocations for counsel are not even ambiguous/equivocal. They are simply not invocations at all, and as such do not require any effort to clarify from the police interrogators.

The Court tackles the invocation for counsel and clarification discussion once more in the seminal case of *Davis* v. *United States* (1994). This case erodes the last vestiges of broad or "ordinary" interpretations of invocations for counsel, and it removes the need for police clarification altogether. Parting from *Davis*, police interrogators are not required to clarify an invocation for counsel they deem ambiguous or equivocal.

In *Davis*, the petitioner (Davis), who was a member of the United States Navy, initially waived his Miranda rights when he was interrogated by Naval Investigative Service agents about the murder of a sailor. About an hour and a half into the interview, Davis said, "Maybe I should talk to a lawyer" (p. 466). The agents followed up by asking Davis if he was asking for a lawyer to which Davis replied that he was not. The interrogators took a short break and then reread Davis his rights and the interrogation continued for another hour. At this point, Davis asked to have a lawyer present: "I think I want a lawyer before I say anything else" (p. 466). The interrogation ended. The military court denied Davis's motion to suppress statements made during the interrogation on the grounds that Davis's mention of a lawyer was not a request for counsel. The Court of Military Appeals affirmed.

Davis is the first time the Court considered the degree of clarity needed for a custodial suspect to invoke counsel after a Miranda waiver. The Court's ruling narrowed the scope in which a suspect can reasonably invoke legal counsel. In this ruling, invocations for counsel must be performed in a manner that a reasonable police officer deems unequivocal before they are given any legal effect. The ruling, as past ones, does not define what a reasonable police officer would understand as an unequivocal invocation for counsel. The Court stated simply that if a police officer believes that the suspect may not be invoking the right to counsel, the officer does not need to cease questioning. Justice O'Connor delivered the majority opinion for the Court:

> The rationale underlying Edwards is that the police must respect a suspect's wishes regarding his right to have an attorney present during custodial interrogation. But when the officers conducting the questioning reasonably do not know whether or not the suspect wants a lawyer, a rule requiring the immediate cessation of questioning "would transform the Miranda safeguards into wholly irrational obstacles to legitimate police investigative activity, . . .," because it would needlessly prevent the police from questioning a suspect in the absence of counsel even if the suspect did not wish to have a lawyer present. Nothing in Edwards requires the provision of counsel to a suspect who consents to answer questions without the assistance of a lawyer. (p. 460)

O'Connor adds:

> In considering how a suspect must invoke the right to counsel, we must consider the other side of the Miranda equation: the need for effective law enforcement. Although the courts ensure compliance with the Miranda requirements through the exclusionary rule, it is police officers who must actually decide whether or not they can question a suspect. The Edwards rule – questioning must cease if the suspect asks for a lawyer – provides a bright line that can be applied by officers in the real world of investigation and interrogation without unduly hampering the gathering of information. But if we were to require questioning to cease if a suspect makes a statement that might be a request for an attorney, this clarity and ease of application would be lost. Police officers would be forced to make difficult judgment calls about whether the suspect in fact wants a lawyer even though he has not said so, with the threat of suppression if they guess wrong. We therefore hold that, after a knowing and voluntary waiver of the Miranda rights, law enforcement officers may continue questioning until and unless the suspect clearly requests an attorney. (p. 461)

Justice O'Connor also reminds the Court that *Miranda* rejected the assumption "that each police station must have a 'station house lawyer' present at all times to advise prisoners" (p. 460). She reiterates that police officers must inform the suspects of their right to counsel and that they may not be questioned after such invocation is made, as long as the invocation is clear. If the suspect is "indecisive in his request for counsel" (p. 460), the police officers may not need to cease questioning.

In an attempt to address the limitations inherent in *Davis*, Justice Souter, who delivered the *Davis* concurrence, advocated for the clarification standard whenever the degree of clarity of a suspect's invocation is at question. Souter argued that interrogators have the legal obligation to clarify a custodial suspect's ambiguous statement if the statement could be interpreted as a desire to consult with legal counsel. This standard, according to Justice Souter, would ensure a suspect's choice for counsel as well as address possible misunderstandings that may arise during custodial interrogation:

> I agree with the majority that the Constitution does not forbid law enforcement officers to pose questions (like those directed at Davis) aimed solely at clarifying whether a suspect's ambiguous reference to counsel was meant to assert his Fifth Amendment right. Accordingly I concur in the judgment affirming Davis's conviction, resting partly on evidence of statements given after agents ascertained that he did not wish to deal with them through counsel. I cannot, however, join in my colleagues' further conclusion that if the investigators here had been so inclined, they were at liberty to disregard Davis's reference to a lawyer entirely, in accordance with a general rule that interrogators have no legal obligation to discover what a custodial subject meant by an ambiguous statement that could reasonably be understood to express a desire to consult a lawyer. (p. 466)

Souter adds:

> While the question we address today is an open one, its answer requires coherence with nearly three decades of case law addressing the relationship between police and criminal suspects in custodial interrogation. Throughout that period, two precepts have commanded broad assent: that the Miranda safeguards exist "to assure that the individual's right to choose between speech and silence remains unfettered throughout the interrogation process, . . . ", and that the justification for Miranda rules, intended to operate in the real world, "must be consistent with . . . practical realities," (Kennedy, J., dissenting). A rule barring government agents from further interrogation until they determine whether a suspect's ambiguous statement was meant as a request for counsel fulfills both ambitions. It assures that a suspect's choice whether or not to deal with police through counsel will be "scrupulously honored, . . . " (White, J., concurring in result), and it faces both the real-world reasons why misunderstandings arise between suspect and interrogator and the real-world limitations on the capacity of police and trial courts to apply fine distinctions and intricate rules. (pp. 468–469)

Souter's attempt to include real life (linguistic challenges) to the application of the law reflects some of the justices' concerns for good police practices during custodial interrogation: "In the abstract, nothing may seem more clear than a 'clear statement' rule, but in police stations and trial courts the question, 'how clear is clear?' is not so readily answered. When a suspect says 'uh, yeah, I'd like to do that' after being told he has a right to a lawyer, has he 'clearly asserted' his right?" Souter also warns that the primary arbiters of "clarity" will be the police officers, who will be in a position of advantage, particularly "when an inculpatory statement has been obtained as a result of an unrecorded, incommunicado interrogation" (footnote 7, p. 475).

Souter's opinion about the limitations inherent in the "threshold-of-clarity" standard, coupled with the lack of a definition for what constitutes an unequivocal invocation for counsel in *Davis*, opened the door for state and federal courts to utilize and apply, at their discretion, the clarification standard to post-waiver invocations. Notable (recent) cases in which the clarification standard was invoked include: *United States* v. *Rodriguez* (2008), *United States* v. *Fry* (2009), and *State* v. *Blackburn* (2009). In these cases, the courts ruled that the burden of obtaining clarification before proceeding with an interrogation lies with the interrogating officer(s) and not with the suspect(s). These rulings, however, are not in line with Justice O'Connor's *Davis* opinion:

> To recapitulate: We held in Miranda that a suspect is entitled to the assistance of counsel during custodial interrogation even though the Constitution does not provide for such assistance. We held in Edwards that if the suspect invokes the right to counsel at any time, the police must immediately cease questioning him until an attorney is present. But we are unwilling to create a third layer of prophylaxis to prevent police questioning when the suspect might want a lawyer. Unless the suspect actually requests an attorney, questioning may continue. (p. 462)

O'Connor's majority opinion has legal standing. Justice Souter's concurring recommendations do not. They are merely suggestions for good police interrogation practices.

The *Davis* ruling becomes the standard for courts to review and rule on the (un)equivocalness of a suspect's invocation for counsel and the police's behavior when suspects invoke counsel. The key points to take from this ruling include: (1) the treatment/analysis of invocations for counsel; (2) the clarification standard; and (3) the matter of "initiation" addressed in *Edwards*. Prior to *Davis*, the courts ruled that invocations for counsel should be interpreted as "ordinary people would," and in cases in which the request for counsel may be equivocal allow for a broad interpretation. The police's use of clarification was also encouraged with these types of invocations. In *Davis*, the courts leave it up to the police to determine whether the request for counsel is equivocal "as a reasonable police officer would understand it," while also stating that police do not need to clarify equivocal or ambiguous invocations for counsel, albeit it may be good practice. The Court, as with prior rulings, does not define what constitutes an equivocal or ambiguous invocation for counsel. It simply leaves it as a judgment call of the police. The use of clarifications, also not defined, are encouraged, rather than expected, in the concurrent ruling. This is a recommendation, not a requirement or expectation, aimed at protecting the *Miranda* and *Edwards* "bright-line rules."

In addition, the *Davis* ruling does not address how suspects know that they have invoked council unequivocally during a police interrogation. There are no provisions in the ruling (or other rulings for that matter) for suspects to be informed of the status of their invocations for counsel. This matter is highlighted in a prior Court ruling, whose majority opinion was also delivered by Justice O'Connor:

> we have never read the Constitution to require that the police supply a suspect with a flow of information to help him calibrate his self-interest in deciding whether to speak or stand by his rights . . . Once it is determined that a suspect's decision not to rely on his rights was uncoerced, that he at all times knew he could stand mute and request a lawyer, and that he was aware of the State's intention to use his statements to secure a conviction, the analysis is complete, and the waiver is valid as a matter of law. (*Moran* v. *Burbine*, 1986, pp. 422–423)

Of note, the dissenting opinion in *Moran* v. *Burbine*, delivered by Justice Stevens with Justice Brennan and Justice Marshall joining, shows the Court's, then and still, differing views on *Miranda*, society's interest in interrogating suspects, and suspects' ability to make an informed invocation for counsel:

> The Court concludes that the police may deceive an attorney by giving her false information about whether her client will be questioned, and that the police may deceive a suspect by failing to inform him of his attorney's communications and efforts to represent him . . . For the majority, this conclusion, though "distaste[ful]," . . . is not even debatable. The deception of the attorney is irrelevant, because the attorney has no right to information, accuracy, honesty, or fairness in the police response to her questions about her client. The deception of the client is acceptable, because, although the information would affect the client's assertion of his rights, the client's actions in ignorance of the availability of his attorney are voluntary, knowing, and intelligent; additionally, society's interest in apprehending, prosecuting, and punishing criminals outweighs the suspect's interest in information regarding his attorney's efforts to communicate with him. Finally, even mendacious police interference in the communications between a suspect and his lawyer does not violate any notion of fundamental fairness, because it does not shock the conscience of the majority (*Moran* v. *Burbine*, 1986, p. 435).

The debate in *Davis* raises important ethical and legal concerns. That is, if the police are not legally obligated to tell suspects they have or, alternatively, have not invoked counsel unequivocally, suspects may (and do) continue to talk to police (or as argued in *Edwards* "initiate talks with police"), after invoking counsel. Moreover, suspects who may be unaware of the effectiveness of their invocations may subsequently waive their rights and provide a statement, even if they were not overtly "tricked" or "coerced" into doing so:

> Social science confirms what common sense would suggest, that individuals who feel intimidated or powerless are more likely to speak in equivocal or nonstandard terms when no ambiguity or equivocation is meant ... Suspects in police interrogation are strong candidates for these effects. Even while resort by the police to the "third degree" has abated since *Miranda*, the basic forms of psychological pressure applied by police appear to have changed less. (Justice Souter's *Davis* concurring opinion, footnote 4, p. 470)

The next section proceeds to examine a representative selection of federal court rulings post-*Davis* (1994–2021) that show the judges' application of this case. The cases, which are part of the corpus, explore the legal standing of a suspect's invocation for counsel as well as the effect of *Davis* on vulnerable populations (e.g., juveniles, persons with intellectual and/or cognitive disabilities) and L2 speakers of English. These populations and their potential inability to speak assertively due to being overwhelmed by the uncertainty of the situation are raised in Justice Souter's concurring opinion, and other pre- and post-*Davis* rulings with concern.

2.5 Post-*Davis* to Present: 1994–2021

Cases in this section will explore the impact of the *Davis* ruling on judges' assessment of a suspect's invocation for counsel. These cases, which are representative of the corpus, will serve to illustrate the treatment of an invocation for counsel and its effect on other aspects of a case, such as the voluntariness of a suspect's statement, the use of clarifications and follow-ups by police during interrogation, and the harmless error doctrine. In addition, a few of the cases will feature members of vulnerable populations (e.g., juveniles and L2 speakers of English) in order to assess how judges have incorporated these variables into their rulings on Miranda invocations for counsel.

2.5.1 Invoking Counsel: Where Do Judges "Draw the Line"?

Post-*Davis* judicial rulings reflect the effect of *Davis* on judges' assessments of what constitutes an unequivocal invocation for counsel. As discussed previously, pre-*Davis* judges often took a broader approach, including the police's use of clarifications, when interpreting suspects' invocations for counsel. Since *Davis*, and potentially due to the lack of clarity and guidance of the ruling, judges have narrowed the interpretation of an invocation for counsel. Common themes include: (1) the "talismanic" meaning of "attorney"; (2) the use of hedges (e.g., "think" and "might") or indirect questions (e.g., "Can I?"/"Can you?"); and (3) the use of inquiries (e.g., "Should I") to request counsel. A broad interpretation is often replaced with narrower interpretations of what constitutes an unequivocal invocation for counsel. Some of the rulings also provide a reinterpretation of "how ordinary people would understand" an invocation for counsel to mean literal rather than indirect.

In *United States* v. *Cheely* (1994), the Ninth Circuit examined the talismanic effect of a suspect mentioning "attorney" during the reading of Miranda. Cheely, who was serving a lengthy sentence for murder, was questioned regarding a mail bomb explosion. The inspectors who conducted the interrogation advised Cheely of his rights. Cheely acknowledged that he understood them, but he declined to sign the waiver. At trial, the interrogators were examined, and the exchange shown in Excerpt 2.4 took place.

The interrogation lasted approximately two hours. Cheely did not confess, but he made several incriminating statements.

In the circuit court's *de novo* review of the district court's decision on Cheely's Miranda rights violation claim, the court ruled that Cheely was under custodial interrogation by government agents. Regarding Cheely's invocation, the court argues:

> Of course, Cheely does not necessarily invoke his rights simply by saying the magic word "attorney"; that word "has no talismanic qualities," and "[a] defendant does not invoke his right to counsel any time the word falls from his lips." ... Similarly, an express written or oral waiver of the right to counsel "is not inevitably either necessary or sufficient to establish waiver ... ." (p. 1448)

Excerpt 2.4

1 Q: [by the prosecutor] Did [Cheely] say anything with regard to declining to sign the waiver portion of the form?
2 A: He did tell us that he – his attorney had advised him not to talk to us.
. . . .
3 Q: Well, did you read it to him?
4 A: I read him the waiver, yes.
5 Q: And then what happened after you read it to him? Did you ask him anything?
6 A: Well, he told me that he didn't think his attorney would want him talking to us, and I said to him, "With that in mind, would you still want to talk with us?"
7 Q: What did he say?
8 A: He said he sure – he said he appreciated the postal inspectors coming to visit with him, and then he started to tell us, back in October of 1990, that he'd wanted to talk to Anchorage Police Department regarding the homicide case at that time, and they refused to talk to him.

The court, however, noted that the combination of Cheely's acknowledgment, his refusal to sign the waiver form, and his explanation for wanting to do so: "my attorney does not want me to talk to you," needs to be taken into consideration in light of *Davis*: "We now reaffirm the district court's grant of Cheely's motion to suppress. The factual differences between the two cases are striking. Davis waived his right to counsel both orally and in writing. Cheely declined to waive his right to counsel either orally or in writing" (p. 1448). The differences between Davis and Cheely's case led the court to affirm the district court's ruling of granting Cheely's motion to suppress his statements, since he had invoked counsel.

Cheely is an early post-*Davis* case. The courts' interpretation that Cheely invoked counsel evolves over time with other rulings, particularly with certain types of invocations, as for example those that are formulated as inquiries. These types of invocations are observed often in the corpus, hence, the next cases will show the judges' differing perspectives on invocations for counsel that are formulated as inquiries to police, *United States* v. *Ogbuehi* (1994), or inquiries through third parties and/or for someone other than an attorney, *United States* v. *Posada–Rios* (1998). In these cases, the focus of the analysis is on the invocation rather than the interrogators' follow-ups or alleged attempts at clarification. The latter will be discussed further in the next section.

In *Ogbuehi*, also a Ninth Circuit ruling, the suspect inquires to the police about the need for counsel. These types of requests are particularly interesting because in the corpus courts often view them as falling short of invoking counsel or not requesting counsel at all. In this case, after the police read the suspect the Miranda form and informed him of his right to counsel, the suspect asked: "Do I need a lawyer?" or "Do you think I need a lawyer?" (p. 813). The police interrogator provided a fairly standard response: "that was a question that only he could answer," and "I can't answer that one for you." Another police interrogator noted: "You can go ahead and answer questions and . . . stop and ask for a lawyer later if you like" (p. 813). After these exchanges, the suspect signed the waiver form and waived his rights. The suspect contended that his statements should be suppressed because the police interrogators' responses to his question regarding counsel were improper. The court disagreed and referred to case law: "Looking at the words as 'ordinary people would understand them,' *De La Jara* . . ., Teague asked Deal for his opinion on the need for an attorney. Deal responded correctly. Teague asked for advice, not an attorney. Therefore, failing to suppress Teague's statements was not error" (p. 814). The court added that the police were also not required to clarify Ogbuehi's inquiry.

In *Posada–Rios*, the Fifth Circuit took a similar stance to the suspect's request: "might have to get a lawyer then, huh?" The suspect contends that her confession should not have been admitted and it was involuntary. As in *Ogbuehi*, the court disagreed, but with the added caveat that the court relied on the *Davis* ruling rather than: "Looking at the words as 'ordinary people' would." The Fifth Circuit ruled in *Posada–Rios* that: "A confession is voluntary if under all the circumstances it is the product of the defendant's free and rational choice" (p. 866). The court rejected the suspect's contention that her confession was involuntary due to a "false friend" interrogation, an interrogation in which the police create an atmosphere of sympathy and trust, which by law are not considered coercive. The suspect's argument that she invoked counsel through a third party and after when she commented to deputy Porter that she "might have to get a lawyer then, huh?" were also considered groundless. The suspect alleged that she asked her mother to contact an attorney (by name) and the police officers at the scene overheard such request. The court ruled that this type of invocation did not reach the *Davis* standard of unequivocalness, nor did it require clarification from the police interrogators. Asking for a parent, or another person, to make a request for counsel on behalf of the suspect or requesting to "make arrangements" to obtain counsel has been ruled in this case and others as not reaching *Davis*'s standard of unequivocalness.

The use of indirectly formulated invocations for counsel is also highlighted in numerous cases in the corpus. The next cases show how the courts have approached the indirect/direct invocation for counsel legal dilemma in light of *Davis*. The role of context and the type of invocation itself (e.g., formulated as "Can I" or "I think" as opposed to "Maybe I should" or as an inquiry) are central to the discussion. The case of *United States* v. *Salazar-Orellana* (2010), reviewed by the district court for the Northern District of Georgia, provides some interesting insights. In this case, the defendant, Salazar-Orellana, requested an attorney after being Mirandized, but not formally arrested. The police officer testified that the defendant then "asked me if I could get him a lawyer to come over and talk to him" (p. 2). The officer told the defendant that once he was arrested and booked into the county jail, he would receive a court-appointed attorney. This request did not cease the interrogation. At trial the interrogating officer testified that when the suspect made the request for counsel, he interpreted the request as whether he "was able to personally go and obtain a lawyer for Defendant at that minute" (p. 2). The court was not convinced of this interpretation. Judge Duffey, who delivered the opinion for the court, provided a linguistic justification for the suspect's unequivocal invocation for counsel:

> Thus, because Defendant's request for an attorney was unambiguous, all of Defendant's statements after his request for an attorney must be suppressed. If Defendant had said, for example, "Can you get me a glass of water?" the clear and unambiguous meaning

would be that Defendant wanted a glass of water and was asking for a glass of water. Officer McCollough, however, did not interpret Defendant's request to be a request for an attorney. (p. 5)

The judge's ruling takes a linguistic, usage-based, approach that stands out in these types of rulings. Although this is not a definition for unequivocal/unambiguous invocations for counsel, it provides a parameter of sorts from which to measure the effect of a speech act in context. This approach is adopted in other rulings in this section, although it is not supported by those that take a more literal definition of the unequivocalness standard, per *Davis*.

The case of *Wood v. Ercole* (2011) also shows how the courts often debate whether invocations for counsel have direct or indirect meaning/intent based on how they are formulated. In this Second Circuit case, the court reviews whether "I think I should get a lawyer" constitutes an unequivocal invocation for counsel and whether the admission of Wood's statements at trial constituted harmless error. On the observance of Fifth Amendment protections, the court ruled:

Wood clearly expressed his belief that, before making a videotaped statement, he should speak with an attorney. As Arnao testified, Wood "asked for a lawyer." Wood's language was unambiguous: he did not say "perhaps I should get a lawyer" or "maybe I need a lawyer." The statement "I think I should get a lawyer" evidences no internal debate whatsoever. Though Wood may have used a few extra words, we refuse to require criminal defendants to "speak with the discrimination of an Oxford don," . . . . (p. 91)

The court's opinion on the unequivocalness of an invocation for counsel and whether the court should grant a motion to suppress a suspect's statements is also addressed in *Wood* from two differing perspectives. First, the majority opinion delivered by Judge Lynch:

When a reviewing court has "grave doubt about whether a trial error . . . had 'substantial and injurious effect or influence in determining the jury's verdict,' that error is not harmless. And, the petitioner must win." . . . Here, where the wrongfully admitted evidence was an inculpatory statement by the defendant central to the prosecution's case, we can confidently say that the error was not harmless. (p. 99)

Second, the dissenting ruling argued by Judge Livingston. The judge's ruling is consonant with the majority's Fifth Amendment violation ruling, but it departs from the majority's assessment of harmless error. The judge argued that other evidence of Wood's guilt in the case, excluding his confession, was very strong and, hence, as the previous courts have ruled, the introduction of Wood's statements at trial was harmless error. This perspective is not uncommon in rulings dealing with the admissibility of statements obtained in violation of *Miranda*.

In *United States* v. *Hunter* (2013), the Seventh Circuit provides an extensive analysis of the unequivocalness standard post-*Davis*, specifically the role of "can," "should," and "maybe," in qualifying an invocation for counsel. In *Hunter* the suspect asked, "Can you call my attorney?" The majority opinion, led by Judge Tinder, referred to the Oxford dictionary for guidance:

> In the present case, the text of Hunter's statement is more definitive than the statements by the defendants in both Davis and Shabaz, and as a result, is readily distinguishable. As discussed in the previous section, Hunter used the decisive word "can" when he asked Detective Karzin to call his attorney. In contrast, the defendant in Davis used the indecisive words "maybe" and "should." "Maybe" means only "perhaps" or "possibly," while "should" is "used to . . . ask advice or suggestions . . . ." (p. 944)

The court added that context should also be considered in making a determination of equivocalness. In this case, the court ruled: "Following the Supreme Court's directive in *Smith*, we have often looked to prior context when determining whether a defendant unambiguously invoked his right to counsel" (p. 946). The court opined:

> we noted that Hunter used decisive language like the word "can" – as opposed to indecisive words like "should" – indicating that Hunter's request, "Can you call my attorney?" was inherently unambiguous. Hunter's request becomes particularly unambiguous when read in light of what had occurred previously. (p. 946)

The majority ruling is followed by Judge Tharp's dissenting opinion. The judge, who takes a more literal stance, argues that the majority rests its opinion on the suspect's use of the word "can." For the judge, it is not clear that the suspect's question is an unequivocal statement: "of one's desire to consult with an attorney ... Ability is not a synonym of desire; viewed in isolation, 'can I have a lawyer' does not necessarily mean the same thing as 'I want a lawyer.' It might, but that question cannot be answered simply by consulting a dictionary" (p. 950). Furthermore, the judge noted that although the cases cited in the majority's ruling support the use of "can" to invoke counsel, there are other cases that do not support this interpretation: "If, as the majority maintains, 'can I have a lawyer' is an unambiguous invocation of the right to counsel, how can so many courts – including this one – have found equivalent statements to be ambiguous?" (p. 950). The judge also disputes the majority's "talismanic" interpretation of the suspect's use of the term "attorney" and its interpretation of the context as overreaching in its analysis. The judge reminds the majority that: "the Supreme Court held in *Davis* that it is the suspect's burden to make an unambiguous assertion of the right to counsel: to avoid forcing police officers 'to make difficult judgment calls about whether the suspect in fact wants a lawyer even though he has not said so, with the threat of suppression if they guess wrong'" (p. 952). The divide between judges that deem indirectly formulated invocations for counsel as not rising to the standard of *Davis* and those that deem some indirect invocations as potentially having a direct meaning/intent in context also frames the discussion of whether it is good practice for police interrogators to use clarifications when in doubt of the intent of a suspect's invocation for counsel.

2.5.2 A Closer Look at Post-Davis Rulings: Invocations for Counsel, Police "Clarifications," and Voluntariness of Waiver

As the previous section highlights, the *Davis* ruling did not settle the question of what constitutes an unequivocal invocation for counsel. On the contrary, these cases added to the law's inconsistent treatment of these types of invocations. *Davis* has also not settled the question of the role of clarifications and/or police follow-ups after a suspect invokes counsel, particularly if done so equivocally. Prior to the *Davis* ruling, courts often encouraged police interrogators to attempt to clarify a suspect's equivocal or ambiguous invocations for counsel. In *Davis*, this encouragement is simply a suggestion (part of the concurrent ruling) rather than binding. In the rulings shortly after *Davis*, however, many judges still ascribed to the clarification standard and deemed it an appropriate measure when the equivocalness of a suspect's request for counsel is at question. This perspective, for the most part, changed with time. This section will examine the matter of police clarification post *Davis* as well as the courts' evolving perspective on police interrogators' follow-up responses to a suspect's invocation for counsel, particularly as it relates to the matter of voluntariness of waiver.

In *Lord* v. *Duckworth* (1994), the Seventh Circuit reviewed Lord's claim that police interrogators violated his right to counsel by continuing to question him after being Mirandized and having requested counsel. Lord contended that the police interrogators elicited a confession by promising him leniency. Excerpt 2.5 shows how during the defendant's interrogation one of the police interrogators (Vetter) suggested that he talk to the county prosecutor (George):

Excerpt 2.5

1 Mr. Vetter: . . . If I could get George down here right now and tell him the truth, if I could get him down here and you were willing to tell him the truth, and I could cut him a deal, would you . . . would you talk to him? If I could promise you . . . if I could promise you . . . if I could promise you he'd cut a deal with you, would you then talk and tell the truth? You better hurry. It's getting close to quitting time. It's 4:50. If I could get George down here and he'd cut you a deal.

After some turns of talk in which the defendant asked the interrogator questions regarding what would happen if he talked to the prosecutor, among other concerns, the defendant stated: "I don't know, I just need to talk to somebody" (p. 1218). The interrogation continued and the defendant provided a statement that included incriminating admissions. At some point after providing the statement, the exchange illustrated in Excerpt 2.6 transpired between the defendant and Officer Sibbitt.

The court addresses first whether the defendant's claim that his statement "I can't afford a lawyer but is there any way I can get one?" constituted a request for counsel, and second whether the police interrogation should have ceased after the defendant made this statement. The court ruled:

> In Davis, the Court clarified what constitutes an invocation of the right to counsel during a custodial interview. Unwilling to create a "third layer of prophylaxis to prevent police questioning when the suspect might want a lawyer," a majority of the Court held that "after a knowing and voluntary waiver of the Miranda rights, law enforcement officers may continue questioning until and unless the suspect clearly requests an attorney." . . . The Court acknowledged that its approach might disadvantage some suspects who, for whatever reason, cannot articulate clearly their desire for counsel, but found the requirement that a suspect knowingly and voluntarily waive his Miranda rights prior to questioning sufficient to protect the integrity of the interrogation process. (*Lord* v. *Duckworth*, 1994, p. 1220)

Considering *Davis*, the court determined that Lord's statement "I can't afford a lawyer but is there any way I can get one?" was a "clear request" for counsel, yet when examining case law on the matter of unequivocal invocations for counsel the court finds that Lord's statement was not sufficiently clear to meet case law standard. The police interrogators, hence, did not have to stop the interrogation. The court also notes that the context in which Lord's invocation was made also supports this interpretation. The court adds, however, that although per *Davis* the police interrogators were not obligated to seek clarification "it would have been entirely appropriate for them to clarify whether Lord in fact wanted a lawyer, either immediately or at trial" (p. 1221). This argument, also seen in other rulings, puts forth two potentially conflicting

Excerpt 2.6

1 Defendant: I can't afford a lawyer but is there any way I can get one?
2 Mr. Sibbitt: Yeah. (Nods head yes.)
3 Defendant: Is there anyway I can talk to some doctor or someone too?
4 Mr. Sibbitt: Well, that will be up to the . . . that will be up to the Court or up to your attorney.

notions: on the one hand, the invocation for counsel, per case law, is not sufficiently clear to cease an interrogation, on the other hand, the invocation may be a request for counsel and as such benefits from clarification.

Another point that is raised in *Lord* is the factual and psychological factors that may affect a suspect's invocation for counsel and/or providing a confession. In *Lord*, the suspect's age (he was thirty-five at the time), the fact that he was not deprived of his basic needs "and had experience with the criminal justice system by virtue of two prior felony convictions" (p. 1222) was integral in the court denying his petition for *habeas relief*. In the corpus, the role of a suspect's prior experience with the criminal justice system is a recurrent theme in determining whether a suspect should be able to navigate successfully custodial interrogation.

The police interrogators' use of follow-ups, including "clarifications," when a suspect has invoked counsel is the focus of the next court rulings. These cases will provide insights into the possible mindset of the police interrogators, the effect their training in police interrogation and experience with the law has on their follow-up responses to suspects' invocations for counsel, and the courts' perspective on police interrogators' linguistic behavior.

In *United States* v. *Feyler* (1999), a United States District Court of Maine ruling, the issue at hand is whether the defendant (Feyler) voluntarily waived his rights and confessed. As part of the legal examination of Feyler's case, the court also examined whether he was invoking his right to counsel when he asked the law enforcement agent conducting the interrogation "what was the right thing to do?" and whether the agent violated that right by responding that "he should tell the truth." The defendant asked several questions expressing concern about his circumstances and also about whether his cooperation would assist him to which the interrogator responded that "it always helps to tell the truth" (p. 57).

In *Feyler*, the court ruled that the defendant waived his rights after being properly Mirandized and his statements were voluntary. Feyler's question to the interrogator was also ruled equivocal and the police interrogator was in no obligation to clarify the request, albeit it is noted that often it is good police practice to do so when in doubt. The court also stressed that the defendant was an adult and experienced with the criminal justice system, due to his prior arrests, and was not coerced. The court opined that the police interrogator's statement that "the right thing is always to tell the truth" (p. 58), was not psychological coercion, as the defendant contends, and the defendant's stress or anxiety "was not greater than that which is experienced by suspects generally when considering their post-arrest alternatives" (p. 60). One important point in the court's argument is the notion that the right not to talk, because it may put the suspect/defendant at a disadvantage, is so "transparently self-evident that constitutional and legal protections assure him the right not to say anything" (*United States* v. *Feyler*, 1999, footnote 5, p. 61). In essence, barring blatant police coercion or psychological factors that interfere with a suspect's psyche, a suspect should know the downfalls of "telling the truth" without first consulting with counsel and/or the prosecutor.

But what happens when police interrogators are candid about their use of persuasive interrogation tactics? The next case examines the use of pressure tactics, and their potential effect, on a suspect's custodial interrogation. In *Soffar* v. *Cockrell* (2002), the Fifth Circuit reviewed the actions of the police interrogator, Clawson, who provided what the court described as a candid account of his private conversations with the petitioner, Soffar. Soffar's interrogations, for reasons that befuddle the court, were not video or audio taped. The legal and factual aspects of the case were evaluated based on the police interrogator's testimony.

According to the police interrogator, Soffar made the following statements: he asked whether he should get an attorney, how he could get one, and how long it would take to have an attorney appointed. The police interrogator explained in the *habeas* proceedings that when he interrogated Soffar he felt pressure from the Houston detectives not to screw up and "derail their investigation" by having their only solid lead ask for counsel, and that he suspected that the detectives did not want him to interfere in their investigation. He added that the pressure he felt led him to take steps to keep Max talking instead of seeking to slow things down for him so that he could understand what was happening. He also noted that he knew Soffar could not afford private counsel and was aware of Houston's seventy-two-hour rule under which a suspect had to be either charged or released within seventy-two hours of arrest. Getting "Max to talk," so Soffar could "follow his lead" was the interrogator's main objective. Despite the interrogator's candid account of his interactions with Soffar, the court focused on Soffar's statements:

> Courts have rejected each and every one of these questions as procedural, and too equivocal to constitute a clear invocation of the right to counsel. First, courts have rejected as ambiguous statements asking for advice on whether or not to obtain an attorney ... Second, a suspect's question about how to obtain an attorney does not constitute an unambiguous assertion of his right ... Third, a suspect's inquiry into how long it would take to get an attorney is not a clear invocation. (p. 595)

The court ruled that Soffar's questions did not rise to the level of an unambiguous invocation of his right to counsel under *Davis*. Of note, the police interrogator's follow-ups when interrogating Soffar were not addressed in the majority opinion. They are addressed in detail in the dissenting opinion.

The dissenting opinion, led by Judge DeMoss, highlights the effect and significance of the police interrogator's follow-up responses. Excerpt 2.7 shows two of the questions for which the judge provided commentary about the "essence" of the right to counsel:

Excerpt 2.7

1 Question No. 1:
2 Soffar asked: "Should I get an attorney or talk to the detective?"
3 Clawson answered: "If [you were] involved in the crime, you should tell the detective [you were] in it; otherwise [you] should get a lawyer."
4 Commentary:

There is nothing in Miranda itself, nor in any of its progeny, which draws any distinction between guilty and innocent suspects as far as being entitled to the Miranda protections. The only requirement for the protections contemplated by Miranda is that the suspect be "in police custody," which Soffar clearly was in this case. Clawson's answer to this question is completely inaccurate, inappropriate, and inconsistent with his obligations under Miranda. I would suggest that a reasonable answer by a reasonable police officer would be:

> You have a constitutional right to have a lawyer present to help you during this interrogation whether you are guilty or innocent. On the other hand, you may talk to the police without a lawyer if you so choose. The choice is up to you and I can't make that choice for you; but if you want a lawyer, you need to clearly say so as otherwise the police may assume you don't want a lawyer.

5 Question No. 2:
6 Soffar asked: How do I get a lawyer?
7 Clawson answered: Can you afford to hire a lawyer on your own?
8 Commentary:

This answer is directly contrary to the language and spirit of Miranda. Clawson knew that Soffar didn't have enough money to hire his own lawyer when he gave this answer and, in my view, Clawson gave this answer not to inform Soffar but to put Soffar in a position of dependency as he had been as an undercover informant for Clawson. Therefore, Clawson's answer is totally non-responsive to the question asked by Soffar. In my view, a reasonable answer by a reasonable police officer would have been:

> You can get a lawyer by hiring one of your own choice and agreeing to pay that lawyer's fees and expenses yourself. If you don't have enough money to pay for your own lawyer, you can sign an affidavit which says that; and the court will then appoint a lawyer to help you and the fees and expenses of this appointed lawyer will be paid for by the state.

These suggested responses provide information about the right to counsel to suspects in custody. The added content may be of assistance to custodial suspects. Yet, as noted previously, police interrogators, by law, are not required to provide further information than the reading of the Miranda rights themselves. This is also the minimum that is done in practice in our corpus: what the law requires.

The dissenting opinion also included the judge's commentary on what would be appropriate responses to Soffar's questions, such as the time it may take to get a court appointed attorney (with "It could take as little as a day or as long as a month" (p. 605), as an inappropriate and inaccurate response), and, in response to Soffar's question: "So you are saying that I have to deal with this on my own?" (p. 606), reiterating that he had a constitutional right to an attorney and did not need to deal with "it" on his own.

In addition to addressing the police interrogator's behavior and follow-up responses to Soffar's questions and requests, the dissenting opinion comments on the matter of ambiguity raised in the majority's opinion: "First, from a pure language and grammar standpoint, there is nothing 'ambiguous' at all about Soffar's questions. They are each clear, unequivocable requests for information relevant and material to Soffar making an intelligent and informed decision as to his desire for counsel" (p. 606). The dissenting opinion also includes a lengthy evaluation of the law applied in this case and strongly disagrees with the majority's assessment of the interactions between Soffar and the police interrogator. This concern over the police interrogator's discursive behavior during custodial interrogation takes a different turn in a court ruling of the United States District Court, South Dakota, *United States* v. *Smith* (2008).

In *Smith*, the defendant (Smith) was given his Miranda rights and he initiated each of the rights on the form, including signing the waiver portion of the form. He was placed in jail overnight and was not questioned. The next day, government agents in charge of interrogating the defendant introduced themselves. The defendant follows up by stating: "Can I get a lawyer here?" to which one of the agents responded: "Sure you can" (p. 3) and proceeded to tell the defendant that they (interrogators/agents) just wanted to talk to him. The defendant was advised again of his Miranda rights, he signed the waiver of rights form, and was interrogated. During the interrogation he provided incriminating statements, while maintaining his innocence. The issue at hand is whether the defendant's statements should be suppressed, because he invoked his right to counsel unequivocally. The court sided with the defendant ruling that the defendant had made "a sufficiently clear and unequivocal request to invoke his Miranda right to counsel" (p. 6) and all questioning needed to cease.

The court cited numerous case law in which invocations like the defendant's "Can I get a lawyer here?" had been ruled as unequivocal invocations for counsel. The court also stressed in its ruling the troubling behavior of one of the interrogators (Ramirez) after the defendant had invoked counsel:

> Although not dispositive to the Court's decision, the conduct of Ramirez, after Defendant requested counsel, is troubling. Ramirez illusively made statements, not

> to discern Defendant's actual intent, but to persuade him not to invoke his right to counsel and to impel him to give up that right. Indeed, Ramirez's responses to Defendant's request for counsel look more like they were designed to coax Defendant into submitting to an interview than to clarify that request. By his own admission, Ramirez was attempting to obtain incriminating statements from Defendant that could later be used in court against Defendant. Ramirez misleadingly explained the potential effects of invoking the right to counsel, seemingly confused the issue, purposefully downplayed and minimized what he and Clifford wanted to do and successfully muddied Defendant's perception of the availability of his rights. Ramirez's supposed "clarifying" comments appear to be a contrived attempt to get around the Miranda/Edwards rule and to keep the interview alive in hopes of getting a confession from Defendant. (p. 9)

The court proceeds to impeach the interrogator for using "biographical questions" (p. 10) in order to get around the defendant's Miranda rights. A tactic deemed by the court as "close to running afoul of Miranda" (p. 10). The use of biographical questions has been at the center of numerous cases, since this stage of the interrogation can be Miranda-exempt (see *Rhode Island* v. *Innis* (1980)). The issue is how and when biographical questions are used. In this case, the court deemed the interrogators' use of biographical questions as part of a broader tactic to dissuade the defendant from invoking his right to counsel.

The final case in this section is *Sessoms* v. *Runnels* (2012). This Ninth Circuit case also deals with a suspect's invocation for counsel and the police interrogators' use of follow-up responses. The case makes an important distinction in the law: pre waiver versus post waiver invocations. The former has been deemed *Davis*-exempt, since *Davis* does not address invocations for counsel that are made prior to the reading of Miranda rights. Of note, the applicability of *Davis* in pre-waiver cases has been considered in other cases (see Gee 2009 for a discussion of applicable case law).

In *Sessoms*, the petitioner, who was a nineteen-year-old black man, turned himself into the local police. His father told his son prior to turning into the police that he "must ask for a lawyer before talking to the police" (p. 1056). Sessoms followed his father's advice when the police interrogators entered the room, as illustrated in Excerpt 2.8:

Excerpt 2.8

1 Sessoms: There wouldn't be any possible way that I could have a – a lawyer present while we do this?
2 [Detective]: Well, uh, what I'll do is, um.
3 Sessoms: Yeah, that's what my dad asked me to ask you guys . . . uh, give me a lawyer.

The police interrogators did not cease the interrogation and convinced the defendant "that the only way to tell his side of the story was to speak to them without an attorney" (p. 1056). Sessoms stated that he was concerned that the police interrogators would "end up switching your words afterwards" (p. 1057), to which Woods, one of the interrogators, responded that he had no intention of playing any "switch games" (p. 1057) and would even tape record the conversation to allay Sessoms' fears. Additionally, Wood mentioned that they wanted to "get his version of it" (p. 1057) and most attorneys advise against making statements to police. The defendant agreed to talk to the police interrogators and provided incriminating statements.

The circuit court reviewed the case *de novo*. The court relied on *Miranda* and *Edwards* for their analysis of the defendant's interactions with the police interrogators. The court argued that "Miranda recognized that overzealous police practices during a custodial interrogation create the potential for compulsion in violation of the Fifth Amendment . . . Indeed, some of the tactics of which *Miranda* warns were employed by the interrogators in this case" (p. 1059). The court reminds of the spirit of *Miranda* protections against police interrogators' use of psychological ploys, in the form of follow-ups, to exploit a suspect's vulnerabilities. The court also stressed that all interrogation must cease after a suspect invokes counsel unless a suspect reinitiates talk with police (per *Edwards*).

Reviewing the applicability of *Davis* to this case, the court recognized the principle raised in *Davis* that equivocal or ambiguous invocations for counsel do not require cessation of custodial interrogation. The court rules that this principle, however, does not apply to Sessoms' invocation for counsel: "*Davis* clearly limits its holding to statements made after a suspect has waived his Miranda rights" (p. 1061). Sessoms made his request for counsel prior to being read his Miranda rights. The court also addressed the lower (state) court's argument that the Court's ruling in *Berghuis* v. *Thompkins* (2010) applied to Sessoms' invocation for counsel: "Relying on Davis, the Court held that an invocation of the right to remain silent, like the right to counsel, must be unambiguous" (p. 1061). In *Sessoms*' case, the Ninth Circuit rejected the applicability of *Davis*. The court argued that for *Davis* to attach, the suspect must have been read his Miranda rights: "Sessoms requested an attorney before receiving a clear and complete statement of his rights and, therefore, knowledge of his rights cannot be ascribed to him. In this circumstance, the clear invocation rule simply should not have been applied" (p. 1062). The court ruled that a broad interpretation of the defendant's invocation for counsel, as was often the standard prior to *Davis*, was needed.

The dissenting opinion, led by Judge Murguia, did not support the court's assessment of the inapplicability of *Davis* in this case or the court's determination that the defendant's invocation for counsel was unequivocal. In the dissent, the court raised the question of whether the defendant was asking for counsel or whether the defendant was inquiring about the possibility of having legal representation, two diametrically different requests whose interpreted intended effect after *Davis* is often determined by the police interrogator's assessment of a suspect's invocation for counsel rather than by a broad interpretation of a defendant's invocation.

2.5.3 Invocations for Counsel with Added "Layers": Written versus Oral Waivers

The next cases deal with the legal standing of invocations for counsel that are asserted in writing, such as in the waiver of rights form or as a letter from an attorney. Of note, these cases are not common in the corpus. The court's assessment of these invocations for counsel, however, provide additional insights into the judiciary's view of what constitutes a suspect's unequivocal invocation for counsel, including whether written assertions meet the standard of unequivocalness, per *Davis*, that is sufficient to require cessation of a custodial interrogation.

In *United States* v. *Brown* (2002), a Tenth Circuit ruling, a suspect's Miranda advisement and waiver form raises questions about the unequivocalness of an invocation for counsel. In this case, the defendant (Brown) who was in custody with Tribal Police, responded "yes" when asked if he would answer questions without a lawyer present, but also answered yes when asked "if he wanted a lawyer" and "if he wanted to talk to a lawyer." The questions in the Miranda advisement and waiver form, as cited in the case footnotes, are shown in Excerpt 2.9. Of note, the defendant did not invoke counsel orally, as other cases discussed in prior sections.

The defendant concedes on appeal "that his responses to the Miranda warnings were not clear and unambiguous" (p. 3), he nonetheless argues that his statements to Agent Hammergren should have been suppressed, contending

Excerpt 2.9

The form provided in pertinent part as follows:

1 Keeping your rights in mind, do you wish to answer questions now without a lawyer present? Yes______ No______
2 Do you want a lawyer? Yes______ No______
3 Do you want to talk to a lawyer? Yes______ No______

the police should have made an effort to clarify his responses. The court examined the merits of the defendant's motion to suppress statements through the lens of the *Davis* ruling: "Although the Court in Davis observed that 'when a suspect makes an ambiguous or equivocal statement it will often be good police practice for the interviewing officers to clarify whether or not he actually wants an attorney,' the Court declined 'to adopt a rule requiring officers to ask clarifying questions'" (p. 4). The court agreed that it would have been desirable for the police officer to clarify the defendant's responses to the questions in the Miranda form. Yet, the court restates the Court's ruling regarding clarifying questions after an equivocal/ambiguous request for counsel. The court concluded that the defendant's responses in the Miranda form were ambiguous, hence the defendant did not invoke counsel and the police interrogator was not required to cease questioning.

In another Tenth Circuit decision, *United States* v. *Santistevan* (2012), the court reviewed whether the defendant's (Santistevan's) handing of a letter from an attorney to an agent constitutes an unequivocal invocation of the right to counsel. The case examines whether there were any *Edwards* bright-line rule violations and whether the defendant's invocation for counsel, per *Davis*, was unequivocal.

The agent received a phone call from a public defender, Katherine Spengler, who informed the agent that she represented Santistevan. The agent noted that he intended to visit and ask Santistevan "if he wanted to make any statements or answer my questions" (p. 1291). The attorney informed the agent that she had given Santistevan a letter to give to the agent if he went to the jail. When the agent visited Santistevan, he handed him the attorney's letter (it was not entered into evidence): "My name is Katherine Spengler. We spoke last week. I have been in touch with Sue Fisher from the Federal Public Defender's Office. At this point, Mr. Santistevan does not wish to speak with you without counsel. However, he is not foreclosing that option in the future" (p. 1291). The agent after reading the letter initiated the following exchanges noted in Excerpt 2.10:

Excerpt 2.10

1 Agent: You have been advised by an attorney not to talk to me today, but it's totally up to you on whether you want to talk to me or not. Do you want to come back to my office and answer questions about these robberies?
2 Mr. Santistevan: Yes.
3 Agent: Are you sure, without a lawyer present?
4 Mr. Santistevan: Yes, I want to.

On review *de novo*, the court ruled on whether the agent violated Santistevan's request for counsel by revisiting the Court's *Edwards* ruling in *Davis*:

> The Court explained that "this is an objective inquiry[;]" a suspect "must articulate his desire to have counsel present sufficiently clearly that a reasonable police officer in the circumstances would understand the statement to be a request for an attorney." ... Absent this "level of clarity, Edwards does not require that the officers stop questioning the suspect." ... However, when the statement is clear, all questioning must stop; this bright-line rule "preserve[s] the integrity of an accused's choice to communicate with police only through counsel, by preventing police from badgering a defendant into waiving his previously asserted Miranda rights." (*United States* v. *Santistevan*, 2012, p. 1292)

The court concluded that Santistevan invoked the right to counsel, when he handed the letter drafted by his attorney to the agent. The court also made some insightful remarks about their assessment of the validity of the claim that the defendant changed his mind about talking to the agents, hence making his request for counsel through the attorney's letter "at best" equivocal:

> we note that it would be unfair to penalize Mr. Santistevan for changing his mind about speaking with the agent. It is well settled that a defendant, who has previously invoked the right to counsel, may change his mind and speak with police so long as the defendant "(a) initiated further discussions with the police, and (b) knowingly and intelligently waived the right he had invoked." ... If a defendant can change his mind to speak with police, it is only fair to allow him to do the opposite. (p. 1294)

The dissenting opinion of Judge Tymkovich reverts to classic *Davis* posture in that the defendant needed to do more to unequivocally invoke his Miranda rights: "Although attorneys generally speak for their clients, they do not necessarily do so in this context, and for sound reasons. Our justice system has no interest in establishing unnecessary barriers to cooperation with and confession to the police" (p. 1297). The judge further argued that the district court's analysis does not sufficiently address whether Santistevan "articulate[d] his desire to have counsel present sufficiently clearly that a reasonable police officer in the circumstances would understand the statement to be a request for an attorney" (p. 1299). The judge added that the ruling "reiterates the judiciary's conflicting views on acceptable police conduct in light of an 'ambiguous/equivocal' invocation for counsel" (p. 1300). The judge concluded that Santistevan did not unequivocally invoke counsel and the police interrogator could "reasonably question whether the act of handing over the letter in response to a request to see the letter is meant to invoke the right to counsel" (p. 1300). The judge holds that per *Davis* and *Edwards*, the police did not have to cease questioning and the suppression order should be reversed.

Santistevan's case illustrates the dissonance that persists since *Miranda*, laying bare the problems that arise when notions such as equivocalness/

ambiguity are not defined and police interrogators are left with the task to "define" it in practice. When police interrogators make an assessment as to whether a suspect has invoked counsel, unequivocally, a judgment call that defines the nature of an invocation for counsel has been made. This judgment call will remain unless the case is appealed and the court(s) reviewing the case agree with the police's assessment (per *Davis*) or take a different yet, potentially, less common perspective. The judge(s) reviewing the case will also play an important role in determining whether the police's interpretation of a suspect's invocation for counsel is reasonable while not in conflict with *Davis*. For the suspects whose cases are appealed, the outcome appears to be tilted to accept the police interrogators' assessment, per *Davis*, with the exception of judges who favor broader interpretations or review fairly egregious cases of police misconduct.

2.5.4 Invocations for Counsel and L2 Speakers of English

There are cases in the corpus, albeit a small number, that deal with suspects who are not native speakers of English. In these cases, as will be discussed in more detail in Chapters 4 and 6, the police interrogators often decide the level of proficiency of the defendant as well as their own level of proficiency to conduct linguistic mediation, if needed. The Ninth Circuit provides some perspective in *United States* v. *Garibay* (1998):

> We are troubled by the circumstances surrounding Garibay's alleged waiver. It is hard for us to discern any justification for the agents' failure to ask Garibay whether he preferred Spanish or English and their failure to seek the assistance of bilingual agents in questioning Garibay . . . The right to remain silent and the right to have counsel present during questioning are indispensable to the protection of the Fifth Amendment privilege against self-incrimination. Written waivers coupled with oral recitations help ensure that the necessary procedures are in place to protect such constitutional rights which all officials are sworn to uphold. In the circumstances of Garibay's custodial interrogation, we find that the steps taken to protect these essential rights were deficient. (p. 540)

The lack of clear and consistent standards for assessing L2 speakers' ability to comprehend Miranda rights, the admissibility of statements taken from L2 speakers, and the lack of a requirement for suspects to receive the assistance of a certified/professional interpreter during custodial interrogation, as the cases in this section will show, raise a number of linguistic, legal, and potentially ethical questions.

The first of two cases analyzed is *United States* v. *Alamilla-Hernandez* (2009). The United States District Court of Nebraska conducted a *de novo* review of the record, including revisiting whether the defendant's, Alamilla-Hernandez's, statements should have been suppressed. At the time of the defendant's arrest for drug-related charges, the arresting officers realized

Excerpt 2.11

1 Agent Slater: You have the right to talk to a lawyer for advice before we ask you any questions and to have a lawyer with you during questioning. Do you understand?
2 Defendant: Yes.
3 Agent Slater: If you cannot afford a lawyer, one will be appointed for you before any questioning if you wish.
4 Defendant: I can't afford an attorney.
5 Agent Slater: If you are hungry, lunch will be provided for you.
6 Defendant: I am hungry.
7 Agent Slater: Lunch is over there.

that no Spanish-speaking officer was present to communicate with the suspect. The next day Agent Slater went to the jail to talk to the suspect. According to the record, Agent Slater, who was a Special Agent with the Drug Enforcement Agency (DEA), had completed a six-month Spanish language training course and had worked in Columbia, South America, for two years. Agent Slater testified that he was not fluent in Spanish, but had working knowledge of the language. He also noted that he and Alamilla-Hernandez spoke different dialects of Spanish, but were still able to communicate with each other. Per the agent's testimony, he stated that he read the defendant the Miranda rights in Spanish. The exchange illustrated in Excerpt 2.11 ensued.

The agent testified that the suspect seemed to follow the reading of the rights and understood them. Of note, the agent also testified that one of the other police officers had informed him that the suspect could not read or write. The agent did not follow-up on this matter with the suspect. Furthermore, the interrogation was not transcribed or recorded. Regarding the motion to suppress the defendant's statements, the court ruled:

> The court finds that under the circumstances presented in this case, the defendant made a clear and unambiguous request for a lawyer when he responded, "I cannot afford an attorney" to the officer's statement that if he could not afford an attorney, one would be appointed for him ... The court finds that Agent Slater's testimony that he understood Alamilla-Hernandez's statement to merely be an expression of his financial status borders on disingenuous. In the context of the conversation, there would be no reason for Alamilla-Hernandez to make such a statement if not to express a desire for representation. Alamilla-Hernandez would not have told Agent Slater that he could not afford an attorney, which is the condition precedent required for appointment of an attorney, had he not wanted an attorney. (p. 1010)

Addressing *Davis*, the court argued that a reasonable police officer would have understood the defendant's statement "I cannot afford an attorney," as an unequivocal invocation for counsel. The court adds that the defendant did not knowingly and voluntarily waive the right to counsel and the agent's continued interrogation of the defendant was improper. The court, however, did not address whether the agent who conducted the interrogation had the expertise to determine the defendant's linguistic proficiency and level of comprehension of the Miranda warnings. This broader issue which would transcend one "egregious" case, as with other matters relating to Miranda waivers, seems to be unexplored by the courts.

The next case also shows what seems to be an egregious violation of a suspect's right to counsel, but with the added caveat that an expert witness provided testimony aimed at establishing the suspect's understanding of the Miranda rights. In *United States* v. *Al-Saimari* (2013), the United States District Court of Utah reviewed the defendant's motion to suppress statements provided during custodial interrogation. At the time of the defendant's arrest, the agent conducting the interrogation began questioning him. Excerpt 2.12, which was recorded, shows the agent reading the defendant his Miranda rights:

Excerpt 2.12

1 Agent Anderson: Okay, Hani. I've got some questions for you, okay, but I've got to – I've got to advise you of your Miranda rights. Okay? Are you familiar with what those are?
2 Mr. Al-Saimari: No (inaudible).
3 Agent Anderson: Not really? What – what they are is you have rights here –
4 Mr. Al-Saimari: Uh-huh.
5 Agent Anderson: In America. We have to read these to you. These are your rights as a – as a person here, okay, before we can talk to you and interact with you. Okay?
6 Mr. Al-Saimari: Okay.
. . .
7 Agent Anderson: Now, Hani, you have the right to remain silent. Anything you say can and will be used against you in a court of law. You have the right to talk to a lawyer and have him present with you while you're being questioned. If you can't afford to hire an attorney, one will be appointed to represent you before any questioning, if you wish. You – you can decide at any time to exercise these rights and not answer any questions or make any statements. Do you understand these rights I've explained to you?
(No audible response)
8 Agent Anderson: Having these rights in mind, do you wish to talk to me today about what's going on?
9 Mr. Al-Saimari: I don't know, you know. I'm just surprised, you know.
10 Agent Anderson: You're just surprised?

(cont.)

11 Mr. Al-Saimari: Yeah.
12 Agent Anderson: Okay. I – I do need kind of a definite answer of a yes or a no, whether I can ask you questions and interact with you, because you do have these rights. So –
13 Mr. Al-Saimari: Okay.
14 Agent Anderson: – is it okay if I talk to you today?
15 Mr. Al-Saimari: Okay.
16 Agent Anderson: You're okay with that?
17 Mr. Al-Saimari: Yeah.
18 Agent Anderson: Okay.
19 Mr. Al-Saimari: Sure.

After the exchange, the agent asked the defendant several questions. The defendant provided incriminating statements that he sought to suppress on the grounds that he did not voluntarily or knowingly waive his Miranda rights.

The court held an evidentiary hearing that provides some important insights about law enforcements' perspective on L2 speaker proficiency and understanding. The agent testified that "he has previously come into contact with suspects who do not speak English as a first language and that he believes he is able to tell whether these people understand him" (p. 1288). In terms of the defendant's understanding of the Miranda warnings, the agent stated "that Mr. Al–Saimari could understand him because he did not observe any blank stares or other indications of confusion" (p. 1288). The agent's testimony is in contrast with the testimony of a linguistic expert (Professor William Gregory Eggington). The expert witness testified that based on his language proficiency tests, the Oral Proficiency Interview and the Elicited Oral Response with Automatic Speech Recognition exam, "Mr. Al–Saimari has 'survival language proficiency,' meaning that Mr. Al–Saimari can only understand simple sentences in English involving basic necessities, and not complex ideas or concepts" (p. 1288). The expert also provided testimony that is consistent with other research on L2 speaker's understanding of Miranda rights and linguistic proficiency in legal settings: "many second language learners who have low proficiency will 'fake comprehension' in conversations, even when they do not understand what they are hearing . . . One indicator of fake comprehension in a speaker with low proficiency is the use of responses such as 'yes, uh-huh, okay'" (p. 1288). These were most of the defendant's responses to the agent's queries.

The court's ruling shows a consideration of the expert's and agent's testimonies, as well as a concern not to place "an undue burden on police officers who are attempting to perform their jobs while respecting a suspect's constitutional rights" (p. 1292). The court acknowledged the difficulties police officers sometimes face when attempting to determine whether suspects have knowingly waived their rights. The court concludes:

> the court does not believe that its decision requires that police officers become linguistic experts. Instead, the Fifth Amendment merely demands that an officer ask follow-up questions as necessary to establish a knowing and voluntary waiver when, as was the case with Mr. Al–Saimari, a suspect expresses or manifests confusion, or fails to state affirmatively that he understands the Miranda warnings. An officer cannot simply obtain a suspect's consent to speak, but must adequately determine that a suspect understands that he has the right not to speak. Without this assurance, the reading of a suspect's Miranda warnings is a mere formality that does not adequately protect the person's constitutional right against self incrimination. (p. 1292)

The cases in this section show fairly egregious behavior from the police interrogators, but there are instances in the corpus in which the suspects' L2 comprehension is at question, linguistically, but not legally. It does not raise to a standard the courts would find problematic and, thus, interfering with a suspect's ability to invoke Miranda rights.

The next chapters will delve further into the relationship between common interrogation techniques used in the United States and the, at times, conflicting applications of the law in the corpus. A comprehensive linguistic and statistical analysis of the variables that make up the rulings in the corpus will also provide further insights into the effect of pre- and post-*Davis* rulings on judges' assessments of custodial interrogation and suspects' invocations for counsel. The analysis of the linguistic and strategic features of police interrogation will also be essential to understanding how the law, and its unsettled *Miranda* debate, facilitates the invocation game of police interrogation.

3 Police Interrogation in the United States: From the Reid Technique to the High-Value Detainee Interrogation Group Report

[T]he very fact of custodial interrogation exacts a heavy toll on individual liberty and trades on the weakness of individuals.

(Chief Justice Warren, *Miranda* v. *Arizona*, 1966)

The history of police interviewing in the United States, as in other countries, has a checkered past that includes physical coercion. This was called the "third degree" which was endemic in early twentieth-century policing. It consisted of literally beating confessions out of suspects if they were not deemed cooperative. This brutal approach is inhumane and often lead to involuntary and false confessions. With time the "third degree" became a less commonly adopted procedure, but incidences of this type of practice were still reported into the early 1960s. The Commission on Civil Rights, for example, found that in 1961 some police officers still engaged in the practice of using physical coercion to obtain a confession. Other instances of police brutality were also reported during this time, such as in *People* v. *Portelli* (1965).

Since the 1960s, behavioral analysis approaches to police interviewing, such as the Reid interrogation technique, have been adopted in United States policing. This approach was a response to the "third degree" and was based on the general notion that it is best to use "one's wits than one's wrists" (*Miranda* v. *Arizona*, 1966). At close examination behavioral analysis approaches, such as the Reid technique, place a premium on obtaining statements from suspects, albeit not through physical force but through psychological trickery, deception, and/or pressure. All of which, to an extent, are legally acceptable in the United States.

Regarding its popularity, the Reid technique appears to be widely used in United States police stations, yet its actual use is not well understood. Among self-reported studies with police investigators, the use of the Reid technique appears to be prevalent (Cleary & Warner, 2016). In addition to Reid, there are rapport and cognitive-based techniques currently in use by police and law enforcement agencies in the United States, such as the Federal Bureau of

Investigation (FBI), United States Drug Enforcement Administration (DEA), and military branches of the United States Armed Forces. Although, as with the Reid technique, it is unknown how often these agencies and the military use rapport-based interviewing. The latter interviewing style is espoused as being part of interviewing reforms in federal law enforcement agencies to reduce coercion and rates of false confessions (see Meissner et al., 2017).

The corpus shares the legal requirement of suspects being read their Miranda rights prior to being subject to any type of custodial interrogation method. No significant differences were observed in the corpus between police or other law enforcement agencies in the invocation of rights stage of an interrogation. In the corpus, regardless of the type of interrogator, the reading of the rights stage is often tackled as a deterrence to interrogation (see also Mason 2020, 2016, 2013), which opens the door to a variety of techniques and approaches used by law enforcement to obtain statements from suspects. Some of the techniques are more enlightened than others, but when applied to United States custodial settings, they are all moored in the legal framework of Miranda guarantees.

Thus, it is worth discussing broadly the methods applied by law enforcement and the military to interrogate custodial suspects and evaluate how these methods may fit with the Miranda rights. To accomplish this task, the next sections will discuss the Reid technique and the operational mandate of the High-Value Detainee Interrogation Group (HIG) (herein the HIG Report, 2016). Of note, while the HIG was developed to collect human intelligence in a counter-terrorism context (HUMINT), the HIG has expanded to achieve a "broader understanding of effective interviewing and interrogation methods – including those that occur in criminal, military, and intelligence settings" (Meissner et al., 2017, p. 446). As Meissner et al. (2017) note criminal and counter intelligence contexts diverge with respect to their purpose: to obtain a confession as evidence for criminal prosecution as opposed to obtain information about the past, present, or future related to a national security investigation. They add, however, that the basic processes that facilitate cooperation and elicitation are shared by both contexts, including the interrogation methods applied by professionals in the field. Hence, how police investigators approach the Miranda rights stage of the interrogation across the corpus, and potentially across interviewing styles, will provide insights into the possible connection between the law and how interviewing styles are used and implemented in the United States.

3.1 The Reid Technique of Interrogation: A Look at the "Manuals"

In the landmark case *Miranda* v. *Arizona* (1966), the justices refer to "the manuals." These manuals were used in the 1960s to train officers in police interrogation techniques. As Justice Warren, who delivered the majority opinion in *Miranda*, states:

It should be noted that these texts professedly present the most enlightened and effective means presently used to obtain statements through custodial interrogation. By considering these texts and other data, it is possible to describe procedures observed and noted around the country. (p. 449)

Justice Warren was skeptical of the training "manuals" and provided a lengthy discussion of the now Reid technique in his *Miranda* opinion. Hence, portions of his and other justices' opinions will be incorporated in the chapter's discussion of the Reid technique of interrogation. This will situate the Court's view on police interrogation and invocation of rights within the often chosen mode of interrogation in the United States, past and present.

The Reid technique was developed in the 1950s by John E. Reid, a psychologist, polygraph expert, and former Chicago police officer, who reformed police interrogation practices in light of the Wickersham Commission (see Drizin and Reich, 2004). Since its inception, training in the Reid technique has been commercially available to government, law enforcement, and, subsequently, business entities. The technique has also received some support in Court rulings. These mentions are part of Reid's marketing strategy. According to Joseph Buckley, president of John E. Reid and Associates, Inc. (2012), the Court recognized the Reid technique in *Stansbury* v. *California* (1994) and in *Missouri* v. *Seibert* (2004).[1] Buckley notes that these cases referenced the Reid technique as an example of proper law enforcement interrogation training: "Courts throughout the country have recognized The Reid Technique as the leading interview and interrogation approach used today in both the law enforcement and business communities" (Buckley 2012, p. 2).

The Reid technique consists of three phases: factual analysis, the investigative interview, and the interrogation. The factual analysis stage consists of reviewing the case facts and evidence. This stage is similar to what Walton (2003) describes as the "preparatory" interview stage. During the "preparatory" stage police officers formulate questions to ask the suspect. These questions often serve to confirm the police officers' suspicions. The latter may arise during the evidence gathering stage of an investigation, which often includes information obtained during the questioning of witnesses and/or alleged victims of a crime (see Mason, 2016).

In the investigative interview stage of Reid, also referred to as the Behavior Analysis Interview, police officers are trained to assess the "guilt" of suspects by analyzing their verbal and nonverbal responses. At the onset of the interview, as noted in the John E. Reid & Associates website:[2] "the investigator must be sure to comply with all legal requirements, such as the appropriate

[1] https://reid.com/about#:~:text=About-,John%20E.,question%20subjects%20in%20the%20world.

[2] https://reid.com/resources/investigator-tips/a-description-of-the-reid-technique.

advisement of rights. It is imperative that throughout the interview, the investigator maintains an objective, neutral, fact-finding demeanor" (Reid, 2018, para. 7). Regarding the presence of counsel during questioning, Inbau appears to have considered it obtrusive and interfering with privacy: "Opening the interrogation process to public scrutiny-for example, by allowing an attorney to sit in with a suspect or by requiring prompt delivery of suspects to magistrates for questioning-would cripple the ability of police to obtain confessions. To Inbau, such outside interference was unnecessary" (Drizin & Reich, 2004, p. 629).

The Behavior Analysis Interview generally consists of three types of questions, such as those concerning the subject's background, specific issues that are under investigation, and behavior-provoking questions. Police investigators trained in Reid often use the latter type of questioning to detect whether suspects are truthful or deceptive in their responses. Leo (2008, p. 95) provides some examples of the types of questions police investigators use in the Behavioral Analysis stage. These include: (1) Who do you think committed (alleged crime)?; (2) Have you ever thought about doing (alleged crime)?; and (3) What do you think the results of our investigation will show with respect to your involvement in (alleged crime)? These questions are often meant to elicit a response, either verbal or nonverbal, which the police investigator will mark as truthful or deceitful, based on what Reid trainers characterize as most consistent with how truthful or deceitful individuals would respond.

The relationship between nonverbal behaviors and deception proclaimed in the Reid manuals, however, has been rejected in numerous studies on verbal cues and deception. This is an important point considering the potential for obtaining unreliable information. As Vrij (2018) notes, Reid's examination and assessment of nonverbal cues has limitations:

> More than 100 deception studies – brilliantly summarized by Bella DePaulo and her colleagues (2003) in their meta-analysis – have shown that the cues Reid and Arther claimed to be diagnostic of deception are actually unrelated to deception. Yet these undiagnostic cues to deceit are presented as diagnostic cues in the Reid training manual (Inbau et al., 2013). Unsurprisingly, observers who paid attention to the cues promoted in the Reid training manual performed less well in lie detection tests than did their counterparts. (p. 160)

Once the Behavior Analysis interview stage of the Reid technique concludes and officers establish the "guilt" of the suspect, the interrogation stage begins. The third stage of the Reid technique is the interrogation. Only those deemed "guilty" in stage 2 are interrogated. Of note, it is unknown how often persons are deemed guilty in stage 2 and are subjected to interrogation. The Behavior Analysis stage consists of the Nine Steps of Interrogation: (1) initial confrontation, (2) theme development, (3) handling denials, (4) overcoming objections, (5) procurement of the subject's attention, (6) handling the subject's passive mood, (7) presenting an alternative question, (8) developing the details of the admission, and (9) converting the verbal confession to a written or recorded document. The use of maximization and minimization describes how these steps are incorporated and used in police-suspect exchanges (see Kassin & Kiechel, 1996).

Minimization involves presenting the suspect with a theme that reduces the import of the crime. Themes usually convey the interrogator's opinion that the crime was not so serious, that the victims deserved their fate, or that anyone else would have acted in the same way. Suspects may understand minimization as implicit promises of leniency. Maximization, on the other hand, involves presenting the case against the suspect as being full proof. The implicit message is that the crime is serious and the suspect faces very harsh consequences and punishment. Being cooperative is portrayed as the only possible way to mitigate the direness of the suspect's situation (see Gaines, 2020).

The discursive actions of minimization and maximization in police interrogation are carried out using strategies, such as "confrontation," "appeals to self-interest," and, "sympathy/minimization" (see Mason, 2013, 2016, 2020; Dixon, 2010). In a self-report survey of police practices and beliefs in the United States, Kassin et al. (2007) found "the typical interrogation often, but not always, includes confronting the suspect with evidence of his or her guilt and appealing to his or her self-interests. Somewhat less frequently, interrogation sometimes includes offering the suspect sympathy, moral justifications and excuses" (p. 389). From a linguistic perspective, these findings suggest that police officers tend to favor discursive actions that emphasize "separateness" or distance between the suspect and the police (i.e., the adversarial nature of interrogation), with an occasional preference for establishing "connectedness" with the suspect, as when employing "sympathy/minimization" (Mason, 2013). The following sections will illustrate some of these techniques, starting with the reading of Miranda rights, using excerpts from actual police interrogations cited in the corpus.

3.1.1 Setting the Tone of the Interrogation: Reading of Rights and Invocation of Counsel

The interrogation phase of the Reid technique is often preceded by the reading of Miranda rights, as illustrated in Excerpt 3.1.

In Excerpt 3.1, the suspect is attempting to invoke counsel while also determining whether it is necessary, or prudent, to do so. This discursive strategy, herein the start of the invocation game (see Chapter 4), is reflected in the questions and statements the suspect makes regarding the uncertainty of

Excerpt 3.1

1 Detective Holliday: So you understand each of your rights?
2 Brandon Johnson: Yes.
3 Detective Holliday: Are you willing to give up these rights and answer questions or make statements at this time?
4 Brandon Johnson: Ah, I really would like to have a lawyer present.
5 Detective Holliday: Okay.
6 Brandon Johnson: Because I know how serious this is.
7 Detective Holliday: Hm-hm.
8 Brandon Johnson: And I don't have anything to hide. I will talk to you guys. You know, I'll tell you any and everything I know, you know. But, um, I just wondered what like what kind of questions would you like to ask me or anything?
9 Detective Holliday: Well you, for, for you to find that out though.
10 Brandon Johnson: I gotta answer these questions though on paper.
11 Detective Holliday: Pardon?
12 Brandon Johnson: You said I gotta, I gotta answer these questions on the paper.
13 Detective Holliday: No. Well no, no. You answered them [Miranda warnings]. But you just said you wanted a lawyer which means I can't ask, tell you what the questions are gonna be without a lawyer being present. Now do you wanna waive your right to a lawyer? You understand that at any time, you can change your mind and stop talking and stop answering questions. You can ask for that lawyer at that time, whatever. But because you're thinking about asking for a lawyer – .
14 Brandon Johnson: Well I understand that.
15 Detective Holliday: Alright. That, I, I don't, you're in control here guy.
16 Brandon Johnson: Right, alright, alright. I understand that. You can, um.
17 Detective Holliday: You're in control. Brandon Johnson: _______, you can, you can.
18 Detective Holliday: You wanna waive your rights and talk to us right now?
19 Brandon Johnson: I can talk to you, yes.
20 Detective Holliday: Okay. So the answer's yes?
21 Brandon Johnson: Yes.

(*Johnson* v. *Booker*, 2014)

the process, the charges (e.g., Johnson does not know what the police officers have on him), and the custodial process in general. The detective, on the other hand, is observed managing two contrasting goals: making sure the suspect acknowledges comprehension of the rights, as read to him, and aiming for the suspect to waive such rights, not invoke counsel, and provide a statement to the police interrogators, while not overtly responding to the suspect's questions or acknowledging the suspect's invocation of the right to counsel.

Waiving of the Miranda rights allows the police interrogator to conduct the interrogation and, thus, apply an array of strategies aimed at obtaining a statement from the suspect. These strategies run the gamut of maximization–minimization and include police officers confronting the suspect with evidence of guilt, using time-limited offers, and/or showing empathy toward the suspect.

3.1.2 Confronting the Suspect

In the Reid technique, police interrogators often confront suspects with evidence that supports their claims and corrodes the suspects' denials. As noted previously, some of the interrogators' alleged evidence may be gathered during the investigative interview of witnesses and/or victims of crime. When using this strategy, the questioner formulates questions to ask the suspect, such as those that confront the suspect with evidence of guilt. Police interrogators may also use false-evidence ploys to extract a confession when confronting the suspect (Leo 2008). Excerpt 3.2 illustrates police interrogators' use of confrontation.

In Excerpt 3.2, the detectives use confrontation, such as "Dude, believe me, we've already questioned [Pena's mom.] … she didn't know where you were," and "She denied even knowing you," to establish their knowledge of the "facts" of the crime and the suspect's alleged involvement. As illustrated in Excerpt 3.2, in the confrontation stage of police interrogation, most of the police-initiated exchanges are formulated as statements of fact, often followed by a short pause that prompts the suspect to respond.

Excerpt 3.2 also shows how police interrogators use confrontation to break down suspects' possible perceptions that the police do not have a strong case against them (and/or will not continue to pursue the case). When Detective 2 says: "How do you know that? You told us you can't remember that day?" the detective is attempting to get the suspect to stop resisting the interrogation and provide statements that corroborate and expand on the interrogators' alleged knowledge of the crime. The asymmetry of knowledge between the police and suspects, coupled with the isolation caused by custodial interrogation, are highlighted in several judicial opinions, among them Justice Warren's *Miranda* majority ruling:

> To highlight the isolation and unfamiliar surroundings, the manuals instruct the police to display an air of confidence in the suspect's guilt and from outward appearance to maintain only an interest in confirming certain details. The guilt of the subject is to be posited as a fact. (p. 450)

Throughout the police interrogation, the "guilt" of the suspect is at the center of the discursive exchanges. Establishing the suspects' guilt may require lying to suspects or what Warren describes as the use of "trickery" in police

Excerpt 3.2

1 Detective 1: [Pena] told Garcia that the person the shot was [Vargas], from El Monte Flores.
2 Detective 2: That dude. You know who he is, right?
3 Petitioner: Yeah, I've seen him before.
. . .
4 Detective 1: . . . Look, I can go on in the statement and [Garcia] says a lot of shit in here.
5 Petitioner: Mmm hmm.
6 Detective 1: But you get the meat of what I'm sayin' right?
7 Petitioner: Yeah, because it's not true. I never talked to him and told [Pena] all that.
. . .
8 Petitioner: Well, is [Pena] telling you this?
9 Detective 1: I ain't gonna tell you what he said . . . Just like I ain't gonna tell [Pena] what you said . . . And I ain't gonna tell nobody else what you said.
10 Petitioner: I just talked to an attorney, sir, because that's nonsense.
11 Detective 2: Well, let me explain to you, you have a unique position. You understand the difference between a suspect and a witness?
12 Petitioner: Yeah, I know that, sir, but it – you're coming at me with this all mixed up stuff.

When the detectives said they had video footage from nearby stores of Petitioner at the crime scene on the night of the murder, Petitioner stated that, although he was unsure when the murder occurred, he was not present at the time because he was at a barbeque at a friend's house. The detectives suggested that Petitioner's phone was not in the vicinity of his friend's house but rather in the vicinity of the murder, and that contrary to Petitioner's allegations, Petitioner had not been seen by witnesses at or near the barbeque:

13 Detective 2: Where were you?
14 Petitioner: I was, I was at my [friend's] house.
. . .
15 Detective 2: How do you know that? You told us you can't remember that day?
16 Petitioner: It had to be like towards the weekend, cuz we were barbequing.
17 Detective 2: Okay
18 Petitioner: His mom always barbeques.
. . .
19 Petitioner: Have you talked to [Pena's] mom? . . . That night she seen me – at [the friend's] house.
20 Detective 1: Dude, believe me, we've already questioned [Pena's mom.] . . . she didn't know where you were.
21 Detective 2: She denied even knowing you.
. . .
22 Detective 1: . . . She didn't see you that night . . .

(*Renteria* v. *Foulk*, 2016)

interrogation. As with the police officers' treatment of invocation of rights, the law provides a great deal of latitude to police officers who lie and misrepresent the strength of the evidence against suspects during police questioning. The use of deception is often ruled as an accepted practice in police interrogation and does not automatically render an interrogation coercive or the product of such interrogation, such as a confession, involuntary (see *Frazier* v. *Cupp*, 1969; *Clanton* v. *Cooper*, 1997).

Another common strategy in the Reid technique of interrogation is police officers' use of pressure tactics with/without time-limited offers. This is an effective strategy to manage suspects' denials: an undesirable outcome of police interrogation (see Mason, 2020).

3.1.3 Time-Limited Offers

In the Reid technique, police interrogators may attempt to persuade suspects that they are trapped and powerless (Kassin et al., 2007). The police officers stress the urgency of the suspect speaking to police and providing a statement. The officers use pressure tactics, such as time-limited offers, to get the suspect to speak to them and stop denying the "evidence." This strategy often follows "confronting the suspect." Excerpt 3.3 illustrates this type of police interrogation strategy.

Excerpt 3.3

1 Q1: Tell the truth, tell the truth.
2 A: Tell the truth about what?
3 Q1: The dairy.
4 A: Well . . . I heard about the dairy.
5 Q1: Let's start there. Again, just try it again. Try again. Just try again.
6 Q1: Who were you there with?
7 A: I'm done talking.
8 Q: Y–You think we're bullshitting you?
9 Q1: Denying it, denying it.
10 Q1: Here's your chance.
11 Q: Jesus? Look at me please. You think I'm bullshitting you about this?
Petitioner continued to deny any special knowledge of or involvement in the incident. After detailed further questioning, the following exchange occurred:
12 Q: . . . You just gonna show us no respect, even though we go out of our way to show you respect? You can answer us something.
13 A: I just want to go back to my cell.
14 Q: You want to go back to your cell?
15 A: Yeah.
16 Q. Okay. You will very shortly . . ..

(cont.)

However, Petitioner did not go back to his cell. The officers continued to question him, and Petitioner continued to deny involvement in the shooting. Eventually, the officers began speaking to each other regarding arresting Petitioner for murder. (Lodged Doc. 8 at 23.) They asked Petitioner what color the victim's eyes were and to describe the sound the victim's screams made. They told Petitioner they didn't want to go to his mother and tell her he was a cold blooded murderer. Eventually, an officer asked, "But how responsible are you? How cold blooded of a killer are you?" (Lodged Doc. 8 at 25.) Plaintiff responded, "It just happened." (Id.) After further questioning, Plaintiff provided additional details regarding the shooting.

(*Flores* v. *Muniz*, 2018, p. 18)

Excerpt 3.3 is a classic example of the police officers' use of confrontation and pressure tactics, such as "Here's your chance." The latter implies that suspects have only a limited amount of opportunities to talk about the case, talk to the police officers, and so on. Of note, this is not consistent with the law. The excerpt also shows how police officers present the seriousness of the charges and the best option for the suspect: cooperate with them. The police officers, here Q and Q1, intimate their knowledge of the case and the suspect's (A's) involvement. They use face threatening strategies that emphasize the police officers' perception of the suspect as a liar who thinks he can "bullshit" them and, hence, is acting disrespectfully. In Excerpt 3.3, the strategy does not change the suspect's initial stance not to talk to police, and the suspect asks to be returned to his cell. The police officers acknowledge the suspect's request, but do not acquiesce. The police officers proceed to question the suspect further until the suspect states: "It just happened."

The next strategy, empathy, is less confrontational and relies on police interrogators establishing some level of solidarity and rapport with suspects.

3.1.4 Empathy

The use of empathy as a police interrogation strategy serves "to instill hope of minimizing the consequences of guilt, thereby paving the way for the interrogator to suggest how one might be able to do so" (Davis et al., 2010, p. 442). This technique often follows the confrontation stage of police interrogation and may be "recycled" if the suspects deny involvement in the crime of which they are accused.

Common questions and statements used with empathetic strategies include flattering the suspect, showing empathy (an affective response) toward the suspect, and optimizing legal outcomes contingent on the suspects admitting guilt. The latter strategy is shown in Excerpt 3.4.

Excerpt 3.4

1 Porter: Okay cool. With these rights in mind are you willing to talk to me?
2 Petitioner: About what?
3 Porter: Well about the shooting that happened last night. We can stop whenever you want.
4 Petitioner: I don't know even know what you're talking about but [unintelligible] wait until an attorney's present or something.
5 Porter: Well that's up to you. I mean that's a decision you've got to make.
6 Petitioner: Yea. Yea cause I don't know what you're talking about a shooting.
7 Porter: Well like I said it's your call[,] you've got to be clear about this. You have the absolute right to talk to us or not talk to us.
8 Petitioner: Yea.
9 Porter: Um but, but we're legally required to make sure we have absolute clarification. Do you want to talk with us? Do you not want to talk with us? Do you want to wait for an attorney? Do you not want to wait for an attorney? The decision falls on you. We obviously want to hear your side of the story. I mean I know you're in a bad position and everything but you know it is what it is now.
Petitioner asked whether charges would be brought against Campbell, and Detective Porter said that both he and Campbell would be charged with attempted murder. He told Petitioner the police had heard the deputy's story and Campbell's story, but they had not yet heard from him. Porter said, however, that Petitioner should not feel pressured and that the decision to talk was up to him. (Petitioner protested that Campbell hadn't done anything.) The following colloquy then took place:
10 Porter: Well hold on nobody's putting any pressure on you. Haven't the cops been decent with you up here so far?
11 Petitioner: Yea. Yea.
12 Porter: And we're going to continue to be. I mean but again if you're going to talk to us the law requires that we protect your rights. Right? The law requires that if you want to talk to us it's something that you want to do freely, voluntarily and I'm not going to[,] you know[,] if you feel like you said you think you want to wait for an attorney or whatever the case is [,] that's up to you. Now all I can do is encourage you that we obviously want to hear the other half of this. But that's a decision that you've got to make, not us. So what do you think?
13 Petitioner: Can I take a couple of minutes to think about it?
14 Porter: Sure, absolutely. Just remember that we'll never know your side of this unless, unless you're the one to tell us. Right? We'll step out and let you think about it. What do you think?

(*Lopez* v. *Janda*, 2015, p. 2)

The excerpt shows the invocation for counsel stage and the suspect's mention of "wait until an attorney is present or something." This was prefaced with the suspect's statement of not knowing what the police officers were talking about. This type of statement often precedes or follows invocations for counsel (or statements referring to counsel) in the corpus. The statements reflect the asymmetry of knowledge between the suspect and police interrogator and also show the suspect's use of gauging options. In Excerpt 3.4, there is no immediate acceptance of the suspect's statement: "waiting for an attorney or something." On the contrary, the police interrogator engages in multiple follow-up turns of talk that appear to be meant to clarify what the suspect wants. That is, to clarify whether the suspect wants to invoke counsel. These statements include commentary from the police interrogator, such as: "We obviously want to hear your side of the story. I mean I know you're in a bad position and everything but you know it is what it is now." The police interrogator's statement also suggests some empathy toward the suspect's predicament: "I know you're in a bad position."

The use of empathy as a police interrogation strategy is part of minimization (Mason, 2020). The police interrogators' use of minimization may include the use of deception, which, as noted previously, may be considered justified within the law. *United States* v. *Monroe* (2017), a United States District Court for the District of Rhode Island ruling, puts into perspective how some in the judiciary view the use of empathy and minimization during police interrogation:

> While Monroe argues the Reid Technique was used "to discourage [him] from not admitting guilt by presenting socially accepted alternatives . . . in order to prod him into choosing the lesser guilt inferring alternative," there is nothing impermissible as a matter of law with this interrogation approach; it falls within the range of acceptable interrogation tactics sanctioned by the First Circuit. Monroe offers no authority, and the Court could not find any, for the contention that an agent's minimization of crimes, under these facts, renders a suspect's statements involuntary. Thus, Monroe's argument that the Reid Technique violated his Due Process rights must fail. (p. 393)

The ruling captures a legal perspective on the role of minimization in police interrogation. This perspective, however, does not account for the strategic features of minimization, which may lead a suspect from wanting to invoke their rights to waiving them. Going back to Excerpt 3.4, the police interrogator's low-key tone is used when the suspect requests some time to think about his predicament. The police interrogator's response is an ongoing attempt at persuading the suspect to talk to him: "Sure, absolutely. Just remember that we'll never know your side of this unless, unless you're the one to tell us. Right?" In this case, as others in the corpus, the suspect choses to waive his right to counsel and provides a statement to the police.

3.2 Core Principles of the Reid Technique

The John E. Reid and Associates website lists a number of principles that police officers are taught to follow when conducting an investigation. A number of these are correlated with observing the law, particularly the legal concept of "voluntariness." Some examples include: (1) Do not make any promises of leniency; (2) do not threaten the subject with any physical harm or inevitable consequences; (3) do not deny the subject any of their rights; (4) do not deny the subject the opportunity to satisfy their physical needs; and (5) always act in compliance with the guidelines established by the courts. The caveat to these guidelines is that they must be observed following the law and around the main goal of Reid: to obtain a statement from the suspect. The emphasis on obtaining a statement, coupled with the legal parameters in which police interrogators operate, may contribute to the problem of false confessions.

3.2.1 The Matter of False Confessions and the Reid Technique

A false confession is one of the most undesirable outcomes of a police interrogation, since at its worst it may result in innocent persons being convicted of crimes they did not commit. The John E. Reid website emphasizes that the Reid technique does not cause false confessions. On the contrary, the website cites that the technique has a high rate of confession (about 80 percent) and of the remaining 20 percent: "a small percentage of them could have been innocent" (see Inbau et al., 2001, p. 364). This claim has yet to be scientifically verified and has raised serious concerns about the technique's association with false confessions (see Gudjonsson & Pearse, 2011, p. 303).

The Reid website[3] also stresses that if false confessions occur it lies with the police officers' improper use of the interrogation techniques:

> False confessions are not caused by the application of the Reid Technique, they are usually caused by interrogators engaging in improper interrogation procedures – engaging in behavior that the courts have ruled to be objectionable, such as threatening inevitable consequences; making a promise of leniency in return for the confession; denying a subject their rights; conducting an excessively long interrogation; etc. (Reid, 2018, para. 26)

This statement, however, does not address the array of Reid interrogation tactics police officers are trained to use in the field, and which the law allows, including, but not limited to, the use of false empathy, the use of pressure tactics that have coercive undertones, and the role of minimization in potentially deceiving suspects into providing statements. All of these strategies may also

[3] https://reid.com/resources/investigator-tips/a-description-of-the-reid-technique.

affect disproportionally vulnerable populations,[4] L2 speakers of English, and/or racialized groups who may be further disempowered in custodial settings due to cognitive, social, economic, and/or cultural factors. The latter considerations are not a central part of the training, but have been addressed in the literature.

Garrett (2015a),[5] for example, provides empirical data about the rate of false confessions among suspects, including those with intellectual disabilities:

> False confessions plague death penalty cases. I have found that in half of the 20 cases where individuals sentenced to death have later been exonerated by DNA evidence, false confessions occurred. Each of those confessions supposedly included specific details of the crime that only the murderer could have known. One half of the cases also involved testimony by police informants who falsely claimed to have overheard confessions. Intellectual disability is entwined with false confessions; one-third of those exonerated by DNA testing who had falsely confessed were mentally ill or intellectually disabled. (para. 5)

Garrett (2015b) adds that "Judges, defense lawyers, prosecutors, and jurors may have a very hard time believing that a person could confess falsely" (p. 395). He argues that police contamination often explains how an innocent person could have provided inside information about the crime scenes.

Kozinski (2017) also tied false confession rates and the possible role of the Reid technique, among other factors, to the statistics. He notes that in a recent study "approximately 29% of DNA exonerations in the US since 1989 have involved false confessions" (p. 303). He adds that researchers found commonalities among these cases, including the suspect being mentally or intellectually challenged, not having assistance of counsel during the interrogation, and being provided information about the crime by police investigators. As Kozinski notes this raises concerns as to whether the Reid technique may be extracting confessions from both guilty and innocent persons.

The psychological aspects of the police interrogation may also contribute significantly to suspects providing false confessions. Gudjonsson and Pearse (2011) note that false confessions appear to be associated with two main causes: "manipulative/coercive interrogation techniques and suspects' vulnerabilities in interviews" (p. 35). The latter point, in particular, has been raised in legal rulings, including *Miranda*. These rulings describe how the isolation of custodial interrogation, which may render suspects more vulnerable to trickery and deception, coupled with discursive tactics meant to break down the resistance of suspects, create a coercive environment ripe for confession extraction, even a false one:

[4] See also recent case study reporting a high percentage of inmates with mental health and substance abuse problems in the state of Connecticut's prisons: www.ctinsider.com/news/article/CT-prison-inmates-mental-health-substance-abuse-17713051.php.

[5] www.huffpost.com/entry/serving-life-for-a-lie_b_8266012.

Although it is generally not unconstitutional for officers to lie as an interrogation technique, we note that Detectives Rivera and Carrillo employed sophisticated interrogation techniques that likely helped overcome Mr. Rodriguez's will … Pressuring a suspect "to change answers inconsistent with guilt and adopt answers evidencing guilt instead" is a police tactic particularly likely to cause an intellectually disabled suspect to "shift" his answers "to conform to the perceived desires of the interrogator" (*Rodriguez* v. *McDonald*, 2017, footnote 3, p. 924).

The coercive nature of police interrogation is also at the forefront of other high profile cases. One of the most cited cases that mentions, specifically, the alleged coerciveness of the Reid technique is *United States* v. *Jacques* (2014): "In this case, the agents' statements exaggerating the quality of their evidence, minimizing the gravity of Jacques's offense, and emphasizing the negative media attention that would attend Jacques's trial all fall safely within the realm of the permissible 'chicanery' sanctioned by this and other courts" (p. 812). Other notable state and federal cases that have ruled on the legality of police deception include: *Ball* v. *State* (1997); *State* v. *Harris* (2010) (the defendant was interrogated for seven hours while shackled to the floor, denied access to phone to call alibi witness, and the use of "themes and options" as interrogation techniques); *United States* v. *Crawford* (2004) (pretext search); *State* v. *Melton* (1991) (defendant was told it would be cowardly and unmanly to blame the crime on a dead person); *State* v. *Carrillo* (1988) (pretext arrest); *United States* v. *Boyce* (1979) (appeal to loyalty); and *State* v. *Rettenberger* (1999) ("false friend" technique).

Legal precedence in the United States suggests a balance tipped more toward the police officers being able to investigate crimes, with legal avenues to do so, than a concern for protecting suspects from coercive police interrogation tactics. As Simon (2012) argues police investigators must "cease relying on physical cues in attempting to detect deceit." He recommends a shift from a "reliance on accusatorial and coercive methods … toward less confrontational procedures that focus on information gathering" (p. 161). Simon adds that this change will require agents of the criminal justice system: police officers, attorneys, and judges to "recognize fault lines in the system as they become apparent to us and do our best to correct them" (p. 162). This sentiment is captured in the shift of some police stations moving away from accusatorial interrogation techniques to more information and rapport-based interviewing methods, such as PEACE.

3.3 Information-Gathering Interview Approach

The information-gathering interview approach does not have its origins in the United States. It came about police reforms in the United Kingdom. Since the mid-1980s after the introduction of legislation, such as the Police and Criminal Evidence Act (PACE), the questioning of suspects in the UK underwent major transformations. The new legislation prompted changes as to how police conducted interviews with witnesses and suspects of an investigation. The confession culture of the past was replaced with a new model called PEACE. This was later adopted, with variations, in many territories in Australia where the investigative interview is used, as well as in territories in Canada, as a PEACE hybrid called the Phased Interview Model for Suspects, and in Norway, as a modified version of PEACE called KREATIV. These are examples of the role of PEACE in shaping police interviewing reforms in Australia, Europe and Canada, among other countries, some of which widely used the Reid technique prior to implementing police interviewing reforms.

The PEACE model is an acronym for "Preparation and Planning," "Engage and Explain," "Account, Clarification, Challenge," "Closure," and "Evaluation." These phases (in sequence) refer to: the planning and preparation conducted prior to the interview; the reading of legal requirements and the opportunity to build rapport between the interviewer and suspect; the interview phase where open-ended questions are used to facilitate the suspect's account of the events being investigated, including further probing and clarification if needed; the final/end of the interview; and the evaluation, or reflection, that occurs after the interview has been conducted. This model of interviewing emphasizes rapport building, empathy, and conversation management. Interviewers are encouraged to be fair and open-minded and to pursue reliable, true, and accurate information during the interview of suspects. The investigative interview, hence, is approached with an investigative, rather than prosecutorial, mindset. The information obtained should be accurate and reliable, withstanding court scrutiny, and suspects must be approached ethically and within the bounds of the law. This includes explaining in the "engage and explain" phase of the interview process and informing the suspects of their rights and ensuring that they understand such rights prior to the start of the interview. Of note, in many countries, such as the UK, the reading of rights includes the right to silence but not counsel. This does not preclude suspects from requesting an attorney and being allowed to contact one. The attorney may give advice and be present during any questioning in many jurisdictions outside of the United States.

In the "account, clarification, and challenge" phase of PEACE, police engage in the investigative interview of the suspect. In this phase, police interviewers are trained to build rapport with the suspect and ask questions in a manner that enhances the objectives of questioning, such as discovering the truth about the matter under investigation, gathering information, and obtaining evidence. This can be accomplished by using appropriate questions. Open-ended questions, for example, elicit more free recall and this is considered the most accurate form of remembering. These types of questions also minimize interviewer bias. Examples of open ended questions include "wh" questions and T.E.D. questions: Tell, Explain, Describe. Closed probing questions are also effective in the clarification and challenge phase of the investigative interview, since they can be used when the interviewee has omitted some detail in the free recall phase.

The role of memory and recall are also part of the PEACE method. Interviewers may utilize different techniques to enhance the suspect's memory. The use of conversation management is one of those techniques that may improve eliciting statements from a potentially guilty suspect. Suspects may also be interviewed using the Cognitive Interview (CI), although this type of interview is often reserved for interviewing witnesses due to its emphasis on recall and truth detection:

> During police and forensic investigations, interviewing witnesses is often a key procedure that frequently determines the outcome of the investigation (Milne, 1997). However, what witnesses report rarely fully corresponds with what they remember. The commonly used questioning techniques may produce a reduced amount of valuable information, as well as some incorrect information. To manage this difficulty, Geiselman et al. (1984) developed the Cognitive Interview, which is now commonly accepted as one of the most successful procedures for enhancing witness recollection. (Paulo et al., 2013, pp. 190–191)

There are a few experimental studies using CI with college students acting as suspects that have shown mixed results (see Geiselman, 2012). In these studies, CI was modified for use with suspects (CIS) to maximize the opportunity to detect deception. The focus on memory recall and truth detection with suspects, however, has raised some concerns, if not controlled properly. An emphasis on truth detection may bias the interviewer and limit the use of questioning that provides a free narrative that can be challenged or probed further with the evidence. As Geiselman (2012) notes: "As a word of caution, each element of the CIS, as well as the more reliable indicators of deception, can provide the interviewer with 'red flags' or 'hot spots' only. Detection of any one indicator of deception during the interview should not be taken as sufficient evidence to conclude that the subject is being deceptive" (p. 11).

In the United States, law enforcement agencies have placed a premium on the use of CI, and related techniques, with high-value detainees and military personnel. Given the inclusion of military and nonpolice interrogators, such as federal agents, in the cases that comprise the corpus, the next section will examine the High-Value Detainee Interrogation Group (2016) report, which includes an extensive review of the literature on rapport-based interviewing.

3.4 The High-Value Detainee Interrogation Group Report

In 2009, Executive Order 13491 established a task force to review the interrogation and transfer policies of the US government. The task force recommended the creation of the High-Value Detainee Interrogation Group to improve the interrogation of those deemed dangerous terrorists by the United States government. The National Defense Authorization Act for Fiscal Year 2016 required HIG to submit a report on best practices for interrogation. This extensive report aims "to provide a systematic review and evidence synthesis of the science related to interrogation. It is not intended as a manual or practitioners' guide" (2016, p. 1). Law enforcement agencies in the United States, such as the FBI, have applied techniques in the HIG report that focus on two core principles: rapport building and enhanced (cognitive) recall. Studies using data from state police interrogations are also cited in the report, such as the Good Stranger study among others. Moreover, studies that examine high-value detainees, suspects of crime, and witnesses are discussed throughout the report, often in the same categories (under type of technique). Hence, this section will discuss the main points addressed in the HIG report with a follow-up section reflecting on the role this report may play in shaping practicing interrogators in a variety of law enforcement agencies.

3.4.1 What Is in the HIG Report?

The HIG Report provides a comprehensive discussion of past and current interrogation practices. These include preparation, context, managing first impressions, countering resistance, developing and maintaining rapport, active listening, use of free narrative and open questions, assisting in the recall of memories (e.g., tell the story in reverse order), language style matching, among other techniques. Some of these work in tandem with each other and/or reinforce other strategies.

To counter resistance, an essential component of the HIG report, the Cylindrical Model (CM) is presented. CM:

> is based on research that shows successful negotiations and interrogations can be understood in terms of the extent to which the interrogator and subject are "in sync"; that is, how they align their dialogue over the course of the interaction. The framework of the Cylindrical Model and research on resistance and counter resistance provides a roadmap for transitioning a subject being resistant to being cooperative. (2016, p. 9)

The interactants' ability to align their framing of dialogue is correlated with level of success in an interrogation. One example of synchronized language use is Language Style Matching (LSM). Research on the coordination of interrogators' and suspects' verbal behavior suggests that higher rates of the suspect matching the interrogators' language style resulted in interrogations containing a confession (see Richardson et al., 2014). The goal of these strategies is to establish a context of cooperation in which the suspect is working in tandem with the interrogator. The interrogator's ability to influence the suspect and remove barriers, such as the suspect's resistance to cooperation, also benefit from rapport building.

In the HIG, rapport is described as playing a central role in the successful interrogation of high-value detainees (see also HUMINT model for noncriminal, threat to national security suspects). The research in the report suggests that interrogators can establish rapport through coordination, such as mimicry, mutual attention, positivity, and activities that foment a working relationship between interrogator and interviewee. With witnesses, interrogators establish a positive relationship. The latter requires, among other steps, that the interviewer explain to the witness why they are being interviewed, what will happen in the interview (e.g., using active listening and nonverbal cues), and encourage the subject to recall as much information as possible, through the use of memory enhancing techniques. Similar methods are applied in the interrogation of high-value detainees. The methods laid out in the HIG report are reportedly used by a number of government agencies and some branches of the military to interrogate a variety of suspects. These methods appear to be modeled on rapport based interviewing (see Collins et al., 2002; Alison et al., 2020).

The HIG Report states that building rapport is considered one of the most important components of an interrogation, since it has been shown to increase the amount of information provided by subjects, improve trust, and produce cooperation. The report cites examples from police interrogations in which the officers used rapport to interview suspects. One of the examples is from video recordings of interrogations from the Los Angeles Police Department in the United States. These interrogations suggest that rapport behaviors increased for those sessions that ended in admissions and remained low for those sessions that ended in denials. As with other studies on rapport behaviors with suspects (see Hartwig & Meissner, 2014), it is unclear how rapport was measured or evaluated in the study.

The use of influencing strategies in forensic interviewing is also addressed in the HIG Report, which states that: "Empirical observations have found that police in the U.S regularly employ poor interview techniques that either reduce the amount of information elicited or entice subjects [witnesses, victims and suspects] to provide incorrect information" (2016, p. 24). Hence, the report notes that CI methods may improve communication between interrogators and interviewees through rapport-building behaviors. The goal of this type of communication dynamics is to improve the amount and quality of information disclosed by the interviewee. To accomplish this task, enhancement of recall and memory retrieval is featured extensively in the report:

> In addition to asking for the full story, the interviewer does not interrupt the subject until he has completed his narrative. The goal is to provide opportunities for the subject to

recall as much as possible; interruptions will only impair that process. The subject is also encouraged not to guess at what he may not know, but to freely admit to lapses in memory. This avoids a too-cooperative subject guessing at what the interviewer wants to know and inserting such into his narrative, and is a recognition that memory about a particular event at any one time is frail and incomplete . . . . Once a full narrative is provided, the interviewer may ask the subject to go through the story again, this time enhancing his ability to recall. (2016, p. 24)

The HIG Report further highlights rapport-based interviewing techniques, including: Observing Rapport-Based Interview Techniques (ORBIT), Motivational Interviewing, the Scharff technique, and Strategic Use of Evidence (SUE). ORBIT and Motivational Interviewing Techniques identify interpersonal interrogator-detainee interactions, one of which is adaptive and the other maladaptive, between interpersonal circles and along two dimensions: a "Cooperation–Confrontation" axis and a "Capitulation–Control" axis (see Alison et al., 2013). Interviewers that showed adaptive behaviors (for example, in charge, supportive and conversational) did not affect information yield, whereas maladaptive behaviors (for example demanding and rigid) significantly decreased information retrieved.

Another technique developed to improve the collection of intelligence information is the Scharff technique (see Granhag et al., 2020). This technique applies a number of tactics, including employing a friendly (adaptive) approach, not pressing for information, using the illusion of "knowing it all," presenting claims for the source to confirm or deny, and giving the impression of ignoring new information to downplay its importance. In experimental research, one consistent finding of the Scharff Technique is that it resulted in subjects thinking that they had revealed less information than they actually did and believing that the interviewers were more informed than they actually were.

Interrogating across cultures is another factor considered in the HIG Report. The emphasis, however, is on the effect of cross-cultural and linguistic differences in the interviewing and truth detection process rather than on improving communication and subject comprehension in these contexts. The report provides research and case studies showing how misunderstandings in cross-cultural communication, social encounters, intelligence interviews, and police interviews can interfere with social dynamics. Points that were addressed in this section of the report, include the role of face, role/authority, and the need for third party mediation, such as interpreter-mediated exchanges:

research on the use of interpreters in clinical settings has shown that an interpreter may also serve as a cultural consultant, community advocate, or even co-therapist . . . and that therapeutic alliance is not adversely impacted by the presence of an interpreter. In simulated interrogations, interviewees who spoke truthfully or lied through an interpreter about their current occupations reported that the presence of an interpreter had no effect on the rapport they felt with the interviewer. (2016, p. 30)

Two points that stand out are (1) the view of the interpreter as a potential cultural advocate or even cotherapist, without consideration of the professional standing of the interpreter in a legal setting or the ethical canons of the profession, and (2) the theme of truth detection/cooperation and its possible effect on interpreter-mediated exchanges. Of note, in community interpreting, as may be the case with high-value detainees in the field, the interpreters may engage in cultural mediation and may not be professional/certified interpreters. The HIG Report, however, does not address the role of the interpreter once the person is in custody in the United States and subjected to interrogation and other legal procedures. The emphasis is on the possible effect of the interpreter on truth detection and interviewer rapport building, rather than on the role of the interpreter in providing accurate interpretations and cultural mediation, if required.

The HIG Report also includes a discussion on truth detecting techniques that rely on imposing cognitive load on suspects. Statement Validity Analysis (SVA), which was designed originally for use with children, is one of the techniques cited that assess the validity of adult suspects' statements. This technique is particularly interesting since it is, or at least was, used by the FBI prior to the HIG Report's release. The technique, called Statement Analysis (Klopf & Tooke, 2003) shares some similarities with the Behavioral Analysis stage of the Reid technique. The goal of the Statement Analysis Field Examination Technique, or SAFE-T, is to assist the investigator in identifying areas for further investigation and truth detection. SAFE-T was designed to identify whether suspects' statements are accurate and complete by focusing primarily on two elements: lack of conviction (personal) and extraneous information. Klopf and Tooke's (2003) study, albeit includes a small corpus, suggests that statement analysis has the potential to detect deception and do so at a higher rate than police interrogator's "gut feelings."

Other studies featured in the HIG report also examine the effect of increasing cognitive load on suspects' recollections. Truth tellers, for example, seem to provide more details in their accounts than liars. Forensic statement analysis studies argue that deceptive narratives are shorter than truthful ones, as well as less lexically diverse (Vrij, 2015). Some studies (e.g., Calderon et al., 2018) found that drawings of false intentions were rated as more abstract than drawings of true intentions. These studies point to the potential role for abstractness in detecting deceit. As with other studies discussed in this section, research on truth detection has limitations ranging from small data sets to the use of experimental versus real life data. As Vrij (2018) notes on the current, and growing field, of truth detection in interviewing:

> The few studies examining multiple interviews have shown that differences between truth tellers and liars in consistency are modest at best. When differences exist, liars appear to be more consistent than truth tellers, which is at variance with the stereotypical belief that liars are more inconsistent than truth tellers . . . However, this finding is in line with the repeat versus reconstruct hypothesis . . . Liars need to keep track of their lies and try to repeat what they have said before, whereas truth tellers rely on their memory of the event. The latter leads to changes because memory is a reconstructive process. (p. 165)

Vrij warns that a "liar's" consistency will also depend on the interview style used. A consideration that needs to be accounted for in future research on cognition, truth detection, and interviewing, particularly with criminal suspects. The question of whether a focus on truth detection and increasing cognitive load, as opposed to information gathering, is appropriate with criminal suspects also needs to be examined further due to the potential implications of creating suspect bias, particularly in legal frameworks that permit the use of trickery and deception and which require Miranda invocations to be unequivocal. A matter discussed in the next section.

3.5 Reid, PEACE, and the HIG Report: Additional Considerations in Light of United States Law

The Reid technique continues to be part of the fabric of United States policing. As previously noted, the technique emphasizes behavior analysis and the use of maximization and minimization, which are aimed at getting the suspect to confess rather than provide quality information that may further the investigation of a crime. The Reid technique has also been criticized for its potential to lead to false confessions: a possible outcome of confrontational, police driven interrogations (Meissner et al., 2014). As Brimbal et al. (2021) note, the lack of collaboration between researchers and practitioners and "empiricism has prolonged the use of a coercive accusatorial approach for suspect interviewing that is not the most effective at eliciting accurate and actionable information" (p. 5).

Contemporary research on the effectiveness of information-gathering and rapport-based approaches, on the other hand, have provided insights into the role of training in the application of these methods in the field. The PEACE model, for example, has been evaluated demonstrating mixed results: some showing post-training skill improvement (McGurk et al., 1993; Griffiths & Milne, 2006) whereas others showing less, or no significant, improvement of interviewing practices and rapport building (see Clarke et al., 2011; Griffiths et al., 2011; Walsh & Milne, 2008). Brimbal et al.'s (2021) quasi-experimental research is noteworthy since it takes a different approach attempting to bridge the gap between research and practice to investigate whether police investigators are more likely to use the rapport building approaches they were trained in, and whether those tactics are effective in developing rapport, establishing cooperation, overcoming resistance, and eliciting information from interviewees. The study shows that the use of productive questioning and conversational rapport (see also Griffiths & Milne, 2006; Brimbal et al., 2019) supports interviewee cooperation. The study concludes that police investigators can be effectively trained to perform evidence-based interviewing. In Brimbal et al.'s (2019) prior study this interviewing style facilitated the development of rapport and indirectly increased subjects' cooperation and disclosure of information.

The CI model highlighted in the HIG report also emphasizes the role of rapport and productive questioning in the interrogation of high-value suspects. Despite its potential benefits improving recall and rapport building, this interview style raises a number of questions when applied to custodial, criminal, settings. As discussed previously, CI has traditionally been applied to witnesses, rather than suspects (see Geiselman, 2012). This interview model aims to facilitate memory recall and detect possible deception. Witnesses' statements, in particular, are key in the planning stages of a police interview as well as in the interview/interrogation phases of both Reid and PEACE. Hence, improving the odds of obtaining truthful information from witnesses may enhance the effectiveness of the investigative interview, and the probing/clarification stage of PEACE. Yet, the model may not be appropriate, in mission and objective, to the interview of custodial suspects, particularly in the United States. At present, there is also no available research that tests how either PEACE or CI would stand in the Miranda stage of a police interview, specifically in light of the *Davis* ruling. The emphasis on truth detection may also be a factor that affects the observance of the right to counsel. This takes us to a fairly new and controversial method called the Complex Investigation Phased Engagement Model (CIPEM) that is worth noting giving its potential to provide some clues as to how rapport building in CI and PEACE could fail when applied to custodial suspects in the United States.

CIPEM allegedly aims to get suspects who are not forthcoming with statements to open up to police investigators. This is accomplished by replacing normal police interview scenarios with a "fireside chat" environment. This includes the use of comfortable chairs, no desk or note-taking, shared food, and police seeming empathetic and understanding with the suspect's plight. It is unknown how often this fairly new technique has been used, but in a recent high profile criminal case in New Zealand it resulted in the police interrogators breaking numerous guidelines when interviewing one of the suspects, such as not video recording important discussions, failing to advise the suspect of his legal rights on two occasions, engaging in persistent questioning aimed at wearing the suspect down, and misrepresenting the facts of the case (see Ensor & White, 2022). CIPEM has recently been renamed PEACE Plus, yet it is not clear how this model is consistently implemented in the field. More research is needed to assess the uses of PEACE Plus, but what is notable is that the use of rapport interviewing can be as problematic as Reid, if the interviewer does not observe the suspect's legal rights (as in a "friendly" exchange) and fakes empathy toward the suspect in order to get a statement. This point needs to be considered if law enforcement agencies in the United States are utilizing information gathering and rapport based interviewing with criminal suspects in a manner that is inconsistent with the core goals of these methods.

In addition, as discussed previously, United States law allows (to an extent) the use of trickery and deception in police interviews. This is unlike other jurisdictions abroad, such as in the UK and Australia, where legislation was passed deeming it unethical and illegal to confront a suspect with fabricated evidence. The use of rapport to facilitate the interrogation of suspects, even those who have invoked counsel, may be problematic. The Reid technique nor the HIG report comprehensively address the legal needs of suspects (aside from the mandatory reading of rights), such as making legal counsel accessible to suspects, reducing the asymmetry of knowledge between interrogator and suspect, among other important legal and sociolinguistic considerations.

As the law and institutional culture factors stand, the truth detection features of CI and other techniques included in the HIG report, such as Statement Analysis, may bias the police interviewer into trying to "get around" the suspect's rights and focus the interview significantly on detecting deception and/or making the suspect feel at ease and liked, even if the intent is to make the suspect more compliant in order to get a confession. The linguistic manipulation of a suspect during police questioning, as will be discussed in Chapter 4, increases the odds that interrogators will use what the law allows in all interviewing techniques, even those that are less confrontational than the widely used Reid technique. These issues become even more apparent with vulnerable suspects, such as those who may have cognitive and/or intellectual disabilities, as well as L2 speakers of English and juveniles. Furthermore, neither the Reid technique nor the HIG report fully incorporate, or include in the case of the HIG report, extensive research on the role that sociolinguistic factors may play in the interview process (see Shuy, 1998; Heydon, 2005, 2008), including the issue of language bias and profiling (e.g., African American English) and the need for professional/certified interpreters with L2 custodial suspects. The latter has received a good deal of attention in the literature and will be discussed further in Chapter 6.

4 The Invocation Game: The Prelude to Custodial Interrogation

This case is difficult because Clark's statement – "I think I would like to talk to a lawyer" – reflects at least a tentative decision in favor of having a lawyer. It does not, however, indicate unequivocally that a final decision has been made.

(Circuit Judge Stapleton (concurring opinion), *Clark* v. *Murphy*, 2003)

Nonthreatening attempts to persuade the suspect to reconsider that initial decision are not, without more, enough to render a change of heart the product of anything other than the suspect's free will. Thus, what is most remarkable about the Miranda decision–and what made it unacceptable as a matter of straightforward constitutional interpretation in the Marbury tradition–is its palpable hostility toward the act of confession per se, rather than toward what the Constitution abhors, compelled confession ... The Constitution is not, unlike the Miranda majority, offended by a criminal's commendable qualm of conscience or fortunate fit of stupidity.

(Justice Scalia (dissenting opinion), *Dickerson* v. *United States*, 2000)

In the United States, police interrogators are often trained to prioritize getting a custodial suspect's statements (Inbau et al., 2001). What maximizes a police interrogator's strategy is to get incriminating statements from suspects. Now, the law requires that statements be voluntary, knowing, and freely provided, hence police interrogators must read suspects the Miranda rights prior to the onset of custodial interrogation and may not overtly or coercively get suspects to waive them. This chapter challenges the notion that custodial suspects freely and voluntarily waive their Miranda rights. In a police interrogation, perception and preference, such as invoking or not invoking the right to counsel, are subject to manipulation. Manipulation is the process by which an interrogator may alter a custodial suspect's preferences for the benefit of the interrogator.

This chapter provides the theoretical framework for suspects' invocations for counsel in the corpus. The analysis will focus on the discursive features of suspects' invocations for counsel during custodial interrogation, as well as the sequences of talk that follow the suspects' invocations, including the police interrogators' use of requests for clarification. This part of the analysis will apply game theory, specifically hypergame theory (Bennett, 1980), to describe police-suspect exchanges after a custodial suspect invokes counsel. This is a novel approach to analyzing institutional discourse and, in particular, police interrogations.

4.1 Invoking Counsel: A Constitutional Right Handicapped by the Law

There is a presumption in the law that suspects who wish the assistance of counsel must invoke so unequivocally. This creates a distinction between a valid invocation for counsel, that is, one that can stop an interrogation, and an ambiguous one that may not prompt such action from the police. The validity of the invocation is, for the most part, dependent on the police's assessment of the invocation. Hence, police interrogators may end an interrogation at any point when the suspect invokes their rights, albeit directly or indirectly – with indirectly formulated invocations being the most common and least successful at invoking rights (see Mason, 2013, 2020). The manner in which police approach the invocation of rights stage of an interrogation is often guided by the law and training, and strategically framed, rather than by discursive frameworks.

4.1.1 Invocations As a Type of Speech Act

Grice's (1975) theory of conversational implicature examines how speakers convey illocutionary force that the hearers recognize. For Grice, understanding how people mean more than they say is integral to understanding how indirect (nonliteral) meaning is communicated. He proposed the principle of conversational implicature: "make your conversational contribution such as is required, at the stage at which it occurs, by the accepted purpose or direction of the talk exchange in which you are engaged" (1975, p. 45). When speakers abide by this principle, their utterances are of a suitable length (quantity), truthful (quality), clear (manner), and relevant (relation). Speakers, however, do not always abide by these maxims of conversation. If a speaker says at the dinner table, "Can you pass me the salt?," the addressee assumes that the speaker is being relevant, and, thus, has an ulterior motive for not being direct. The violation of one or more of the conversational maxims, such as the maxim of relation in the above example, thus serves as a trigger for the addressee to search for an implied or indirect meaning: its intended perlocutionary effect.

How addressees process and respond to an indirect speech act also lies with the means in which the act is performed. Holtgraves (2002), for example, remarks that there are conventional and nonconventional[1] means of performing a speech act: "a conventional means for performing a speech act means that the literal meaning of the utterance is *pro forma*, not to be taken seriously" (p. 32). An example of this type of pro forma utterance in a legal context is "Can I get a lawyer?," or, in the form of an assertion, "I need a lawyer."

Research on conventional indirect requests suggests that people tend to recognize their meaning in a direct fashion, without the need for a time-consuming inference process (i.e., the idiomatic approach to comprehension). In a conversational exchange, addressees appear to disregard the direct meaning of a speaker's indirect request (see Gibbs, 1983; Holtgraves, 1994; Holtgraves & Ashley, 2001; Jaszczolt, 2019). Thus, the assumption that literal meaning primarily, or alone, plays an important role in the comprehension of conventional indirect requests is not widely supported by psycholinguistic evidence (see Gibbs et al., 1993; Gibbs, 1999; Holtgraves, 2002, 2005). This finding is particularly relevant for invocations for counsel, since judges in our corpus have ruled that conventional invocations for counsel may be equivocal or unequivocal. Excerpt 4.1

Excerpt 4.1

1 Suspect: Can I get an attorney right now, man?
2 Officer 1: Pardon me?
3 Suspect: You can have attorney right now?
4 Officer 1: Ah, you can have one appointed for you, yes.
5 Suspect: Well, like right now you got one?
6 Officer 1: We don't have one here, no. There's not one present now.
7 Officer 2: There will be one appointed to you at the arraignment, ah, whether you can afford one. If you can't one will be appointed to you by the court.
8 Suspect: All right.
9 Officer 1: [Inaudible].
10 Suspect: I'll – I'll talk to you guys.

(*Alvarez* v. *Gomez*, 1999, cited in *United States* v. *Gray*, 2015)

[1] With nonconventional requests, the comprehension of the implied meaning may, on occasion, involve an inference process. For example, the indirect speech act "It's hot in here" used to indirectly request the addressee to open a window may require the addressee to recognize, from the literal (illocutionary) force of the utterance, its conveyed or indirect (illocutionary) force. With these nonconventional requests, "pragmatic duality" may occur and it is up to the addressees to decide whether they can plausibly deny that a request has been made. The latter point is important for invocations for counsel, since police interrogators in the corpus often assess indirect invocations, such as "It might be better that I get an attorney," as equivocal. This may lead police interrogators to use follow-up moves to "clarify" the invocation.

shows an example of a conventional invocation for counsel treated as equivocal by the police interrogators, but ruled as unequivocal by the court.

In Excerpt 4.1, the police officer (Officer 1) requests clarification of the suspect's invocation for counsel – "Can I get an attorney right now, man?" – using a follow-up question "Pardon me?" The police officer seems to either not have heard the utterance correctly or not understood its intent. The latter hints at the possible ambiguity of the suspect's request. The suspect responds to the officer's request for clarification with "You can have attorney right now?" to which the officer responds with "Ah, you can have one appointed for you, yes." The next turns of talk show the suspect asking again for an attorney – "Well, like right now you got one?" – followed by the officer's response "We don't have one here, no. There's not one present now." In these exchanges, the officer's requests for clarification and follow-up moves are not used to address the apparent ambiguity of the request, as for example to verify what the suspect is actually requesting (see Noh, 1998, 2001; Blakemore, 1994; Mason, 2016, 2020), but to establish that the initial invocation was equivocal/ambiguous and it does not rise to the legal standard of unequivocalness needed to cease an interrogation. In the excerpt, the police officer has taken the stance that the suspect was not requesting counsel but rather was inquiring about the availability of counsel at the police station. The next turns of talk serve to remind the suspect of his rights (Officer 2): "There will be one appointed to you at the arraignment, ah, whether you can afford one. If you can't one will be appointed to you by the court." This reminder would require that the suspect attempt to invoke counsel again, despite having been unsuccessful on multiple occasions, and/or inquire about the process to acquire an attorney during the arraignment. The suspect does not take these routes and proceeds to waive his rights and provide a statement to the police. In this case, the suspect's requests for counsel were ruled unequivocal: "Alvarez's repeated questions about the immediate availability of an attorney were a clear and unequivocal invocation of his Miranda right to counsel, and he did not thereafter waive that right" (*Alvarez* v. *Gomez*, 1999).

Directing a suspect's invocation for counsel is also highlighted in Excerpt 4.2. In this excerpt, police officers use, among other tactics, requests for clarification to attempt to thwart the suspect's invocations for counsel and get the suspect "back on track".

The negotiations that occur in requests for clarification, as in Excerpt 4.2, are intended to establish a mutuality of understanding that cannot be fully achieved until the speaker's intent is clear. Often these requests for clarification take the form of partial or full echo questions (see Pöchhacker, 2012) such as "you need a lawyer?" or "lawyer?" or as explicit or implicit confirmation (see Schlangen, 2004) such as "Did you say you need a lawyer?" or "a lawyer?" The request for clarification could also simply ask for specification, such as

Excerpt 4.2

1 Mande: And if you decide to answer questions now, without a lawyer present, you have the right to stop answering questions at any time.
2 Davis: If, if I'm, if I'm going to answer questions, I'm going to need a lawyer here.
3 Mande: Alright, well, this is just so you understand that . . . and then down here, it's just now we're, this is the part where, if you want a way to talk to us and answer questions, that's where you sign there. If you don't want to talk to us, don't . . .
4 Davis: I want to talk to you, but I just need my lawyer.
5 Chaney: Ok, ok, so here's what you're telling us—you do want your lawyer?
6 Davis: I want to talk, yeah. But I need my lawyer present.
7 Chaney: We wanna . . . either you talk to us now . . . if you want to talk to us now, without anybody else present, you have to sign that waiver. If not, all bets are off, you go into the system, ok?
8 Davis: Yeah

(*United States* v. *Davis*, 2018)

(referring to a lawyer) "a what"? As Schlangen (2004) explains: "What the questions in these examples have in common is that, unlike 'normal' questions, they are not about the state of the world in general, but rather about aspects of previous utterances: they indicate a problem with understanding that utterance, and they request repair of that problem" (p. 137). In the police interrogations that comprise the corpus, however, follow-ups that appear to be requests for clarification are often used to deter the suspects from being able to determine their best options. Asking the suspect a "loaded" follow-up request, such as "Ok, ok, so here's what you're telling us – you do want your lawyer?," although may appear to request clarification, and many rulings in the corpus deem these as such, has an alternate purpose: to narrow the suspect's options to either talk to the police officers or "all bets are off, you go into the system." This is an important point, since the law gives police officers wide latitude to clarify and establish whether a suspect wants an attorney. In practice, as seen in the excerpts, this allows the police to insert their own objective into the interrogation and potentially manipulate the suspect into not wanting an attorney present (see Yuncker, 1995).

Asymmetry in police–suspect exchanges may also affect how suspects perceive police follow-ups and use indirectness to gauge their options during police interrogation. In conversational exchanges in which there is asymmetry of knowledge, indirectness may provide a socially conventional way of invoking counsel, albeit not necessarily an effective one. In the United States, police officers do not need to inform suspects of the reasons for their arrest.[2] Once suspects are read their Miranda rights, police officers may not be forthcoming either. Furthermore, legal rulings, such as *Davis*, facilitate police officers not informing suspects whether their invocations rise to an unequivocal standard. The suspects' inability to recognize, at the onset of the police interrogation, whether being indirect is effective when invoking counsel, as it is in other discursive contexts, will sustain the asymmetry of knowledge between police officers and suspects, benefiting those conducting the interrogation.

4.1.2 Maintaining Asymmetry in Police Interrogations

In police interrogations, police officers control the direction of the interrogation, which limits the suspects' ability to introduce topics, ask questions, or give directives. In these types of exchanges, power usually resides with the police officers because they are "vested with such authority by the institutions that employ them" (Berk-Seligson, 2009, p. 71). Police officers are often trained to implement their own linguistic agenda and dominate the agendas of the custodial suspect (e.g., Reid technique). In contexts of asymmetry, lay persons may show an aversion for directness (Busse, 2002; Terkourafi, 2011), resulting in the use of face management and politeness in the formulation of speech acts (Brown & Levinson, 1987; Goffman, 1959, 1967).

Face work (Goffman, 1967, p. 44) is the ritual attention people must give to each other in order to have self-regulating participants in social encounters. Social order is sustained through face work: by supporting one's face the other's face is also supported. Brown and Levinson (1987) expand on Goffman's theory and provide a linguistic realization of face called politeness theory. They argue that face is comprised of both negative face, or the desire for autonomy, and positive face, or the desire for connection with others. Like Goffman, Brown and Levinson argue that face is continuously subject to threat. For Brown and Levinson, many of the acts speakers perform in social interactions are inherently face threatening. Requests, for example, threaten negative face since they restrict an individual's autonomy and freedom from interference. They may also threaten positive face if the request implies a criticism of the addressee which lessens solidarity between the interactants.

In general, all directives (e.g., requests) may threaten the speakers' face and require a strategy that manages the effect of the threat to face on the

[2] In *Devenpeck* v. *Alford* (2004), the Court explained that although it's certainly "good police practice" to let a suspect know the reason for his arrest when taken into custody, there is no constitutional requirement to do so.

conversational participants. Brown and Levinson (1987) lay out this strategy in their theory of politeness. They argue that politeness strategies can be ordered in a continuum. The least polite strategy is bald on-record politeness. This strategy adheres to Grice's maxims and is maximally efficient. An example of bald-on record politeness is the formulation of requests using the imperative (i.e., a direct speech act), such as "Get me an attorney" or "I want an attorney." The other politeness strategies (in their ascending order of politeness) include: positive politeness (e.g., "Can you get me an attorney?"), negative politeness (e.g., "Can I get an attorney?"), and off-record politeness (e.g., "I think I need help here"). Of note, the most polite strategy, off-record politeness, is the prototype of indirect communication since the speech act is not conventional and must be inferred (e.g., a novel indirect request, hints, rhetorical questions, etc.).

In the corpus, a gamut of indirectly formulated invocations for counsel is observed. It is not uncommon for suspects to invoke counsel in a nonconventional manner. The law often tags these invocations as ambiguous or equivocal formulations aimed at gauging the police officers' responses (a type of pre-invocation). Most lay persons (e.g., suspects), however, may not know that invocations for counsel must be formulated directly and "unequivocally" to have any legal effect. This is counter to a suspect's notion of the potential importance of being cordial when invoking counsel, as cited in *Taylor* v. *Jackson* (2017):

> At the beginning of the interview, detectives advised Taylor of his Miranda rights and asked if he would like to talk to them. Taylor said, "I would rather stop. Talk to a lawyer. I mean I'm tryin to be, I'm trying to be cordial, you know what I'm sayin. I'm not about bull shit." After the detectives attempted to clarify whether Taylor wanted to speak with them, Taylor explained, "I really don't want to talk because I may want to stop you know, somewhere." The detectives then explained that Taylor had the right to stop the interview at any time. And Taylor responded, "Well then let's go then," and agreed to speak with the detectives.

In Taylor's police interrogation, Taylor seems to be balancing his desire for counsel with cordialness. He seemed to be attempting to be cooperative, while maintaining his right to secure counsel. The suspect's background knowledge of how to engage speakers in a face threatening, asymmetric context, however, does not conform to the reality of the interrogation room. Taylor's reliance on his knowledge of the normative aspects of speech (see Fox, 2014), which allow for mutuality of understanding between conversational participants, fails him with regard to invoking the right to counsel. Hence, he waives his right to counsel and proceeds to provide a statement to the police officers.

4.1.3 *Mutuality of Understanding in Police Interrogation*

Recent research on the use of requests in institutional settings has shed light on the organization of request sequences in these types of encounters. Some of these studies (Fox, 2014; Raevaara & Sorjonen, 2014) have focused on a type of request traditionally considered pre-requests, such as "do you have X?," "can I have X?," or "can you X for me?" This research suggests that in some institutional settings no distinction is made between pre-requests and requests: all requesting utterances are treated as requests (Raevaara & Sorjonen, 2014). The view that no distinction holds between the function of pre-requests and requests creates a normative expectation for hearing a person's utterances as requests, akin to the discussion on types of conventional requests. The research points to the importance of mutuality of understanding, common ground, and preference for progressivity in discourse. As Fox (2014) notes "we have thus seen that if preference organization is at work in these sequences, it is a preference for progressivity in moving the sequence forward to granting" (p. 60).

The law's current, and common, interpretation of indirect invocations as equivocal is at odds with the notion that certain types of requests aim to move the conversation forward. The judiciary's view of language use, coupled with current police interrogation training, have provided a space in which police officers do not have to share a (discursive) mutuality of understanding or common ground with suspects. This, in turn, interferes with suspects' ability to invoke their constitutional rights during police questioning. For an invocation for counsel to be granted and move forward the talk, the police interrogation must be "cooperatively constituted as a space for a focused joint activity" (Raevaara & Sorjonen, 2014, p. 264). As Excerpt 4.3 further illustrates, in the

Excerpt 4.3

At about 8.5 minutes into the interrogation, Williams asked whether he could call a lawyer:

1 Defendant: Can I call a lawyer, Mr. Howaniec, son, 'cause you're not – you're not telling me . . .
2 St. Laurent: So we're ending this conversation?
3 Defendant: Yeah, you're not telling me what you're charging me with. You're not telling me nothin'.
4 Fillebrown: Well, we're trying to get there with ya, but . . .

(*United States* v. *Williams*, 2015)

corpus the invocation stage of a police interrogation is not a space for a focused joint activity, but rather a space where the police interrogator's agenda is to block the suspect's attempts at performing a request for counsel.

In Excerpt 4.3, the defendant eventually agrees to speak to the police officers. His inability to obtain counsel and information from the officers, in a sense, "wears him out" until he concedes to waive his rights. The judge presiding the case sided with the police officers and ruled that the invocation was equivocal, the suspect was gauging his options, and the defendant knowingly and voluntarily waived his rights.

It is important to note that there are instances in the corpus that could be considered pre-requests (see Levinson, 1983; Schegloff, 2007). Speakers may use pre-requests to find out whether they will get a positive response to their request. In a context where speakers have very little information, such as a police interrogation, this type of pre-request would not be unusual. Suspects may employ a pre-request such as "Do you think I should get an attorney?" or "Should I get an attorney?" to ascertain (or as the judges argue potentially "gauge") whether there are grounds for refusing the request – or getting counsel. The suspect is avoiding making a wrong move that could result in a worse outcome than being interrogated (e.g., being sent to jail for an undetermined period of time, being deemed uncooperative, etc.). These types of requests, hence, require a follow-up move that addresses the suspect's inquiry. In the corpus, these requests are often dismissed (no information is provided) and/or they are "clarified."

The notion that a suspect who is "gauging" their options in a police interrogation invalidates the possibility that they may be requesting counsel is a creation of the law and the standards laid forth in *Davis* and other rulings. In talk, speakers often attempt to achieve multiple functions: politeness, saving face, achieving common ground and mutuality of understanding, etc. These functions may be mediated also by social and cultural factors. As expected, requests and pre requests may be susceptible to misunderstanding and require follow-ups aimed at clarification. These are all potential features of discourse that in practice are handicapped by the law and the limitations it creates when attempting to narrow down the functions of speech in police interrogation.

The next section will examine how police interrogation creates a space of nonmutuality of understanding and noncooperation during the invocation of rights stage of an interrogation. A space that may not conform to the suspects' understanding of shared knowledge in discourse. For this part of the analysis, the chapter will apply game theory methodology to police–suspect exchanges that include and follow a suspect's invocation for counsel. This discussion will address how sequences of talk during the invocation of rights stage represent a type of game where one player (custodial suspect) is strategizing in a manner consistent with how speakers attempt to reach mutuality of understanding in conversation, whereas the other player (the interrogator) is simply responding, based on their training, in a manner that appears to address the other players' turns of talk while invalidating the common knowledge assumption (see Varsos et al., 2021). This creates a type of discursive game where one player (custodial suspect) fails to recognize the game as framed and the other player (interrogator) takes advantage of this failure by employing manipulation and deception to change the other player's discursive preferences.

4.2 Communication As a Type of Game

Linguists have employed game theory to understand how speakers strategically convey meaning and intent in communication. Players have preferences for outcomes that motivate strategic linguistic choices made during the game. Theoretically, in communication as in other games, a player cannot control the outcome of the game just by one's actions. Instead, a player must take the other player's linguistic actions into account. This process has traditionally been studied in linguistics under rationalistic game theory (see van Rooij, 2008). Rationalistic game theory examines "when is it rationalizable to communicate at all" and "how can credibility of messages be established" (Jäger, 2008, p. 410).

Some common approaches to the credibility question include the application of costly signaling games and cheap talk. Rabin (1990), for example, takes a game theoretic approach that is reminiscent of Grice's (1975) cooperative principles that all messages are credible assuming cooperativity. Rabin developed Credible Message Rationalizability (CMR) by combining Crawford and Sobel's (1982) standard equilibrium analysis and Farrell and Gibbon's (1989) rich language assumption that players are rational. Players tend to believe statements that are consistent with rationality, allowing for some meaningful communication to be predicted, including those that require implicature[3] to derive the players' intent.

Other approaches predicting communication include Blutner's (2000) Bidirectional Optimality Theory and Parikh's (1991) Strategic Discourse Model (SDM). Dekker and van Rooij (2000) reformulated Blutner's theory as the exchange of information between sender and receiver characterized as a strategic signaling game of complete information. The actions of speakers are described as the choice of expressions and the actions of the hearers as the choice of interpretations. These models examine cooperative exchanges, focusing on form-meaning relationships.

[3] With implicatures, what the speaker said is distinct from what the speaker meant or implied (see Grice, 1975).

Parikh (1991, 2000, 2001) expanded on the analysis of sender and receiver exchanges by adding the sequential features of a communication game of partial information with a unique solution. Parikh (1991) argues that most languages are "situated" which makes language an efficient system of communication: "Once we allow situations a role in the determination of content, it becomes clear that there are certain aspects of utterances that are constant across utterances and others that vary from one situation to another" (p. 475). He notes that part of the task of a theory of communication is to explain how we can get from meaning to content. His model of strategic communication under conditions of ambiguity introduced the concept of "strategic inference" in communication. The central assumption of Parikh's Strategic Discourse Model (SDM) is that the transfer of information between players involves a strategic interaction between them. When the strategic interaction is common knowledge between the players, that is, when it is a game with a unique solution, the flow will be communicative. Parikh notes "that this game-theoretic structure is situated somewhere, either in the 'minds' of players or in their ambient circumstances or both" (p. 478).

Parikh's SDM, as other models previously discussed, describes how players reach cooperative, meaningful communication, including situations where ambiguity may arise. These approaches, however, do not address noncooperative situations, where players may not have complete information of the signaling strategies of other players (see Rabin, 1990; Farrell, 1993; Asher and Lascarides, 2013). As Pinker et al. (2008) note, models of conversation that only assume cooperative agents fail to explain the dynamics of strategic conversations.

Discursive games have also been modeled through game-theoretic constructs such as Bayesian games (Frank and Goodman, 2012; Stevens et al., 2015; Burnett, 2019; Harsanyi, 1967). In Bayesian games, an agent's utility is determined not only by actions but also by types of the agents. In these types of games, "the existence of private information leads naturally to attempts by informed parties to communicate (or mislead) and to attempts by uninformed parties to learn and respond" (Gibbons, 1997, p. 138).

In the analysis of reference, Stevens (2016) discusses, through a Bayesian and cognitive lens, whether strategic and nonstrategic thinking play independent roles in explaining pragmatic behavior. Stevens notes that a model that explains interaction must account for why people think strategically and, alternatively, why they may not. Stevens argues that the failure of agents to work out the best strategy for themselves may be rooted in reconciling strategic considerations with situational or cognitive biases. Stevens adds that pragmatic behavior does not always tilt toward strategic optimality and, hence, may only provide partial explanations for complex (linguistic) situations where the choices of strategy may not be obvious.

Rational choice theory may not provide a framework for accounting for an agent's variances in preferences owing to misperceptions. According to Tversky and Kahneman (1986), the normative analysis in game theory makes four assumptions to develop expected utility theory: cancellation, transitivity, dominance, and invariance. Cancellation eliminates trivial outcomes in which action does not produce different results. Transitivity has a standard mathematical meaning ($A \succ B$, $B \succ C \rightarrow A \succ C$) in which A is preferred ($\succ$) to B, and B is preferred to C, transitivity implies ($\rightarrow$) that A is preferred to C. Dominance postulates that if one option is better than another in one state and as good as other options in all other states, it is preferred.

Invariance, which assumes that different representations of the same choice problem should yield the same preference, creates a problem for rational choice theory. Because invariance and dominance are normatively essential, Tversky and Kahneman argue rational choice theory cannot provide a description of choice if an agent shifts their preference unless a fundamental change in perception arises. They find that the normative axioms of rational choice are often violated in situations lacking transparency. To illustrate this point, Tversky and Kahneman show that individuals respond differently to alternative frames of a risky choice, first as the prospect of gaining utility, and second as the prospect of minimizing loss. Even though the alternate statements yield the exact same utility, individuals in their study made different choices depending on how the choice was phrased.

Cason and Plott (2014) assert that the absence of an integrated theory of perception masks the existence of a specific form of misperception: the "failure of game form recognition" (p. 1236). Suffering this type of misperception causes a decision maker to fail "to recognize the proper connections between the acts available for choice and the consequences of choice, which, by necessity, are associated with the method of measuring preferences" (p. 1237). They warn that errors in utility maximization, owing to misperceptions of the game form, lose a separate identity when mistakes are considered generically as an error term, as do errors arising from misinformation, opaque rules, and misperceptions of a situated environment.

Parting from framing theory, the analysis of an unbalanced game model, such as a police interrogation, allows for the examination of differences in each player's understating of the game and their choices. In these types of games, a player may not be able to recognize the other player's manipulation of their preference to become that of the other player. Excerpt 4.4 shows a representative excerpt from the corpus that illustrates linguistically how the custodial suspect's, *CS*'s, preferences are guided by the interrogator's, *I*'s, discursive actions.

The interrogation continued with the officer vaguely discussing the crime and possible charges. Information is not forthcoming in police interrogations as

Excerpt 4.4

1 Officer: Okay. You know what, I have to read them to you anyway regardless of whether you know them or not. You have the right to remain silent, do you understand?
2 Rodriguez: Yes.
3 Officer: Anything you say can be used against you in a court, do you understand?
4 Rodriguez: Yes.
5 Officer: You have the right of the presence of an attorney before and during any questioning, do you understand?
6 Rodriguez: Yes.
7 Officer: If you cannot afford an attorney one will be appointed for you free of charge before any questioning, if you want, do you understand?
8 Rodriguez: Yes.
9 Officer: Okay.
10 The officers then questioned Mr. Rodriguez about his involvement in the drive-by shooting . . . Eventually, Mr. Rodriguez asked for an attorney:
11 Rodriguez: Can I speak to an attorney?
12 Officer: Whatever you want.
13 Rodriguez: Can I speak to an attorney?
14 Officer: You tell me what you want.
15 Rodriguez: That is what I want.
16 Officer: That's fine bro we stop because we can't talk to you anymore, okay, so.
17 Officer: You're going to be charged with murder today.
18 Rodriguez: Why?

(*Rodriguez* v. *Mcdonald*, 2017)

a matter of training and strategy. The discussion of the attorney resumed to establish that Rodriguez did not want counsel and he waived his rights.

The discursive analysis of Excerpt 4.4 begins with *I* reading *CS* the Miranda rights. The suspect affirms understanding of the rights and in turn 11 proceeds to invoke the right to counsel: "Can I speak to an attorney?" The invocation is phrased using a hedged indirect request, which may have linguistic moorings in politeness (Brown & Levison, 1987), face (Goffman, 1967), risk aversion, as well as in cognitive frameworks and sociolinguistics (see Gibbs, 1983; Holtgraves, 1994; Brooks, 2000; Holtgraves & Ashley, 2001). It may also be natural in the context of asymmetric bargaining and exchanges. Regardless of the explanation, indirectly invoking the right to counsel shows *CS*'s preference to invoke counsel and do so in a manner that fits *CS*'s understanding of formulating requests in conversation, particularly asymmetric ones (Mason, 2013).[4]

The use of an indirect request, in light of the *Davis* ruling, places *CS*'s ability to invoke counsel in the hands of *I*. As noted previously, *I* is not required by law to inform *CS* that the invocation does not rise to the level of unequivocalness to end an interrogation. *I*, however, cannot coerce *CS* into not invoking rights. Statements must be provided voluntarily or have the appearance as such. This creates a situation in which *I* does not provide information to *CS*, but has to appear to address *CS*'s indirect request.

The next turns of talk (turns 12–15) constitute *CS*'s repeated attempts at invoking counsel and restating his preference, which is met with *I*'s lack of acknowledgment of such attempts. Of note, follow-up moves are commonly used in conversation to clarify, repair, and/or respond to a prior turn of talk. *I*'s "whatever you want" or "you tell me what you want" does not address directly *CS*'s request for counsel or further *CS*'s ability to invoke counsel. *CS*, hence, continues to assert his preference for counsel and repeatedly invokes counsel in turns 11, 13, and 15, albeit successfully only in turn 15.

In turn 16, *I* changes his follow-up response to: "That's fine bro we stop because we can't talk to you anymore, okay, so," which is the first follow-up to address the outcome of *CS* invoking counsel ("we can't talk to you anymore"), but without overtly acknowledging *CS*'s invocation. In turn 17, *I* interjects with: "You're going to be charged with murder today." This statement leads *CS* to inquire "why?," which brings *CS* back to the interrogation table and away from his initial, and sustained, preference to request counsel. The talk continues and eventually *CS* waives his rights and provides incriminating statements. This is *I*'s preferred outcome based on his training: to get a statement from *CS*.

In Excerpt 4.4, *CS*'s continued attempts to invoke counsel indirectly, coupled with *I*'s strategic use of follow-up moves, serve to misdirect *CS* from invoking counsel. The ultimate success of the strategy shows *CS* exhibiting what Gharesifard and Cortés (2010, p. 1077) note is an "imprecise understanding about the objectives and true intentions of other players." *CS* attempts to invoke counsel repeatedly, yet *CS* does not question the follow-ups by *I* that do not address his attempts at invoking counsel, nor does *CS* change strategy to use another type of request for counsel (e.g., invoke directly). These options, otherwise available in talk, are not pursued by *CS* because *CS* does not recognize that *CS*'s utterances were deemed equivocal and *I* does not have to accept (by law) these utterances as invocations for counsel, regardless of the reading of the Miranda rights. *CS* continues to participate as if the conversation

[4] In the analysis, the term "preference" is expressed by discursive action: to invoke counsel, to engage in talk, or to waive rights following the reading of the Miranda rights.

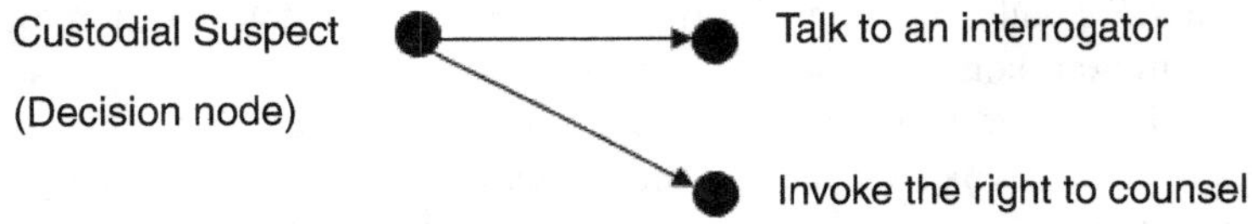

Figure 4.1 The surface game

abides by commonality of understanding where indirectly formulated requests are understood as unambiguous requests.

On *I*'s third attempt at invoking counsel, *I* indirectly acknowledges *CS*'s invocation by stating the consequences of the decision. However, *I* follows up by telling *CS* "You're going to be charged with murder today." This "distracts" *CS* into engaging with *I* as a cooperative conversational participant. *CS* is lured back into conversation because *CS* believes *I* will share information about why *CS* will be charged in the case. The information is not forthcoming, but it did return *CS* to the invocation stage of the interrogation, and, in this case, *CS* waived the right to legal counsel and agreed to talk with the interrogator.

Incorporating perceptions into the analysis of discursive strategies prompts the question of whether Bayesian analysis, commonly used in linguistics, or an alternate model should be considered to describe the actions observed in Excerpt 4.4. Bayesian analysis is based on rational utility maximization measured as the sum of the subjectively assessed utility of each outcome weighted by the probability of its occurrence. The surface game, depicted in Figure 4.1 (Mason & Mason, 2021), is a simplified Bayesian model in which *CS* has 100 percent certainty of obtaining either outcome: choosing to talk to an interrogator or invoking the right to counsel.

If *CS* chooses to invoke the right to legal counsel, shown as the arrow pointing to the lower circle on the right, whenever counsel arrives the invocation game becomes the interrogation game, and all future decisions will be generated from this lower node. *I* has a preference that *CS* chooses the other path, and *I* has strategies to shift *CS's* preference.

The surface game is the game as presented to the *CS*. However, as observed in the corpus (see Excerpt 4.4), something more than the surface game takes place. *I* has institutional powers that grant *I* a choice of outcome, the linguistic and procedural response in conversation with *CS*, to shape *CS*'s perceptions. These powers include *I*'s ability to limit *CS*'s discursive options to express preference; to control new information to influence *CS*; and to impose the least preferred outcome on *CS*. This is accomplished through *I*'s initiated follow-up moves. The observed shifts in *CS*'s responses, from invoking counsel to talking to an interrogator without counsel, may not be the product of individual free will, as cited in numerous legal cases, but the product of *CS*'s "failure of game form recognition" that accommodates misperceptions arising from other psychological, discursive, and deceptive influences.

The nuances that institutional power brings to game theory, as summarized by Prates (2014), incorporates into game theory the use of power by one agent to alter the options of another agent:

> It should be emphasized that the only form of power is the exercise of power, not its mere possession. This means that an agent with power will always exercise it, as generates better results for him. It is also important to highlight that game theory usually encompasses different games when the action-environment changes. For instance, when power is incorporated into a specific game, the use of power by an agent generates a new game, which transforms the options set of the player subjected by the power relation. (p. 286)

Prates points out what is essentially applicable to any successful hypergame employed by *I* and embedded within an invocation game: preferences shift. The shift in preferences can be thought of as new conditions that must be met for *CS* to invoke a particular action because the environment changes and not the assessed risk.

In Figure 4.1, the switch from the lower node to the higher node (i.e., from invoking the right to counsel to waiving that right) entails a different risk environment for *CS*. As Prates notes: new game, new player, new standards. In an extensive form rendition of the game, subsequent action switches from one pathway to another. The shift creates a new game outside of Bayesian sequential analysis. The hypergame creates the shift observed in Excerpt 4.4.

This chapter proposes an alternative to rational choice theory to investigate why discursive preferences shift in real world applications, such as police interrogations (see also Mason & Mason, 2023). The analysis this approach produces will provide insights into the effect of institutional power in framing "the invocation game" as a type of hypergame:

> Figuring out what strategy a player will use is dependent upon not only his or her observation of the game, but also how that player believes their opponent is viewing the game . . . The goal of hypergame analysis is to provide insight into real-world situations that are often more complex than a game where the choices of strategy present themselves as obvious. (Kovach et al., 2015, p. 2)

4.3 Hypergame Dynamics

Hypergame Theory (HgT) expands traditional game theory and noncooperative game theory (see Fudenberg & Tirole, 1991) by incorporating players' perceptions of other players' preferences into their strategic action (see Bennett, 1977; Wang et al., 1989; Başar & Olsder, 1999). HgT accommodates a player with the power to shape the game while it is being played to exercise that power strategically guided by that player's perceptions of other player's preferences. In the invocation game, *I* controls the discursive exchanges, which confers to *I* an advantage over *CS*. During the game, *I* accumulates information on *CS*'s preferences. *I* uses that information strategically in choosing outcomes to influence *CS*'s perception of the invocation game and to shape the game, while it is being played, to shift *CS*'s preferences to conform with *I*'s. Within the invocation game, each turn of talk produces an ordered pair of ranked preferences for *CS* and *I* (P_{CS}, P_I) over *CS*'s choices: (a) waive rights and agree to interrogation, (b) stay silent, (c) engage in talk, and (d) invoke the right to legal counsel. *CS*'s preferences are given initially by nature, are fluid to the situation, and are updated after each turn of *I*'s talk.

For *I*, it is easiest to obtain a statement if no legal counsel is present with the *CS*. An interrogation with a lawyer present is preferable to silence. Talk is preferred to an interrogation with a lawyer present because talk is an opportunity for *I* to persuade *CS* to consent to speak without an attorney. It should also be noted that anything *CS* says can be used against *CS* in a court of law, making all conversation, by default, in the realm of an interrogation without legal counsel, the most preferred outcome of all.

The legal framework in which police interrogation operates creates two hypergames in which at least one player's strategy is determined by their perception of the other player's preferences. The next sections provide the notation and modeling of the hypergames and the application of hypergame modeling to representative excerpts from the corpus.

4.3.1 Hypergame Notation of the Invocation Game

The invocation game adopts Gharesifard and Cortés's (2014) notation where a game $G = (V, S_{outcome}, P)$, consists of a vector of two players $V = \{CS, I\}$, an outcome vector $S_{outcome} = S_{CS}$ with cardinality $N = |S_{outcome}| = 2$, where S_{CS} is one of two outcomes arising from *CS* taking action $X \in (x_1 \ldots x_4)$:

Variable	Description of action
x_1	Agree to an interrogation,
x_2	Remain silent,
x_3	Engage in talk,
x_4	Invoke right to counsel

CS will make a choice to invoke or waive, and both *CS* and *I* will derive utility from *CS*'s choice generating a preference rank (P) of outcomes for *CS* and *I*: $P = (P_{CS}, P_I)$. Preference is measured along a sequence of events.

The surface game is a single move game. The game begins formulaically with the reading of Miranda rights. The choice by *CS* either to invoke x_4 or to waive x_1 generates the outcome preference rank P. Within the game, two other moves x_2 (silence) and x_3 (talk) are allowed, but these additional moves occur around *CS*'s choice: x_1 or x_4. Since both x_1 and x_4 entail conversation x_3, they are subsets of talk: $x_1, x_4 \ni x_3$. Given the specific inclusion of x_1 and x_4 as choices in the game, we distinguish $x_3^{'}$ to be talk that excludes invoking and waiving the right to counsel: $x_3^{'} = x_3 \backslash x_1, x_4$.

I's preference among outcomes, $P_I = x_1 \succ x_3 \succ x_4 \succ x_2$, is assumed constant by training and will guide *I*'s strategy when engaging with *CS*. *I* most prefers an interrogation without a lawyer present because the absence of a lawyer makes obtaining a statement from *CS* easier. *I* prefers conversation (x_3) to a decision by *CS* to invoke the right to a lawyer (x_4) because it leaves open the possibility of persuading *CS* to talk without a lawyer, and *I* least prefers silence as silence does not further *I*'s investigation.

The invocation game situates discourse for *CS*. *CS* has exactly two powers: the right to remain silent and the right to have a lawyer present for questioning. The power dynamics are evident from what transpires in an interrogation: *CS* has lost the right to freedom and faces the possibility of imprisonment. *CS*'s preference rank, $P_{CS} = (x_1, \ldots, x_4)^T$, is fluid to the situation and is updated after each turn of *I*'s talk $T \in \mathbb{N} \geq 0$. Any *CS* who prefers $x_2 \succ x_3$ will end the game by not engaging in the interrogation, albeit while being detained in jail, or, in some instances, with the release of *CS* (e.g., at the discretion of *I*).

For those *CS* willing to talk, *CS*'s preference rankings are given as a state of nature $P_{CS} = x_3 \succ x_2$. Therefore, *CS*'s preferences manifest from nature as either $P_{CS} = x_4 \succ x_1 \succ x_3^{'} \succ x_2$ or as $P_{CS} = x_1 \succ x_4 \succ x_3^{'} \succ x_2$. Both x_1 and x_4 are presumed to be preferred to $x_3{}'$ owing to a preference for relevant conversation over irrelevant conversation, because engaging in talk may lead to providing incriminating statements. Therefore, $x_3^{'}$ is held in reserve until $x_3^{'}$ is perceived to hold strategic value (e.g., request information or clarification) at which point *CS* reveals $P_{CS} = x_3^{'} \succ x_4 \succ x_1 \succ x_2$ or $P_{CS} = x_3^{'} \succ x_1 \succ x_4 \succ x_2$. Once $x_3^{'}$ loses strategic value, preferences revert to their previous state unless the discourse altered *CS*'s preference ranking.

4.4 Two Hypergames

4.4.1 *Type 1 Hypergame: CS Initiates $x_3^{'}$*

Type 1 hypergame originates after *CS* initiates conversation $x_3^{'}$. The strategic value of $x_3^{'}$ for *CS* ranges from human need (e.g., a desire for water) to probing for information. The success or failure of *CS*'s initiative depends on the willingness of *I* to grant such success. Leaving aside human rights violations

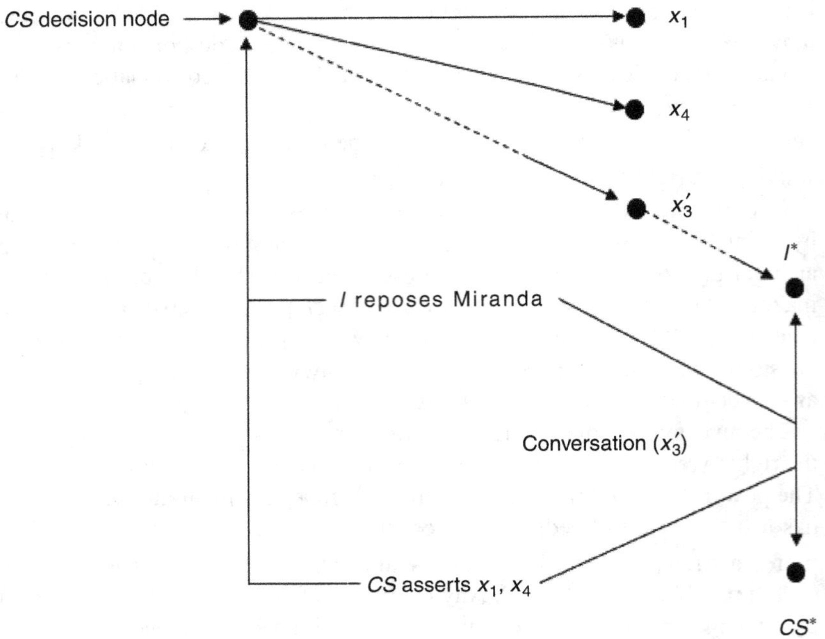

Figure 4.2 Type I Hypergame: *CS* initiates x'_3

(e.g., denying requested water), *I* has the ability to shift the topic of x'_3. This topic shift is the type 1 hypergame depicted in Figure 4.2 (Mason & Mason, 2021). In this subgame, the shifted conversation continues with the participants denoted as CS^* and I^* until either *I* reposes the Miranda question, or *CS* declares x_1 or attempts to invoke x_4 which returns the conversation to the *CS* decision node.

4.4.2 *Type 2 Hypergame: I Initiates x'_3*

In the type 2 hypergame, *CS* makes an indirectly formulated assertion of x_4, and *I* initiates conversation x'_3 to divert *CS* away from x_4. The conversation continues until *CS* asserts x_1 or x_4, or until *I* becomes convinced *CS*'s position has changed at which point *I* reposes the Miranda question. The type 2 hypergame is depicted in Figure 4.3 (Mason & Mason, 2021).

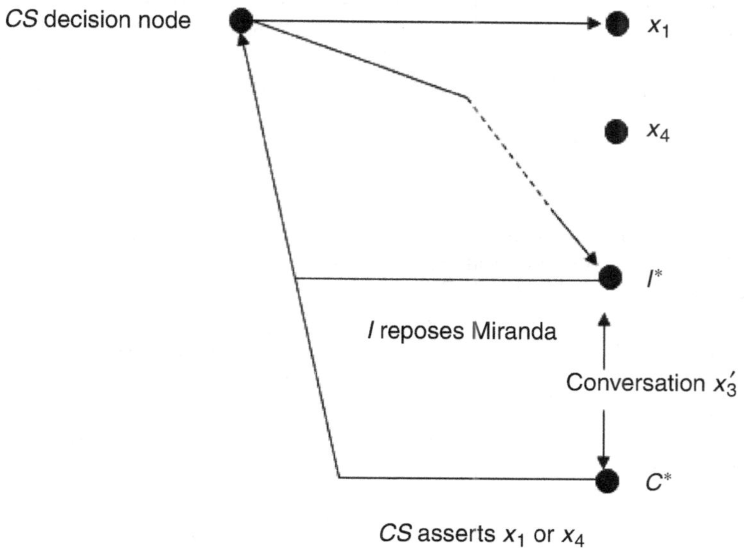

Figure 4.3 Type 2 Hypergame: *I* initiates $x_3^{'}$ to divert *CS* away from $x_4^{'}$

4.5 Analyzing the Invocation Game and Its Hypergames

The two hypergames illustrated in Figures 4.2 and 4.3 show the assertion of power in which *I* takes footing[5] from *CS* to influence the outcome of the game by controlling the topic of conversation. In a noncooperative asymmetric exchange, the person who controls the talk may direct the exchanges without regard for mutuality of understanding. In the invocation game, *I*, guided by perceptions of what motivates *CS*, works to influence *CS* to *I*'s desired preference. *CS* will be handicapped from achieving discursive goals if *CS* does not recognize how the talk is situated. *I* protects *CS*'s misunderstanding instead of eliminating it. An equivocal/ambiguous invocation for counsel allows *I* to ask follow-up questions aimed at "clarifying" the invocation. *I* is not required to take any action, such as initiating the process x_4, making the follow-up an empty rhetorical clarification. The analysis of Excerpt 4.5, previously cited as Excerpt 4.2, will show how *I* manipulates *CS*'s preferences through a series of commonly observed extensive moves, with multiple iterations, to match *I*'s own.

The surface game commences at the end of turn 1. After listening to the Miranda rights, *CS* asserts x_4 in turn 2 revealing $P_{CS} = x_4 \succ x_1 \succ x_3^{'} \succ x_2$. In turn 3, *I* initiates a type 2 hypergame with $x_3^{'}$ in which *I* provides unsolicited

[5] Footing is "the alignment we take up to ourselves and the others present as expressed in the way we manage the production or reception of an utterance" (Goffman, 1981, p. 128).

Excerpt 4.5

1 Mande: And if you decide to answer questions now, without a lawyer present, you have the right to stop answering questions at any time.
2 Davis: If, if I'm, if I'm going to answer questions, I'm going to need a lawyer here.
3 Mande: Alright, well, this is just so you understand that ... and then down here, it's just now we're, this is the part where, if you want a way to talk to us and answer questions, that's where you sign there. If you don't want to talk to us, don't ...
4 Davis: I want to talk to you, but I just need my lawyer.
5 Chaney: Ok, ok, so here's what you're telling us – you do want your lawyer?
6 Davis: I want to talk, yeah. But I need my lawyer present.
7 Chaney: We wanna ... either you talk to us now ... if you want to talk to us now, without anybody else present, you have to sign that waiver. If not, all bets are off, you go into the system, ok?
8 Davis: Yeah.

(*United States* v. *Davis*, 2019)

information. Viewed as a cooperative move, *I*'s "clarification" implies that *CS* can choose x_1 and assert x_4 "at any time" implying x_4 is a subset of $\boldsymbol{x}_1 : \boldsymbol{x}_4 \ni \boldsymbol{x}_1$. This "clarification" reduces the perceived cost of x_1 because, by implication, x_4 is already a part of x_1.

CS responds to *I*'s type 2 hypergame in turn 4 as in turn 2 except *CS* couches this assertion of x_4 by first presenting a cooperative ethos. The effect is a short apology made prior to exercising self-interest. This statement should end the game for a second time, but in turn 5 *I* engages the type 2 hypergame a second time by presenting x_3' that appears at first as a summary but changes into what appears to be a clarifying question. Almost word for word, *CS* repeats the preference expressed in turn 4 and now again in turn 6, and once more the invocation game should end.

In the third iteration of the type 2 hypergame, *I* shifts strategy to employ an ominous tone. After an initial misstep in turn 7, *I* returns the conversation directly to *CS*'s decision node by presenting alternative x_1 with its procedure of signing a waiver, or, if *CS* does not choose x_1, an outcome with no certainty and an unknown procedure which will be no better than x_2. *I* concludes turn 7 by asking "ok?" Here "ok" is a request for *CS* to confirm that *CS* understands *CS*'s choices which do not explicitly include x_4.

I has reshaped *CS*'s perception of the game. In turn 6, *CS* asserts x_4 with conviction, just as in turn 4. In turn 8, *CS* reveals that the perceived value of the alternative to x_1 has become worse than it was in turn 6 because the alternative to x_1 in turn 6 was x_4 but in turn 8 the alternative to x_1 is one of uncertainty, as alluded to with the reference to betting, except instead of a payout of x_4 there is certainty of going into the "system." After turn 8, *CS* signs a waiver revealing the shift to $P_{CS} = x_1 \succ x_4 \succ x_3 \succ x_2$ brought on by *I*'s statement in turn 7.

Excerpt 4.6 provides another example of the hypergames played in a police interrogation.

Excerpt 4.6 is situated at the initial stage of the invocation game initiated by *I*'s reading of the *Miranda* rights. In turn 1, *I* seeks affirmation from *CS* that *CS* understands these rights and warnings. *CS* affirms in turn 2. *I* then imposes a decision on *CS* in turn 3: x_1 or not x_1? *CS* responds by indirectly invoking the right to counsel in turn 4 which reveals $P_{CS} = x_4 \succ x_1 \succ x_3 \succ x_2$. *I* appears to acknowledge the invocation in turn 5.

In turn 6, *CS* initiates a type 1 hypergame with x_3' which reveals a shift in preference $P_{CS} = x_3 \succ x_4 \succ x_1 \succ x_2$. Strategically, it seems that *CS* is apologizing for, or justifying, *CS*'s assertion of x_4, perhaps responding to the perceived power dynamics between *CS* and *I*. *I* acknowledges the expression, then in turn 8 *CS* executes a strategic probe for information. *I* defers providing information, and then *CS* asks a procedural question in turn 10, *I* expresses a need for clarification, *CS* repeats the question in turn 12, and then *I* makes the strategic move in turn 13 to shift the topic back to the question of waiving or invoking the right to counsel, as if *CS* had not expressed an opinion.

Turn 14 shows that in x_3' *CS* has gone from seeker to provider of information by acknowledging the procedure for the dispreferred choice x_1 and that x_1 does not negate x_4. In turn 15, *I* does not acknowledge the lingering invocation and instead asserts that *CS* is in control and must yet decide what to do. In taking this action, *I* asserts a perception of how power is situated in the talk that is contrary to reality. Had *CS* been able to assert footing, the invocation of turn 4 would have been acknowledged. Instead, it stands as a powerless utterance.

CS agrees four times in turn 16 to the illusion *I* gives in turn 15, but then *CS* expresses confusion. *I* provides a (mis)guiding reaffirmation that *CS* is in control. *CS* assumes control by twice starting an assertion of what *I* can do in turn 18 to which *I* helpfully completes the thought asking if *CS* wants x_1. Turn 20 reveals the important change: $P_{CS} = x_1 \succ x_4 \succ x_3' \succ x_2$, and with a request for clarification in turn 20, *CS* confirms in turn 21.

But, why did *CS*'s preferences change? Key to understanding the change is the fact that during the conversation no new information about circumstances or procedure were provided, despite *CS*'s probe for this information. The only notable topic that arises is one of power: who is in control of the situation. Within the conversation, *CS*'s tone changes from one of certainty about

Excerpt 4.6

1 Detective Holliday: So you understand each of your rights?
2 Brandon Johnson: Yes.
3 Detective Holliday: Are you willing to give up these rights and answer questions or make statements at this time?
4 Brandon Johnson: Ah, I really would like to have a lawyer present.
5 Detective Holliday: Okay.
6 Brandon Johnson: Because I know how serious this is.
7 Detective Holliday: Hm-hm.
8 Brandon Johnson: And I don't have anything to hide. I will talk to you guys. You know, I'll tell you any and everything I know, you know. But, um, I just wondered what like what kind of questions would you like to ask me or anything?
9 Detective Holliday: Well you, for, for you to find that out though.
10 Brandon Johnson: I gotta answer these questions though on paper.
11 Detective Holliday: Pardon?
12 Brandon Johnson: You said I gotta, I gotta answer these questions on the paper.
13 Detective Holliday: No. Well no, no. You answered them [Miranda warnings]. But you just said you wanted a lawyer which means I can't ask, tell you what the questions are gonna be without a lawyer being present. Now do you wanna waive your right to a lawyer? You understand that at any time, you can change your mind and stop talking and stop answering questions. You can ask for that lawyer at that time, whatever. But because you're thinking about asking for a lawyer—.
14 Brandon Johnson: Well I understand that.
15 Detective Holliday: Alright. That, I, I don't, you're in control here guy.
16 Brandon Johnson: Right, alright, alright. I understand that. You can, um.
17 Detective Holliday: You're in control.
18 Brandon Johnson: ________, you can, you can.
19 Detective Holliday: You wanna waive your rights and talk to us right now?
20 Brandon Johnson: I can talk to you, yes.
21 Detective Holliday: Okay. So the answers yes?
22 Brandon Johnson: Yes.

(*Johnson* v. *Booker*, 2014)

preference, to a small hesitation in the probe for information in turn 8, to a desire for affirmation of understanding of the procedure in turns 10 and 12, and then to the shift in footing from being a requester of information to a provider.

Perhaps the incongruous nature of an exchange in which the one who gives up information is portrayed as being in control is as confusing as it is comforting. After the reassuring illusion of control, *CS* switches to trust the situation and relinquish all control by waiving the right to legal counsel. It may seem that *CS* has switched from skepticism of *I* to trusting *I*, but in probing for information in turn 8 it shows that *CS* believes *I* is willing to be helpful, an illusion furthered by the illusion of control. *I* has reassured *CS* to see the talk as situated cooperatively with *CS* in the position of power. *I* implies that $x_2, x_4 \ni x_1$ because if x_1 is chosen both x_4 and x_2 remain as options, and x_1 is the way to satisfy the curiosity *CS* expressed in turn 8. *I* affirms the change in preference by requesting clarification consistent with a cooperatively situated exchange in turn 21, and *CS* cooperatively affirms in turn 22.

4.6 Implications of the Invocation Game: Identifying Manipulation of Preferences in Police Interrogation

The application of hypergame theory to empirical linguistic data provides a method for analyzing the strategic aspects of a police interrogation. This game theoretic approach to analyzing linguistic actions describes how *I* develops linguistic strategies that reshape *CS*'s perceptions to shift *CS*'s preferences to conform with *I*'s preferences. This chapter's game theoretic approach expands the analysis of discourse by treating the reading and waiving of Miranda rights as a noncooperative game with potentially multiple preference manipulating moves. When applied to linguistics, the hypergame approach gives manipulation a coherent structure. Its distinct structure accommodates binary states consistent with discursive success or failure as well as a continuum of many states consistent with stages in discursive persuasion. It can incorporate motives, incentives, boundaries, etc., to expand the range of analysis to an infinite number of turns, accommodating any number of digressions relevant or not.

Moreover, this chapter considers the invocation game to be a particular example of a more broadly identified mode of a game which recognizes many avenues by which perceptions may be disturbed causing changes in preferences. This game theoretic approach may also be applied to the minimization and maximization strategies of police interrogation, as well as other types of police interviewing techniques in which changes of preferences are observed. Noncoercive police interrogation techniques are not impervious to police interviewers changing suspects' preferences. The application of hypergame theory to the invocation game presented in this chapter can identify instances of manipulation of preferences at all stages of a police interrogation or interview – broadly defined and applied, including the interview of witnesses and victims of crime.

5 Invocations for Counsel, the Rulings, and the Courts: A Statistical Analysis of the Corpus

The policeman is not a fiduciary of the suspect. The police are allowed to play on a suspect's ignorance, his anxieties, his fears, and his uncertainties; they just are not allowed to magnify those fears, uncertainties, and so forth to the point where rational decision becomes impossible.

(Circuit Judge Posner, *United States* v. *Rutledge*, 1990)

This chapter takes a statistical approach to the analysis of the legal rulings that comprise the corpus. The analysis will provide insights into the possible relationships between the variables that make up the corpus, including types of invocations for counsel, the judges' rulings, the presence of police follow-ups, and the judges' presidential appointments, among an array of other legal and linguistic factors. To frame the discussion and understand the judges' application of the law, the chapter starts with a description of the corpus, the selection of variables, and the research questions posed. The latter will be tested further using statistical analysis, specifically a difference in proportion test.

5.1 The Corpus

The corpus consists of 301 criminal federal cases. The search engine used for the collection of the corpus is Westlaw Edge. This search engine is used by law schools and provides a comprehensive database of federal and state rulings, as well as supplementary documents and opinions on an array of legal matters, including the Miranda rights, the invocation of rights, and legal analysis on police interrogation. Both unpublished and published opinions are included in Westlaw and comprise the corpus, albeit most of the opinions in the study are published opinions. An opinion is considered unpublished (not precedential, except when relevant under doctrine of law) if it is not published in the Federal Reporter. Yet, Westlaw publishes most of these opinions online, as well as in a print series called the Federal Appendix. Of note, the distinction between published and unpublished opinions is not relevant to the analysis of the book's corpus. Both types of opinions were adjudicated, had an impact on the defendant's legal journey, and reveal the judges' stance on legal precedence.

The parameters for the search were limited to the three main levels of the federal court system: district courts (the trial court), circuit courts (first level of appeal), and the Supreme Court of the United States (final level of appeal in the federal system). Military courts were also included in the search since custodial interrogations occur in military settings and custodial suspects must be read their Miranda rights.[1] Cases that are argued in military courts may be appealed at The United States Court of Appeals for the Armed Forces and up to the Supreme Court of the United States (see Chapter 1 for details on the federal court system).

The search terms include "unequivocal," "equivocal," "ambiguous," and "unambiguous" invocations for counsel. The legal standard is for invocations for counsel to be unequivocal and/or unambiguous, hence these parameters (and their counterparts) capture the legal requirements of invoking counsel in the United States. As noted previously, the courts often do not make a clear distinction between the terms, albeit some courts have addressed them interchangeably. The date parameters for the search terms were 1966–2021. The result of this broad search were 1,050 cases. The search terms, however, included other types of "unequivocal," "equivocal," "ambiguous," and "unambiguous" invocations, such as unequivocal invocations for silence and unequivocal *pro se* (self-representation) invocations, among others. Of the 1,050 cases, 316 cases fit the (initial) parameters of the search.

The initial corpus of 316 cases was adjusted to 301 cases, after a careful three-step review process aimed at ensuring (single) rater reliability and accuracy of the corpus entries. First, an Excel file was created to manually enter the variables examined in the study – these are described in detail in the next section. Every variable was entered per initial review of each case. Second, every variable entry was rechecked, per case, against the 316-case corpus. In this second review, the researcher noted fourteen double counted case entries in the database. These were removed from the Excel file, since they could alter the quantitative and statistical results. The revised corpus was reduced to 302 cases. Third, before completing the statistical analysis, the researcher performed an additional (final) check to ensure that there were no other double counts or errors in the corpus file. To accomplish this task, all variables were rechecked individually against the corpus to ensure that the entries were accurate and reflected the corpus to be analyzed. One additional error was noted: the inclusion of one state court criminal case. State court cases were not included in the federal courts' Westlaw search parameters and it is unknown why it was included in the results. The case was subsequently removed from the research corpus. To reduce the possible effect of "tunnel vision" during data

[1] Miranda rights for military members are controlled by Article 31, UCMJ. All members of the military are entitled to Article 31 rights, regardless of whether they are in official custody.

entry and when (re)checking for errors, the three-step review process occurred (approximately) one month apart for the first two checks and approximately six months apart for the third and final check. The review of the corpus resulted in an updated 301 case file, which is 29 percent of the total cases (1,050) that fit the broad search parameters of the study. The final corpus of court rulings constitutes a large data set for statistical analysis.

5.2 The Variables Tested

The variables that comprise the corpus are numerous and include: the courts that reviewed the cases, type of interrogator (police interrogator, FBI interrogator, DEA interrogator, and military interrogator), the date of the case ruling (pre-*Davis*, *Davis*/post-*Davis*), unequivocal/equivocal[2] invocations for counsel (per court ruling,) linguistic formulation of invocation for counsel, vulnerable suspects (e.g., L2 speakers, juveniles, suspects' with limited literacy and/or education), police follow-ups, requests for clarification, *Davis* citation, case ruling (e.g., affirmed, granted, denied), and presidential appointment of lead judge delivering the opinion of the court (majority, concurring, and dissenting opinion appointments, if applicable).

The quantitative composition of the variables, by group/type, follows, starting with the courts. Table 5.1 provides a summarized quantitative account of the types of courts represented in the corpus and the number of cases viewed by each of the courts.

Table 5.1 *The courts*

Court	Total	%
SCOTUS	**10**	**3%**
Circuit Courts	**86**	**29%**
United States Court of Appeals, First Circuit	3	
United States Court of Appeals, Second Circuit	2	
United States Court of Appeals, Fourth Circuit	5	
United States Court of Appeals, Fifth Circuit	10	
United States Court of Appeals, Sixth Circuit	11	
United States Court of Appeals, Seventh Circuit	11	
United States Court of Appeals, Eighth Circuit	1	
United States Court of Appeals, Ninth Circuit	28	
United States Court of Appeals, Tenth Circuit	8	
United States Court of Appeals, Eleventh Circuit	7	

[2] For the statistical analysis, the rulings will be noted as unequivocal/equivocal.

Table 5.1 (*cont.*)

Court	Total	%
District Courts by State/Territory	**196**	**65%**
United States District Court, Alabama	2	
United States District Court, Alaska	1	
United States District Court, Arizona	9	
United States District Court, California	30	
United States District Court, Colorado	1	
United States District Court, Connecticut	2	
United States District Court, Delaware	1	
United States District Court, District of Columbia	2	
United States District Court, Florida	3	
United States District Court, Georgia	5	
United States District Court, Hawaii	1	
United States District Court, Idaho	1	
United States District Court, Illinois	3	
United States District Court, Indiana	2	
United States District Court, Iowa	3	
United States District Court, Kansas	1	
United States District Court, Kentucky	2	
United States District Court, Louisiana	2	
United States District Court, Maine	5	
United States District Court, Maryland	1	
United States District Court, Massachusetts	2	
United States District Court, Michigan	8	
United States District Court, Minnesota	12	
United States District Court, Mississippi	1	
United States District Court, Missouri	6	
United States District Court, Montana	1	
United States District Court, Nebraska	4	
United States District Court, New Mexico	4	
United States District Court, New York	22	
United States District Court, Nevada	3	
United States District Court, North Carolina	2	
United States District Court, Ohio	8	
United States District Court, Oklahoma	2	
United States District Court, Oregon	1	
United States District Court, Pennsylvania	5	
United States District Court, Rhode Island	1	
United States District Court, South Dakota	3	
United States District Court, Tennessee	5	
United States District Court, Texas	8	
United States District Court, Utah	3	
United States District Court, Vermont	1	
United States District Court, Virginia	5	
United States District Court, Virgin Islands, St. Thomas and St. John	2	
United States District Court, West Virginia	4	

Table 5.1 (*cont.*)

Court	Total	%
District Courts by State/Territory	**196**	**65%**
United States District Court, Wisconsin	5	
United States District Court, Wyoming	1	
Military Courts	**9**	**3%**
United States Court of Military Appeals	2	
United States Army Court of Military Review	4	
United States Air Force Court of Military Review	1	
United States Air Force Court of Criminal Appeals	1	
United States Navy-Marine Corps Court of Criminal Appeals	1	

Table 5.2 *Type of interrogator*

Interrogator	Total	%
Police interrogator	244	81%
Police interrogator and FBI interrogator	8	3%
FBI interrogator	33	11%
DEA interrogator	10	3%
Military interrogator	6	2%

Of note, the United States Court of Appeals for the Armed Forces is formerly known as the United States Court of Military Appeals. Furthermore, the district court cases listed in Table 5.1 are not divided by region of the court (e.g., eastern, southern, etc.). Appendix 1 includes a complete count of cases per district court and region.

Table 5.2 shows the five types of interrogators featured in the corpus. The numbers match the cases in which a type of interrogator is used, rather than the number of interrogators present in each case. In some instances, more than one type of interrogator questioned a suspect. The presence of a second police interrogator may affect the interrogation and interview process (see Tkacukova & Oxburgh, 2020), but for the purposes of our analysis the discursive strategies used to change the suspects' invocation preferences are consistent and complimentary across the corpus. For this reason, and to avoid double counting per case, one type of interrogator is recorded. Of note, if two different types of interrogators (e.g., police interrogator and FBI agent) questioned the suspect, each type of interrogator (combination) is accounted for in the corpus.

As observed in Table 5.2 most cases in the corpus featured a police interrogator. There are a few cases in which the police and agents from the Federal

Table 5.3 *The Davis ruling and the corpus*

Ruling	Total	%
Pre Davis	48	16%
Davis/Post Davis	253	84%

Bureau of Investigation (FBI) jointly participated in an interrogation. Interrogators from the Drug Enforcement Administration (DEA) and military branches of the United States Armed Forces are also accounted for, but they are not as common in the corpus. In the cases that featured military interrogators, the suspects were Spanish speakers and Arab nationals. The latter's native language is not part of the court record. A few of the military cases included FBI interrogators. It is unknown whether the Reid technique or one of the other methods listed in the High-Value Detainee Interrogation (HIG) Report (see Chapter 2) were used. Yet, the interrogators' treatment of the invocation for counsel stage was consistent across interrogations irrespective of the interrogation technique employed. This is an insightful finding of the corpus and has important implications when discussing the connection between the law and police interrogation practices during the invocation stage of a custodial interrogation.

In addition to the type of interrogator, the corpus was also divided into two points in time: pre-*Davis* and *Davis*/post-*Davis* rulings. As Table 5.3 shows, most cases fall in the *Davis*/post-*Davis* time frame.

The judges' rulings on type of invocation for counsel, from a legal perspective, are also captured in the corpus. Table 5.4 shows the judges' rulings on invocations for counsel (unequivocal or equivocal) and the linguistic formulation of the invocations for counsel, if one is provided, per court record. These two variables, judicial ruling and type of linguistic invocation, are distinct and will be analyzed further in the statistical portion of the analysis.

A case may have more than one invocation for counsel. The defendant/petitioner, then suspect, may have attempted to invoke counsel more than once either after the reading of rights (per interrogation) or in the middle of an interrogation. If the case record accounts for more than one attempt at invoking counsel and the invocations were of different types (to avoid double counting) these instances were noted in the corpus. This did not occur often in the corpus. Of 301 cases, there are 329 instances of invocations for counsel, as reported in Table 5.4.

Table 5.4 also shows that most of the invocations were ruled as equivocal. When looking at the linguistic formulations of the defendants' invocations, as argued in the court record, we see a different story. The defendants invoked counsel using multiple formulations. Some of the formulations were in-dispute/

Table 5.4 *Judicial ruling and invocation for counsel types*

Judicial Ruling	Total	%
Unequivocal	66	22%
Equivocal	235	78%
Invocation for counsel types		
In dispute-disagreement	15	4%
Unknown/unclear (not reported in citation ruling)	21	6%
Refused to invoke counsel (noted in record)	1	< 1%
Requested other than an attorney	25	8%
Requested a detective and lawyer	1	< 1%
Invoked as a direct statement	20	6%
Invoked as a direct statement (first interrogation), waived rights (second)	3	1%
Invoked as a conditional statement	1	< 1%
Hedged invocation	77	23%
Invoked as a conditional request	19	6%
Requested police to secure an attorney	5	2%
Responded to Miranda waiver	17	5%
Pre-requested with an inquiry	71	22%
Requested with an interrogative (pro forma)	19	6%
(Other) Invoked on behalf of suspect	1	< 1%
Mentioned a specific attorney	4	1%
Signed a waiver form noting the desire for counsel	1	< 1%
Refused to sign a waiver form or to waive rights	8	2%
Noted having counsel (in custody/abroad)	1	< 1%
Requested "phone calls"	3	1%
Requested without mentioning counsel overtly	1	< 1%
Directed officers to do "something" regarding counsel	4	1%
Non-sequitur response to desire for counsel	1	< 1%
"Talismanic" request for counsel	5	2%
Requested to be taken to jail	2	1%
Invocation per se is not addressed (its equivocalness)	2	1%
Invocation ruled as irrelevant	1	< 1%

disagreement or not mentioned overtly in the court record. Yet, the defense argued that the suspect invoked counsel. Other invocations, albeit uncommon, included, the defendant requesting a detective or "phone calls," refusing to sign a waiver form, requesting to be taken to jail, requesting someone other than an attorney (e.g., spouse, parent) or someone invoking counsel on the suspect's behalf (e.g., juveniles) and what some judges refer to as the "talismanic" request for counsel, such as "I rather talk to an attorney." Several invocation types were used more often, such as invoking as a direct statement (e.g., "I want an attorney"), invoking as a conditional request (e.g., "If I can call my mom, I'll talk" or "I'll talk, but it depends on the question"), invoking as a pro forma, indirect request (e.g., "Can I get an attorney?"), and responding directly to the Miranda waiver (e.g., "Yeah, I would like to do that").

The most common invocations for counsel are "hedged" invocations, such as "If possible, can I call my lawyer?" and "I may need a lawyer," and pre-requests (with an inquiry), such as "Should I get an attorney?" and "Do you think I need an attorney?" Invocations for counsel that are hedged were ruled as both equivocal and unequivocal invocations. The latter, particularly, in more contemporary rulings. Pre-requests, or pre-invocations, however, have been predominantly and historically ruled as equivocal, nonrequests. The judges' rationale with these types of invocations is often that they reflect suspects' attempts at obtaining information that improves their situation or as failed attempts at invoking counsel. In either assessment, the judges remind us that police have no legal obligation to provide information to, or advise, custodial suspects. The police, in essence, are not a "fiduciary of the suspect."

As noted in Chapter 4, discursively pre-requests carry an expectation of a follow-up move. This could range from addressing the pre-request specifically, such as "I cannot advise you regarding counsel, but you do have the right to have counsel present during the interrogation," to informing the suspect that they are unable to respond to their request (they are not legally required to do so), but reaffirming the suspect's right to counsel. These responses would, at a minimum, although as the corpus suggests probably inadequately, address the suspect's pre-request, which would allow the suspect to make another attempt at requesting counsel, waive their rights, or simply remain silent.

From the suspect's perspective, the use of a pre-request, such as "Should I get an attorney?" also suggests that the suspect views the police interrogator as a type of fiduciary: the opposite interpretation of the law, per *United States* v. *Rutledge* (1990). In the context of a custodial interrogation, the suspect is often interacting solely with the police and can only seek responses from them, including assessing the question of counsel. This discursive process of seeking information, observed often in talk, including in institutional contexts, has been arbitrarily restricted by the law, as an unsuccessful move to invoke counsel. Consequently, the courts' treatment of pre-requests may penalize suspects who employ these discursive strategies, benefitting in turn the interrogators who are playing the invocation game. This may affect all custodial suspects, but potentially more so vulnerable ones.

Table 5.5 shows the number of vulnerable suspects and nontraditional suspects (e.g., police officers) in the corpus.

Vulnerable and nontraditional suspects account for thirty-one (31/301) or 10 percent of the corpus. Vulnerable suspects include juveniles, persons with cognitive and/or intellectual disabilities, as well as persons with limited education and low (or no) literacy skills (as noted in the court record). L2 speakers of English are also part of the vulnerable population corpus and account for the largest number of suspects in this category. These suspects included Spanish speakers and a few Arab nationals. Nontraditional suspects, on the other hand, included two police officers. The category "cognitive, educational, and/or intellectual considerations" was noted three times in the corpus (two for juveniles and one for L2 speaker). This is a separate category from the other three, hence, it is accounted for individually. The total number of suspects in Table 5.5 is thirty-one, rather than thirty-four, for the purposes of the quantitative analysis. This classification of the corpus is also accounted for in the statistical analysis.

During the Miranda reading stage of a police interrogation, vulnerable populations, across the board, were subjected to identical interrogation strategies as those used with other suspects in the corpus. Of note, the police officer as suspect, albeit a small sample, is particularly interesting because despite stating knowledge of the law and/or familiarity with interrogations (as noted in the court record) they invoked counsel indirectly and ended up waiving their rights. In essence, the two police officers, as other suspects in the corpus, behaved in a similar manner when subjected to police interrogation, even though the police officers potentially had more knowledge of the Miranda rights and/or police interrogation techniques.

After suspects invoked counsel, the police interrogators often followed up the suspects' statements or requests. These follow-up turns of talk did not always serve the linguistic function of requests for clarification, hence distinctions were made between follow-up moves and requests for clarification moves, linguistically defined. The frequency of use of these moves is illustrated in Table 5.6.

Table 5.5 *Vulnerable and nontraditional suspects*

Suspect type	Total
Nonnative (L2) Speaker	23
Cognitive, Educational, and/or Intellectual Considerations	(3)
Juveniles	6
Police Officer	2

Table 5.6 *Invocation for counsel follow-ups and requests for clarification*

	Total
Follow ups	208
Requests for Clarification	84

There were nine instances in the corpus in which the case record did not discuss the police interrogators' response to the suspects' invocations for counsel. A transcript of the exchange was not provided, hence it is unknown whether a follow-up or a request for clarification was employed in these cases.

As discussed in Chapter 4, judges often referred to police interrogators' follow-ups as requests for clarification. Linguistically they were often not formulated as such. Table 5.6 shows the distinction between a discursive follow-up and a request for clarification. This is an important distinction, since the judges in the corpus often argued that despite the police officers not being required to clarify a suspect's ambiguous/equivocal invocation for counsel, they did so showing due diligence on their part. This argument is particularly meaningful after the *Davis* ruling whose concurring opinion encourages police interrogators to err on the side of caution and clarify a suspect's ambiguous/equivocal invocation for counsel.

The corpus also accounts for *Davis* being (overtly) cited in a ruling. This citation occurred in 219 or 73 percent of the cases. The final case rulings divided by type and frequency are shown in Table 5.7.

The cases sometimes have "universal" rulings that account for all motions and grounds for appeal. Some cases, however, have specific/separate rulings per motion and grounds for appeal. The rulings in Table 5.7 account for those that relate solely to a violation of the right to counsel, such as motions to suppress statements and/or requesting *habeas* relief due to Miranda violations. In addition, the distinction against and in favor of defendant was made since the

Table 5.7 *The case rulings*

Type of ruling	Total	%
Affirmed (against defendant)	62	21%
Affirmed (in favor of defendant)	6	2%
Dismissed	12	4%
Denied	130	43%
Denied and dismissed	16	5%
Granted (in favor of defendant)	19	6%
Granted in part	23	8%
Remanded	2	1%
Vacated and remanded (in favor of defendant)	2	1%
Reversed (in favor of defendant)	5	2%
Reversed (against the defendant)	4	1%
Reversed and remanded	16	5%
Reversed (against defendant/finding invocation legal)	2	1%
Deferred	1	< 1%
No ruling on invocation for counsel per se (invocation issue noted)	1	< 1%

Table 5.8 *Authoring opinions*

Opinions	Total
Concurring	20
Dissenting	21
Concurring or dissenting in part	5

appeals, although mostly filed by the defense, also included a small number of cases brought by the prosecution. These include cases that were reversed. Only one ruling that deals with the invocation for counsel matter is noted to avoid introducing extraneous variables that are not relevant to the analysis.

The rulings noted in Table 5.7 include affirming a lower court's ruling, as valid and correct, dismissing a court ruling without imposing liability on the defendant, denying a motion for the court to review a case on appeal (a court may also rule to deny and dismiss), granting a motion, such as a motion to suppress statements or a writ of *habeas corpus* (the ruling may be granted in part), remanding the case to a lower court, vacating a ruling making a prior legal judgment legally void, reversing the judgment of a lower court because it was incorrect (the case may also be reversed and remanded), and deferring a judgment to a lower court. Some rulings also included dissenting, concurring, and dissenting/concurring in part opinions, as noted in Table 5.8.

A concurring opinion is an opinion that agrees with the majority opinion but does not agree with its rationale. Concurring opinions are not binding since they do not receive the majority of the court's support. Dissenting opinions are a separate judicial opinion in which a judge who disagreed with the majority's decision explains the disagreement. Opinions may also be concurring and/or dissenting in part. These were not common in the corpus. Agreement among the judges seems to be the norm, yet some of the most important cases tried in the Court, such as *Miranda* and *Davis*, had concurring and/or dissenting opinions that provide insights into the justices' viewpoint on the protection of custodial suspects' rights against the police's ability to question suspects.

Finally, the analysis also looks at the presidential appointments of the judges who wrote the lead opinion for the courts. These appointments are listed in Table 5.9.

Now, some opinions were *en banc* (two) or *per curiam* (six). The former occurs when all judges of a particular court hear a case. The latter is a court opinion issued in the name of the Court rather than specific judges. In three cases tried in a military court, the presidential appointment of the judge who presided the case could not be established. The term "other" accounts for these eleven instances in which there is no presidential appointment.

Table 5.9 *Judicial appointments*

Appointment	Total	%
Dwight D. Eisenhower	2	1%
John F. Kennedy	4	1%
Lyndon B. Johnson	5	2%
Richard Nixon	4	1%
Gerald Ford	2	1%
Jimmy Carter	23	8%
Ronald Reagan	49	16%
George H. W. Bush	38	13%
Bill Clinton	51	17%
George W. Bush	38	13%
Barack Obama	26	9%
Donald J. Trump	4	1%
Magistrate Judge	42	14%
Operation of Law	2	1%
Other	11	4%

The decision as to which judge writes the opinion(s) for the court varies by federal court. At the Court level, after the votes have been tallied, the Chief Justice, or the most senior justice in the majority (e.g., if the Chief Justice is in the dissent,) assigns a justice in the majority to write the opinion of the Court or writes the opinion themself. The most senior justice in the dissent can assign a dissenting justice to write the dissenting opinion or write the opinion themself.

At the federal appellate (circuit) court level, cases are decided in a panel composed of three judges. These judges do not always work together, but rather they rotate periodically. The panels are assigned cases using a mathematical formula, so that each judge hears one civil, criminal, and other types of cases within a specified period.

In the federal district court, judges are assigned cases following an order, which may be altered if the case, for example, requires specialization, such as with death penalty cases. A district court judge who specializes in those types of cases may be assigned to hear the case outside the prescribed order.

With regard to the presidential appointment of the lead judge writing the court's opinion, the most common appointments include: Bill Clinton (17 percent), Ronald Reagan (16 percent), George H. W. Bush (13 percent), and George W. Bush (13 percent). These percentages are reflective of the total judgeship appointments from 1901–2021.[3] Bill Clinton had the highest number of appointments, followed closely by Ronald Reagan and George W. Bush.

[3] https://ballotpedia.org/Federal_judicial_appointments_by_president.

Ronald Reagan made four appointments to the Court during his presidency. He also had the highest number of appointments in the Regional Court of Appeals. Bill Clinton made the most appointments to the district courts, with Ronald Reagan and George W. Bush following close behind. These facts are interesting, since the divide between the *Miranda* and the *Davis* Court, for example, may have political overtones. The *Miranda* (majority) opinion was delivered by justices who were deemed more liberal, starting with Chief Justice Earl Warren (Dwight D. Eisenhower appointment), whereas the *Davis* (majority) opinion was led by more conservative justices, such as Sandra Day O'Connor, who wrote the opinion for the Court, Chief Justice, William Rehnquist, and Justices Antonin Scalia (concurring), Anthony Kennedy, and Clarence Thomas. These justices, except for Justice Thomas (George H. W. Bush), were appointed by Ronald Reagan. The concurring, joining, opinion of the Court was delivered by Justice David Souter (George H. W. Bush), joined by justices Harry Blackmun (Richard Nixon), John Paul Stevens (Gerald Ford), and Ruth Bader Ginsburg (Bill Clinton.) These justices, most of which were appointed by Republican presidents, were considered ideologically moderate (e.g., Souter) or liberal (e.g., Ginsburg).

The presidential appointment of the judges in the corpus may also prove to have statistical bearing, yet it is important to note that some past (older) studies that have examined the possible relationship between Republican presidents, such as Reagan, and the conservative makeup of the federal courts, have shown:

> that while Republican judges overall are much more conservative than their Democratic colleagues, Reagan appointees are not significantly more conservative than other Republican judges. In fact, the decision making of federal judges in the Reagan era reflects the divergent attitudes represented by the mainstreams of the two major parties and not, at least so far, the extremism of the far right. (Tomasi & Velona, 1987, pp. 792–793)

More recent studies on the ideological makeup of federal circuit courts also show that although there appear to be "differences between circuits that we can characterize as ideological . . . , knowing who appointed the judges on a federal appeals panel, and which circuit the panel is located in, improves our ability to predict case outcomes only marginally" (Broscheid, 2011, p. 189). The statistical analysis of the corpus will examine the possible effect of the judges' presidential appointments on their rulings, including more recent appointments to the federal courts.

Table 5.9 also shows other types of appointments that are not presidential. Two of the judicial appointments were by operation of law. Here a judge who was confirmed by the Senate to serve on a circuit court is reassigned without the need of Senate approval to another circuit court. The corpus also included magistrate judges (14 percent of the corpus).

The next section will consist of a statistical analysis of the corpus. This analysis, and the research questions posed, will reveal the characteristics that make it more or less likely an invocation for counsel will be ruled as equivocal.

5.3 Method and Research Questions

The statistical analysis of the corpus consists of a difference in proportion test. A test of proportion will assess whether a sample from a population represents the true proportion from the entire population. In this test, an interval is created by subtracting the population proportion from the sample proportion plus and minus a margin of error based on a 0.95 confidence interval:

$$\overline{p}_1 - \overline{p}_2 \pm z_{\alpha/2}\sqrt{\frac{\overline{p}_1(1-\overline{p}_1)}{n_1} + \frac{\overline{p}_2(1-\overline{p}_2)}{n_2}}$$

Where $\overline{p}_1$ is the subgroup proportion, $\overline{p}_2$ is the population proportion, n_1 is the size of the subgroup, n_2 is the population size, and $z_{\alpha/2} = 1.96$ standard deviations associated with a 95 percent confidence interval.

This test is appropriate for analyzing a corpus that consists of binomial data indicating membership (1) or no membership (0) in one or two categories. In the corpus, rulings of unequivocal invocations for counsel (0) and equivocal invocations (1) are the two possible outcomes, since all cases fall under one or the other category (the population). The subgroups (characteristics) of the corpus are represented in the tables and include: case rulings, presidential appointments, interrogators' use of follow-ups, and linguistic formulation of the invocation for counsel.

The difference in proportion test will measure the effect of characteristics on case outcomes (indirectly) through the measure of invocations for counsel ruled as equivocal. The following questions were tested:

(1) Do types of court rulings exhibit a different proportion of invocations being ruled as equivocal than the general population of cases?
(2) Are cases involving police asking follow-up questions ruled differently than the population's proportion, in terms of invocations being ruled equivocal? Are cases involving police requesting clarification ruled differently?
(3) Does the proportion of invocations ruled equivocal vary by whether follow-ups or requests for clarification were used by police or nonpolice interrogators?
(4) Is there a difference in proportion between invocations ruled equivocal and pre-*Davis*/*Davis*-post-*Davis* for (a) all cases, (b) just police interrogators, (c) nonpolice interrogators?
(5) Does the linguistic formulation of the invocation affect the proportion of cases with invocations ruled equivocal?

(6) Do cases involving specific subgroups of suspects exhibit a different proportion of invocations ruled equivocal than the population?
(7) Does the presidential appointment of the lead judge writing the opinion for the court affect the proportion of cases with invocations ruled equivocal pre- and *Davis*/post-*Davis*? Does the presidential appointment of the lead concurring judge and the lead dissenting judge provide different results than those for the lead majority judge?

5.4 Results

There are three possible outcomes with the difference in proportion test: higher than the population proportion, statistically equal to the population proportion (the null hypothesis), or lower than the population proportion. If the low end of the interval is negative and the high end of the interval is positive, the subgroup is not significantly different from the population for this characteristic (null is accepted). If the interval is entirely negative, the subgroup has a significantly lower incidence of the characteristic than the population (null is rejected). If the interval is entirely positive, the subgroup has a significantly higher incidence of the characteristic than the population (null is rejected).

For question 1, the difference in proportion test shows that in none of the comparisons of types of rulings against the population proportion (see Tables 5.4 and 5.7), did any type of ruling deviate significantly from the population. This means that each of the following case outcomes is different from the judicial ruling on unequivocal/equivocal invocation, and the null hypothesis is accepted.

The results for question 2 show that the subgroup proportion is different from the population proportion (see Tables 5.4 and 5.6) with regard to police using follow-up moves, hence the null hypothesis is accepted. When the distinction is made for requests for clarification, the test shows that this subgroup is significantly lower than the population proportion. Thus, cases that have requests for clarification have a lower rate of invocations for counsel being ruled equivocal than unequivocal, as reported in Table 5.10.

Question 3 shows that neither subgroup proportion, except for nonpolice requests for clarification, is different from the population proportion (see Tables 5.2 and 5.4). Of note, the subgroup of military interrogators was excluded due to its small sample. The test on nonpolice requests for clarification (excluding military) shows that cases with this characteristic have a significantly lower rate of having invocations for counsel ruled equivocal. The sample size is small (16), so results may not be robust; that is, if another sample were taken of 301 cases this result may not hold. Still, this result is statistically significant, as noted in Table 5.11, hence the null hypothesis is rejected.

Table 5.10 *Police interrogators' requests for clarification and invocations ruled equivocal*

Population Size	Population Incidents (=1)	Sample Size	Sample Incidents (=1)
301	235	84	52
Population Proportion	Sample Proportion		Expected Value
0.7807309	0.6190476		65.58139535
	Standard Deviation		
	3.7920936		
Interval	+/–	Low Range	High Range
–0.16168	0.113886	–0.27557	–0.04779715

Table 5.11 *Nonpolice requests for clarification and invocations for counsel ruled equivocal*

Population Size	Population Incidents (=1)	Sample Size	Sample Incidents (=1)
301	235	16	8
Population Proportion	Sample Proportion		Expected Value
0.780730897	0.5		12.49169435
	Standard Deviation		
	1.655005322		
Interval	+/–	Low Range	High Range
–0.280730897	0.249419053	–0.53015	–0.031311844

In question 4, the subgroup pre- and post-*Davis* is not statistically different for invocations for counsel ruled equivocal (see Tables 5.3 and 5.4). The test was repeated for: all interrogators (pre and post), police interrogators (pre and post), and nonpolice interrogators (pre and post). No significant differences between subsamples and population proportions were found. Differences were found for some of the subgroups tested in question 5 (see Table 5.4).

The results for question 5 show that some of the linguistic formulations of an invocation for counsel affect the proportion of cases with invocations ruled equivocal. Each of the linguistic formulations (subgroups) that showed differences with the population proportion will be discussed individually, starting with "invoked other than attorney," in Table 5.12.

"Invoking other than attorney" is statistically above the population proportion. Thus, fewer cases with this subgroup were ruled unequivocal invocations and more were ruled equivocal. For the custodial suspects this translates to having less of a chance of being successful with this type of argument in court.

Table 5.12 *Linguistic formulation: invoked other than attorney*

Population Size	Population Incidents (=1)	Sample Size	Sample Incidents (=1)
301	235	25	24
Population Proportion 0.780730897	Sample Proportion 0.96 Standard Deviation 2.068756652		Expected Value 19.51827243
Interval 0.179269103	+/– 0.089919752	Low Range 0.08934935	High Range 0.269188855

Table 5.13 *Linguistic formulation: invoked directly*

Population Size	Population Incidents (=1)	Sample Size	Sample Incidents (=1)
301	235	30	11
Population Proportion 0.780730897	Sample Proportion 0.36666667 Standard Deviation 2.266209369		Expected Value 23.42192691
Interval –0.41406423	+/– 0.178666423	Low Range –0.592730662	High Range –0.235397799

"Invoked directly," on the other hand, is statistically lower than the population proportion, as shown in Table 5.13.

As Table 5.13 reports, the subgroup "invoked directly" is statistically lower than the population proportion. For custodial suspects, fewer cases with this subgroup were ruled equivocal invocations and more were ruled unequivocal. Hence, custodial suspects have a higher chance of being successful with this type of argument in court, a finding that is consisting with prior research.

Regarding "hedged" invocations, this subgroup is statistically higher than the population proportion, as shown in Table 5.14.

These results indicate that "hedged" invocations are ruled more often as equivocal than the population proportion. For suspects who employed this linguistic formulation to make their invocations for counsel, this translates to fewer successful outcomes in court.

Invocations for counsel formulated as "pre-requests" were also common in the corpus. This subgroup was ruled as equivocal at a higher rate than the population proportion, as reported in Table 5.15.

Invocations for counsel formulated as "requested with an interrogative (pro forma)" were also ruled as equivocal at a higher rate than the population proportion. The results are shown in Table 5.16.

Table 5.14 *Linguistic formulation: hedged invocations*

Population Size	Population Incidents (=1)	Sample Size	Sample Incidents (=1)
301	235	77	71
Population Proportion	Sample Proportion		Expected Value
0.780730897	0.922077922		60.11627907
	Standard Deviation		
	3.63065319		
Interval	+/–	Low Range	High Range
0.141347025	0.075957471	0.065389554	0.217304496

Table 5.15 *Linguistic formulation: pre-requested with an inquiry*

Population Size	Population Incidents (=1)	Sample Size	Sample Incidents (=1)
301	235	71	68
Population Proportion	Sample Proportion		Expected Value
0.780730897	0.957746479		55.43189369
	Standard Deviation		
	3.486330679		
Interval	+/–	Low Range	High Range
0.177015582	0.066139827	0.110875755	0.243155409

Table 5.16 *Linguistic formulation: requested with an interrogative (pro forma)*

Population Size	Population Incidents (=1)	Sample Size	Sample Incidents (=1)
301	235	19	18
Population Proportion	Sample Proportion		Expected Value
0.780730897	0.947368421		14.83388704
	Standard Deviation		
	1.803500237		
Interval	+/–	Low Range	High Range
0.166637524	0.110753482	0.055884042	0.277391006

The next question addresses whether cases involving specific subgroups of suspects (see Table 5.5) exhibit a different proportion of invocations ruled as equivocal than the population. The results are reported in Table 5.17.

The results for question 6 show that for L2 speakers of English invocations for counsel were ruled more often as directly formulated. Of note, the sample size of this subgroup was small and the discursive behavior of the police interrogators was also fairly egregious, as discussed in Chapter 4. For the

Table 5.17 *Subgroups of suspects and invocation ruling*

Population Size	Population Incidents (=1)	Sample Size	Sample Incidents (=1)
301	235	23	13
Population Proportion 0.7807309	Sample Proportion 0.5652174 Standard Deviation 1.9842817		Expected Value 17.95681063
Interval −0.21551	+/− 0.207921	Low Range −0.42343	High Range −0.00759291

Table 5.18 *Effect of presidential appointment on lead judge (concurrent opinion)*

Population Size	Population Incidents (=1)	Sample Size	Sample Incidents (=1)
301	235	6	6
Population Proportion 0.7807309	Sample Proportion 1 Standard Deviation 1.0134796		Expected Value 4.684385382
Interval 0.219269	+/− 0.046743	Low Range 0.172526572	High Range 0.266011634

other subgroups in the category of nontraditional suspects (including and excluding police officers as suspects), the null hypothesis was accepted.

The final question addresses whether the presidential appointment of the lead judge writing the opinion for the court affected the proportion of cases with invocations ruled as equivocal pre- and *Davis*/post-*Davis* (see Tables 5.3, 5.4, and 5.9). This test was repeated for lead judge writing concurrent and dissenting opinions. Presidential appointments were grouped as either Democrat or Republican for three categories: Majority, Concurring, and Dissenting opinions. Care was taken to eliminate Magistrate Judge, Military Judge, Per curiam, and Operation of Law appointments and decisions. As noted in Table 5.18, only post-*Davis* Democrat appointed judges writing concurrent opinions were different from the null. For this subgroup, the invocations for counsel were ruled as equivocal at a significantly higher rate than the population proportion. This subgroup included only six cases, so small sample concerns prevail.

One remaining question arises with the presidential appointment of the lead judges in the corpus: whether judges appointed by a particular president had a different proportion of rulings of invocations ruled equivocal than the population proportion. The results show that judicial rulings did not vary by presidential appointment when each president was tested individually (e.g., Reagan, Clinton, Obama, etc.). This finding seems consistent with prior research that has shown that despite Republican judges being more conservative than their Democratic counterparts overall, the presidential appointment does not appear to be a significant factor.

5.5 Interpreting the Results in the Context of the Invocation Game

The broader interpretation of these results, in the context of the invocation game, is that often suspects' invocations for counsel are ruled as equivocal. This occurred with a variety of linguistic formulations in the corpus, including pro forma invocations for counsel and pre-requests. The latter formulation is of particular interest since it is observed often in the corpus and requires a follow-up move to achieve mutuality of understanding and move the conversation forward. The law and interrogation training may block this next move to reaching common ground, unbeknownst to the suspects who, despite the opinion of some judges, may view the police interrogator as a fiduciary of the Miranda rights.

The effect of judges' ruling suspects' invocations as equivocal/ambiguous has an additional potential legal cost, if the case goes to trial. As noted previously it is not uncommon for judges to argue that even if the trial court erred by admitting a defendant's statements, the alleged error does not have a substantial and injurious effect or influence in determining the jury's verdict (see *Brecht* v. *Abrahamson*, 1993; *Fry* v. *Pliler*, 2007). This argument, which is not uncommon in the corpus, has an opposite side: the guilty verdict is directly attributable to the defendant's statements, hence the effect on the jury's verdict may be substantial (see *Kyger* v. *Carlton*, 1998).

Given the role of suspects' statements in the investigation of a crime and subsequently in the conviction of such crime, the "preponderance of evidence" argument needs further consideration within the invocation game of custodial interrogation. Otherwise, a suspect's attempt at invoking counsel during custodial interrogation may in effect be nullified a second time in court, if the harmless error perspective is not revisited in light of the high proportion of invocations for counsel, even those that are formulated pro forma, being ruled as equivocal in the corpus.

6 Police Interrogation Reform in the United States: Paths to Consider

In closing this necessarily truncated discussion of policy considerations attending the new confession rules, some reference must be made to their ironic untimeliness. There is now in progress in this country a massive reexamination of criminal law enforcement procedures on a scale never before witnessed . . . It is no secret that concern has been expressed lest long-range and lasting reforms be frustrated by this Court's too rapid departure from existing constitutional standards. Despite the Court's disclaimer, the practical effect of the decision made today must inevitably be to handicap seriously sound efforts at reform, not least by removing options necessary to a just compromise of competing interests. Of course legislative reform is rarely speedy or unanimous, though this Court has been more patient in the past. But the legislative reforms when they come would have the vast advantage of empirical data and comprehensive study, they would allow experimentation and use of solutions not open to the courts, and they would restore the initiative in criminal law reform to those forums where it truly belongs.

(Justice Harlan (dissenting opinion), *Miranda* v. *Arizona*, 1966)

Justice Harlan's dissenting opinion, joined by Justices Stewart and White, suggests that the *Miranda* ruling was untimely, and potentially unnecessary, given the "massive reexamination of criminal law enforcement procedures" taking place at the time of the ruling. In retrospect, the justice's arguments were premature. The manner in which police interact with citizens has sparked past and present debates for the establishment of national policing standards/accreditations aimed at changing the culture of policing in the United States. These calls for police reform have been limited in application and have not included comprehensive (nationwide) police interrogation reform. This is in contrast with police reforms undertaken in other countries, some of which have been discussed previously, as well as measures adopted by the United Nations[1] and the European Union,[2] which include provisions for ethical police interviewing practices, access to legal counsel, and special consideration for the

[1] www.ohchr.org/en/instruments-mechanisms/instruments/international-covenant-civil-and-political-rights.

[2] https://eur-lex.europa.eu/legal-content/en/TXT/?uri=CELEX%3A52018DC0858.

needs of L2 custodial suspects, juveniles, and persons with cognitive and intellectual disabilities (see also Feld, 2006; Cleary, 2014; Antaki et al., 2015).

In light of the issues raised in this book regarding the right to invoke counsel and the use of police interrogation to question an array of suspects, the next sections of Chapter 6 will explore paths to moving forward with police interrogation reform in the United States. Parting from the lessons of other countries that have undertaken reform, it will focus on three key areas: (1) police interrogation techniques, (2) the interview of vulnerable populations, and (3) changes in case law related to the reading of rights, invocation of rights, the use of trickery and deception, as well as the use of confessions to build and prosecute a criminal case. The goal of Chapter 6 is to consider ways in which the issues presented in this book can be revisited to change the current state of police interrogation in the United States. This will require changes across the board: legislative, legal, police interviewing training, and also an acknowledgment of the role of cognitive, cultural, and sociolinguistic factors in police-suspect discursive interactions. Furthermore, this chapter challenges the perception that a suspect's invocation of the right to counsel, and for that matter the presence of counsel during an interrogation, interferes with police work and with obtaining statements from suspects.

6.1 Police Interrogation Reform: Examining Other Paths Taken

Police interrogation reform in the United States benefits from looking outward: to other countries that have treaded, with varying degrees of success, a path for change. In the United Kingdom, as noted previously, the government legislated the Police and Criminal Evidence Act (PACE), which, among other things, mandated that beginning in 1986 all interviews with suspects would be recorded (e.g., on audiotape). Such electronic recordings provided insights as to what actually transpired in police interviews, including the discursive tactics used by police.

In the years immediately following (i.e., the later 1980s), a few studies were conducted based on such recordings and were later published. In 1992 the United Kingdom Home Office published Baldwin's (1993) groundbreaking research. This research, as well as other studies conducted in the 1980s, showed "that although these mandated, nationwide tape recordings revealed few signs of oppressive interrogating, there was evidently a widespread skills deficit" (Bull & Baker, 2020, p. 45). These studies recognized that police interviewing required formal (and sustained) training and oversight. As a result, a number of experienced police investigators and psychologists came together to develop the PEACE method of interviewing (see Chapter 3 for a discussion).

Following the UK PEACE model, countries such as Norway, Australia, and Canada implemented their own legislative and police interviewing changes. In

Norway, "second jumpers" to the UK's move from interrogation to investigative interviewing, or PEACE (see Griffiths & Rachlew, 2018), it was Norwegian police practitioners who undertook psychological study that changed the original PEACE approach into KREATIV (see Fahsing & Rachlew, 2009). KREATIV training was heavily influenced by PEACE, including the use of UK experts to educate Norwegian trainers and making it a requirement for all detectives seeking further specialization.

As Griffiths and Rachlew (2018) note, in addition to being a "second jumper" to police interrogation reform in the UK, faster progress was achieved in Norway due to a combination of factors, including: the role of police in initiating and driving change, the methodology being embraced by the National University Police College, the support of stakeholders, such as the General Prosecutor's Office and a Supreme Court ruling, and that it was driven by police officers who received post graduate studies in forensic psychology:

> Throughout the Norwegian refinement of the PEACE model, it has been argued that investigative interviewing necessitates strategic disclosure of evidence for a variety of reasons . . ., one of them is the suspect's right to be presumed innocent. The fact that detectives need a strategy stimulating both open mindedness and the retrieval of verifiable information is another. (p. 162)

In the Norwegian model, police investigators are encouraged to test alternative hypotheses and to actively seek information indicating innocence. This is in contrast with a guilt-presumptive mindset overly concerned with lie detection. Ethical principles and following an investigative, rather than prosecutorial, interview approach is key to ending coercive, manipulative strategies aimed at obtaining confessions.

Now, the Norwegian and UK models have also shown "that it takes all areas of the criminal justice system to be pulling in the same direction for transformational change to occur" (Griffiths & Rachlew, 2018, p. 172). Investigative interviewing is not an isolated activity. In both Norway and the UK, police reforms, including police interrogation reform, were driven from within the police and/or in collaboration with academics, such as forensic psychologists and forensic linguists.

Other countries, such as Australia and Canada, also followed the path of PACE/PEACE. In Australia, police agencies are state-based.[3] The path to police reforms in the state of New South Wales, Australia is particularly noteworthy since it illustrates possible roadblocks to the implementation of police reforms due to the problematic relationship between police, legal, and political institutions. An issue that may also affect police reform in the United States.

[3] There is a federal police force in Australia that investigates federal offenses, such as immigration and terrorism matters.

In the 1990s, the Wood Royal Commission into the New South Wales Police Service decided that a state of "systemic and entrenched corruption" existed in the police organization. This report led to major reforms that included the appointment of a new Police Commission, changes in police recruitment and education, and increased monitoring and accountability standards. The Commission's reform program was extensive and substantive, similar to the PACE legislation in the UK, but with an added caveat. The Commission highlighted "the complex relationship between police organizations and the volatile political environments in which they increasingly need to operate" (Chan & Dixon, 2007, p. 443). The research notes that: "The Commission's list of topics indicates the scale and range of corruption discovered: process corruption; gratuities and improper associations; substance abuse; fraudulent practices; assaults and abuse of police powers; prosecution – compromise or favourable treatment; theft and extortion . . ., among other circumstances that suggest corruption" (p. 446). For Chan and Dixon, these problems could not be explained in terms of "black sheep" or "bad apples," but rather, as the Royal Commission reported, a state of systemic and deep-rooted corruption. The findings of the Commission were significant, because it shifted the focus of reform from the traditional "bad apples" simplistic explanations, and fixes (e.g., the firing of corrupt police officers) to the institutional contexts that produced and sustained such culture.

To tackle the Commission's recommendations a number of long-term solutions were implemented. These ranged from recruitment (e.g., increasing diversity) and education (the investigative interview has been adopted in most jurisdictions in Australia, albeit inconsistently) to changing the culture of policing itself. Although these were important goals, particularly in light of the Commission's findings, police reform became politicized with police ministers being described as micromanagers. This reflected the Australian government's commitment to law-and-order (Dixon & Maher, 2004), a commitment that reassured police officers that their main job is to fight crime, not implement reform. This potential political interference, despite reform initiatives, raises important concerns for police reform in the United States, including the widespread and consistent implementation/training in ethical and effective interviewing practices (e.g., a version of PEACE) across the country.

Another interesting case study is Canada, due to its history with the Reid technique. Canada, as other countries noted previously, has undergone a number of police reforms that have changed the manner in which police officers are trained and recruited. In 2015, the Council of Canadian Academies (the Council), which is an independent, not-for-profit organization that supports independent expert assessments to inform public policy development in Canada, released a comprehensive report to better understand how policing may be carried out more efficiently and effectively in the future. The report addresses numerous areas that need to improve in "twenty-first century policing," including the changing nature of crime, accountability and legitimacy, improved workforce culture, and safety and security of the web. The latter was an important component of the report, since it addressed cost effective measures in policing as well as present challenges in contemporary policing.

The Council's report represents the efforts being made in Canada to address justice reform and miscarriages of justice. At present, there are provincial independent civilian oversight bodies that are not involved in local politics that carry the sole authority to decide whether criminal charges should be laid against a police officer. There are also forthcoming changes to civilian oversight of the Royal Canadian Mounted Police (RCMP); possible new requirements on how the RCMP tracks use of force incidents; and how the government will reduce the over-incarceration of Indigenous and black people, as well as addressing concerns of racial profiling. The latter has been a pervasive issue in calls for police reform in the United States.

With regard to police interviewing reform, Snook et al. (2010) note that: "Poor interviewing has also been associated with miscarriages of justice in Canada" (St-Yves, 2009). For example, the Lamer Commission of Inquiry (2006) into wrongful convictions in Newfoundland and Labrador identified inappropriate interviewing of witnesses as a major concern. In addition, the Federal-Provincial-Territorial Heads of Prosecutions Committee Working Group (2004) identified poor interviewing practices as a potential contributor to miscarriages of justice in Canada" (p. 213). Until recently, Canadian police officers received training in the Reid technique, or some version of it. The Canadian Police College, one of the country's foremost police-training institutions, now teaches a version of the PEACE method of interviewing. This change was driven by a desire to move away from the accusatory style of the Reid technique of interrogation. In 2015, the RCMP implemented a more conversational style of police interviewing described as a PEACE hybrid that fits the parameters of Canadian law.

The ongoing challenge in Canada, as other countries that have undergone some type of police reform, is to create a standardized approach to police interviewing that is adopted in all jurisdictions. As Snook et al. (2010) argue because policing is a provincial responsibility, the adoption of national standards is a complex issue, yet given the CACP's and CPA's success in promoting reform on other policing initiatives, they are in the ideal position to reform interviewing. Collaboration between researchers and police organizations is also needed moving forward. As Tedeschini (2008) notes the application of effective interviewing techniques with lay persons is essential to the proper administration of justice. The implementation of training programs that reflect scientific findings over conventional wisdom, as well as breaking longstanding traditions of senior police officers passing on their techniques, including interviewing ones, to junior officers (see Ofshe, 2007) also requires change. Combatting the confession culture, a problem also afflicting United States policing, is another essential objective of police reform in Canada:

> With this type of approach being advocated and utilized over the years by thousands of other trained investigators across North America, it should come as no great shock that research has suggested the existence of a confession culture in the police investigative process that has contributed to miscarriages of justice (Savage & Milne, 2007). It has also been suggested that the strict adherence to a confession-oriented style of interrogation not only promotes human rights abuses, it may also conceal what amounts to a lack of competency in interviewing techniques (Williamson, 2006). In this respect, police investigators have, in my opinion, rightly been criticized for their failure to recognize their primary responsibility – that of information-gatherers (Shuy, 1998). (Tedeschini, 2008, p. 2)

The case studies presented in this section suggest that most of the reforms required the implementation of new legislation/changes to case law, the adoption of less coercive interviewing practices, and the collaboration between police investigators, lawyers, criminologists, forensic psychologists, and forensic linguists. Factors that are also critical in achieving police interrogation reform in the United States (see Griffiths & Rachlew, 2018).

In the past, calls for police reform in the United States have resulted in attempts to address concerns regarding police profiling and disparate treatment of racialized groups. One such attempt, was the recent police reform legislation, H.R.7120 – George Floyd Justice in Policing Act of 2020,[4] which ended with no Congressional agreement in 2021. This Act provided a framework to prevent and remedy racial profiling by law enforcement agencies and to limit use of force and use of no-knock warrants, chokeholds, and carotid holds, among other provisions. This legislation, as prior ones, did not make any provisions for police interrogation reform. This despite longstanding research and high-profile cases (e.g., the Central Park Five) in which suspects provided a false confession following police interrogators' use of coercive interrogation tactics (see Kassin, 1997; Leo, 2008; Kassin et al., 2010; Garrett, 2015). Of note, some efforts have been made at the state level regarding the interrogation of juveniles and at the federal and state levels in the adoption of alternative interrogation methods to the Behavioral Analysis Interview.

At the federal level, some substantive efforts have been made to research best interrogation practices in the aftermath of the 9/11 attacks. As discussed in Chapter 2, since 2009 a government led body called the High-Value Detainee Interrogation Group (HIG) has been assessing research on alternative interrogation methods that do not rely on coercion. The findings of the HIG report

[4] www.congress.gov/bill/116th-congress/house-bill/7120.

provide insights into the use of rapport, open ended/narrative style questioning, and active listening, among other interviewing techniques focused on obtaining cooperation, compliance, and truth detection. The report supports many of the interviewing practices recommended and used in information gathering interview methods, such as PEACE and CI. It also raises questions about its application with criminal suspects within the United States legal framework (see Chapter 3).

Despite the recommendations of the HIG, the report does not mention legislation or policy changes (Griffiths & Rachlew, 2018). The HIG report cannot institute changes to the law or to the training provided to officers at state or local levels:

> In order to maximise the influence of psychological theory the HIG research should be targeted at judges and DoJ policy in order to produce real change. The adversarial system only responds to judicial case law. This is shown, in a legal sense by the period before the eventual Miranda ruling (see Leo, 1996b, 2008 for a fuller discussion). Therefore, the HIG's ability to leverage the significant research evidence it has amassed into investigative practice will remain limited unless there is a sea change in the leadership approach. (Griffiths & Rachlew, 2018, pp. 165–166)

Other factors limit the effectuation of police interrogation reform in the United States, such as the lack of national legislation mandating the audio or video recording of police questioning of suspects. The latter is essential for both review of police conduct during custodial interrogation and for training and research purposes. Furthermore, significant change in interviewing practices nationally requires leadership, such as that shown by the UK Home Office's Principles of Investigative Interviewing (Schollum, 2017). The perspective of senior police investigators, prosecutors, and judges, to the extent that the Code of Ethics of United States[5] judges allow, must also evolve to achieve police interrogation reform in the United States. To this end, the next sections will discuss how these reforms can be adopted to address three key areas: interviewing practices, treatment of vulnerable populations, and the judiciary's perspective on the existing laws on custodial interrogation.

6.2 From Interrogation to Interviewing: Changing the Perspective in the United States

In the United States, some police stations have started to adopt aspects of the PEACE method of interviewing. Training consultants, such as Wicklander-Zulawski & Associates,[6] have also discontinued the use of the Reid technique

[5] www.uscourts.gov/judges-judgeships/code-conduct-united-states-judges.
[6] www.w-z.com/.

and adopted their own style of rapport-based interviewing. This change, although not yet embraced across all federal and state law enforcement agencies, is a step toward the implementation of comprehensive, noncoercive interviewing practices that emphasize rapport building, ethical conduct, and the use of conversational/narrative style of interviewing. Interviewing tenets such as these are also embodied in the Mendez Principles (Mendez & Areh, 2021). The latter is an expert-led initiative that recognizes "that the outcome of an interview is interconnected with the full enjoyment of rights by a person at each stage of contact with public authorities – regardless of whether such encounters are labelled as conversations, interrogations, interviews or questioning" (p. 1). The Principles, albeit not designed as a training manual, propose that good interviewing practices should be universalized and shared among professionals in a variety of countries and all legal cultures with the aim to avoid human rights violations and reduce false confessions. As proposed, the Principles can be applied to both suspects and witnesses in military, state, federal, and other types of jurisdictions (e.g., local police stations).

The main areas addressed in the Principles are the Conduct of Interviews, Justice Systems, and Human Rights. The Principles stress that interviewing is instructed by science, law, and ethics. With regard to the conduct of interviews, one of the pillars of the Principles is that interviewers should establish and maintain rapport with interviewees, as building rapport reduces interviewees' anxiety and stress, and leads to interviewers obtaining more comprehensive, accurate, and actionable information. Procedural standards, such as adhering to the detainee's legal rights to access counsel and/or to remain silent must also be consistently followed. Effective interviewing requires the gathering of accurate and reliable information to obtain the truth under investigation. This process will require careful planning, an unbiased attitude toward the detainee, and constant (re)evaluation of the effectiveness of the interview. This includes transparency and accountability (e.g., record keeping of all interviews), external oversight, and the observance of all domestic legal frameworks, drawn from international law, such as the right to silence and access to counsel.

The role of effective and ethical interviewing on vulnerable populations is also highlighted in the Principles. A situation of heightened vulnerability can include factors such as age, gender, sexual orientation, nationality or ethnicity, cultural or religious background, difficulties with communication and understanding (language barriers), inability to read and/or write, intellectual disabilities, as well as other factors that may be present with socioeconomic level and immigration status, among other variables. The next section will discuss the role of ethical and nondeceptive interviewing practices when interviewing vulnerable populations, such as juveniles and L2 custodial suspects.

6.2.1 Vulnerable Populations

One of the questions that arise from custodial interrogation training is whether there are substantive differences between how police question adult and juvenile suspects. Research on child development shows there are psychological differences between adult and juvenile subjects that permeate the context of interrogation (see Kostelnik & Reppucci, 2009; Meyer & Reppucci, 2007). Cleary and Warner (2016) argue that these differences require further investigation in the interrogation room, particularly due to interrogations with juveniles often being excluded from empirical inquiry due to barriers to data access or other complications owing to legal and confidentiality considerations. The authors add that there is also a "training gap" in the literature on how the law enforcement community trains investigators, legally and tactically, to elicit information from suspects: "Systematic reviews or empirical analyses of interrogation training in the United States are not available, and international data are limited. What is known about modern police interrogation techniques is largely derived from the training manuals of commercially marketed interrogation training programs" (2016, p. 271).

In the United States, some programs have been targeted to questioning child victims or witnesses, such as the ChildFirst method (National Children's Advocacy Center, 2019). These programs adopt an information-gathering approach consistent with the PEACE method. The interrogation of juvenile suspects, however, also requires a targeted approach often not covered in training sessions or manuals. This is concerning in the light that police interrogators in the United States appear to be using the same psychologically coercive interrogation techniques with juveniles as with adult suspects (see Cleary & Warner, 2016). This is an issue that could be addressed through training given the apparent association between inadequate police training and practice (see also Meyer & Reppucci, 2007).

Research on custodial interrogation with juveniles also examines the possible relationship between the invocation of legal safeguards and age, as well as other racial and cultural factors. Kassin and Norwick (2004), for example, examine why people, including juveniles, waive their Miranda rights. They note that juveniles may waive their rights due to being "more compliant in response to an investigator's waiver request than adults" (p. 219). Other factors may also contribute to juvenile and adult suspects' compliance with police, including racial background with racialized groups having a higher distrust of local police (Taylor, 2002) and cultural differences (e.g., Asian American Immigrants, Japanese nationals) placing a higher premium on respecting authority (see Landers, 2000). Furthermore, situational influences on the Miranda decision should be considered with juveniles who are subject to sympathy and minimization techniques and contextual factors that may affect invocation of rights, such as amount of in-custody time and access to an attorney or child advocate. The latter is explored in Schoovaerts et al.'s (2021) case study on the role of mandatory legal assistance with juvenile suspect interviews in Belgium.

In 2016, Belgium introduced legislation mandating legal assistance for juvenile suspects. Schoovaerts et al.'s (2021) study examines how lawyers in Belgium fulfill this role in practice. The authors note that there is widespread consensus that juvenile suspects are more vulnerable than their adult counterparts due to their age and, hence, require more protection, particularly during custodial interrogation. In Belgium, frameworks for legal assistance, such as the 2021 Salduz Act (2011), have been implemented in order to minimize the effects, and risks, of interviewing juvenile suspects.

To test whether juveniles benefit from mandated legal assistance, Schoovaerts et al. (2021) analyzed seventeen video-recorded police interviews of juvenile suspects between the ages of twelve and seventeen who were charged with less serious crimes. As the authors note, Belgium is an interesting jurisdiction to consider, since juvenile suspects cannot waive the right to legal assistance and the role of the lawyer is defined as active and specifically trained to provide assistance to juveniles. In this analysis the lawyer's mandatory presence is overall positive. Most of the interviews followed the information-gathering style and the lawyers adopted a stance which facilitated searching for the truth. The authors, however, stress that there were deficiencies in the lawyers' approach to legal intervention, particularly when police investigators used subtle pressure tactics.

Schoovaerts et al. (2021) argue that mandatory legal assistance is not enough and needs to be accompanied by training specific to assisting juvenile suspects in custody. Lawyers must also be able to adopt an active role in the interview and react quickly to prevent coercion or misconduct. These measures should improve the lawyer's effectiveness safeguarding the juvenile suspects' legal rights. Future studies, however, are needed with a larger sample of juvenile suspects, police questioning of juveniles in other jurisdictions, and juvenile suspects facing more serious criminal offenses. The practicality of these measures, when adapted to other jurisdictions such as the United States, needs to be explored also in light of attorney professional code of conduct considerations.

Another population that requires special attention is suspects who are L2 speakers of the institutional language, such as English. Research on suspects' comprehension of Miranda rights, in particular, has shown that both L1 and L2 speakers of English have problems understanding their rights. L2 speakers face additional comprehension challenges. Pavlenko et al. (2019), for example, examined the comprehension of Miranda rights by L2 speakers of English. The authors compared understanding of the Miranda rights among native and advanced L2 speakers of English to establish whether standardized assessments can predict comprehension of the rights.

According to Pavlenko et al. (2019), research suggests that around 80 percent of adults and 90 percent of juvenile suspects in custody waive their rights and talk to police without the presence of counsel:

> Given that 70% of adult inmates function at or below a sixth grade reading level, it is not surprising that they understand only the simplest sentences . . . . Nor do they benefit from prior encounters with the police: detainees perform no better than members of the general population on Miranda comprehension instruments (Rogers et al., 2010) and "frequent flyers" (> 40 arrests) fare no better than those with brief criminal histories (< 5 arrests) (Rogers and Drogin, 2015). When it comes to decision-making, practice does not make perfect either: a study with 80 pretrial detainees revealed that 48.7% did not consider the long-term consequences of waiving their Miranda rights and 43.8% could not generate a single long-term reason for exercising their rights . . . . (p. 183)

Pavlenko et al. (2019) add that these findings also hold outside the United States. The problems are exacerbated among vulnerable populations (e.g., juveniles, persons with cognitive and/or intellectual disabilities) due to limitations in language skills and memory capacity, poor impulse control, as well as a tendency to be easily manipulated by police interviewers.[7]

L2 speakers also face significant challenges during custodial interrogation, yet few studies have empirically investigated L2 speakers' ability to understand the rights and make a decision. Two of the main issues placing a barrier to L2 assessment of Miranda comprehension are the assessment principles themselves and the lack of a mandate to require interpreters in custodial interviews with L2 speakers. In contrast with federal and state courts in the United States, the right to an interpreter does not (legally) extend to custodial interrogations. This leaves police officers or other nonprofessional interpreters to provide linguistic mediation, even if they have basic or intermediate level skills in the suspect's native language. Police officers acting as interpreters also raises questions of biasness, since: "Research shows that officers serving as interpreters still see themselves primarily as interrogators and may perform their add-on duties in a faulty and half-hearted way" (Pavlenko et al., 2019, p. 185).

With regard to Miranda comprehension assessments, Pavlenko et al. (2019) tested the participant's proficiency using established guidelines, such as the American Council on the Teaching of Foreign Languages (ACTFL) and the Common European Framework (CEFR) tests. The authors note that some of the descriptors of high-level (distinguished) proficiency in the ACTFL test conflate proficiency with education and intelligence, a standard many native speakers never attain. The authors, hence, chose Hulstijn's (2011, 2015)

[7] See Fabian (2005) for a discussion on issues regarding intellectual disability and the role of the forensic psychologist in death penalty cases in light of *Atkins* v. *Virginia* (2002).

theoretical framework, which does not relate proficiency with intellectual abilities, and which distinguishes between basic and higher language cognition, BLC (implicit knowledge of linguistic structures) and HLC (peripheral knowledge acquired through education) respectively, and core and peripheral components of proficiency (2015, p. 187). They find that most of the L2 participants in the study failed to understand their Miranda rights and displayed significant disadvantages in both BLC and HLC when compared to native speakers:

> Such weaknesses, however, may be invisible to the untrained eye because our participants did exactly what they were expected to do, according to CEFR standards – faced with unfamiliar words, speakers at the level B1 and higher infer their meanings from context, and, faced with complicated sentences, they extrapolate their meanings, using contextual, syntactic and lexical cues . . . Unfortunately, in the absence of a basic understanding of the US criminal justice system, compensatory strategies useful in academia lead L2 speakers astray in legal contexts – the plausible alternative meanings they infer create "an illusion of understanding." (Pavlenko et al., 2019, p. 201)

The authors add that standardized assessments, including the adaptation of Grisso's (1998) Miranda Rights Comprehension Instruments (MRCI) to L2 speakers, should not be used to make decisions about comprehension of Miranda guarantees, since "there is no proficiency level at which L2 speakers are guaranteed to understand their rights" (Pavlenko et al., 2019, p. 201). These findings are also shared by Urbanik and Pavlenko (2021) who found that even if one proficiency assessment is superior to another, the manner in which rights are delivered, such as the dialogic approach, is key to reducing linguistic guesswork and safeguarding the L2 custodial suspects' rights. For Urbanik and Pavlenko, what needs to change is how rights are communicated to L2 custodial suspects. This includes dual presentation of the warnings (oral and written), asking the custodial suspect to read each warning out loud, adopting the in-your-own-words requirement, simplifying the waiver and avoiding complex legal jargon, electronic recording of custodial interrogations, and the delivery of rights.

The dual presentation of rights is fairly common in United States policing, but the in-your-own words (dialogic) approach is not. The latter consists of the custodial suspect being asked to restate each right in their own words to ensure comprehension. This is in contrast with the traditional request for comprehension "do you understand these rights?," which albeit typical in the reading of rights stage of custodial interrogation, may elicit feigned comprehension in the form of agreement, such as "yes." The dialogic approach was also highlighted in the Guidelines for Communicating Rights to Non-Native Speakers (2012). The Guidelines emphasize that to reduce guesswork, if the custodial suspect is unable to restate in their own words the rights, a professional interpreter should be provided, and the reading of rights stage repeated to ensure comprehension. A point further noted in Urbanik and Pavlenko (2021):

> Since laypeople are rarely able to accurately assess their linguistic needs and the police lack the expertise to determine independently whether the suspect has sufficient understanding of the language in question, the adoption of an in-your-own words requirement offers a working solution to this dilemma. When suspects have difficulties restating the rights in their own words (e.g., when they remain silent or repeat the statement verbatim), a professional interpreter with expertise in legal interpreting should be brought in, even if the suspect had earlier declined the offer of interpreting services. Then, the dialogic procedure needs to be repeated anew, because in and of itself the provision of interpreters and translations does not guarantee comprehension, especially among people unfamiliar with the very cultural assumptions underpinning the right to silence in police interviews. (pp. 108–109)

The recommendation of using professional interpreters in custodial settings is also the focus of a 2006 National Association of Judiciary Interpreters and Translators (NAJIT) position paper *Language Assistance for Law Enforcement*. This paper emphasizes the need for law enforcement to err on the side of caution and provide a qualified, professional interpreter to L2 speakers subject to questioning, such as custodial suspects. As the paper stresses, the use of a professional legal interpreter minimizes lay person's lack of comprehension, increases accuracy of police–lay person exchanges, and reduces conflict of interest that may be challenged in court when a nonprofessional interpreter (e.g., a police interrogator) provides linguistic mediation. Of note, the practicality of providing a professional interpreter needs to consider factors such as availability, particularly with languages of limited diffusion, economic and logistic factors, the use of technology (e.g., remote interpreting), and increased recruitment and training that may facilitate this endeavor. Moreover, the need for additional mediation to ensure comprehension of the rights may also require changes in current practicing standards in legal interpreting.

6.3 Legal Reforms

Effective interviewing is grounded in ensuring human and legal rights. The reading of rights provision, albeit part of most interviewing models, is only as strong as the laws protecting such rights. Police interrogators can use the invocation game to manipulate the preferences of suspects, including invoking rights, because case law facilitates the task. Hence, to reform police interrogation in the United States the Court's perspective on the application of Miranda rights and the use of trickery and deception needs to be revisited.

Legal scholars have approached these legal reforms from a variety of perspectives, ranging from the Court revisiting the *Davis* ruling to requiring the use of corroborating evidence when suspects give a statement to police. This section will focus on the measures that have been proposed to ensure that custodial suspects' rights, in particular the right to counsel, are observed. As Kassin and Norwick (2004) note: "As the gateway to police interrogation and the production of confessions, which can have far reaching and rippling effects on the disposition of cases (Leo & Ofshe, 1998), the invocation or waiver of Miranda is a pivotal choice point in the life of the accused and in the criminal justice system" (p. 213). In context, this statement is particularly noteworthy since past research suggests that four out of five suspects often waive their Miranda rights and agree to questioning (see Leo & White, 1999). From a legal standpoint this finding is significant since it suggests that Miranda warnings, and how police interrogators interpret suspects' invocations of such rights, may not adequately protect suspects from overzealous police investigators – the very purpose of the warnings.

The Court's approach to *Miranda* limits coercive police interrogation tactics, but it is not designed to remove the numerous barriers that prompt custodial suspects, even innocent ones, from agreeing to speak to law enforcement and provide a confession. This book has addressed many of the factors that contribute to the ineffectiveness of the Miranda warnings, as practiced, including the cost of lawyer-free, incommunicado custodial interrogation. This is compounded with the law not requiring police officers to provide custodial suspects with information regarding the interview process or their rights that may help in their decision to either provide a statement or invoke their Miranda rights. A matter that exacerbates the already present asymmetry of knowledge between police and suspects in custodial settings.

6.3.1 The Elusive Right to Counsel and Overcoming Legal Barriers: The Inherent Limitations of Miranda *and* Davis

Since the *Miranda* and *Davis* rulings, legal scholars have provided an array of perspectives regarding the effect of case law on a suspect's invocation for counsel. One perspective is supportive of the *Davis* ruling, as envisioned by the majority opinion of the Court. Yuncker's (1995) assessment of *Davis*, shortly after the ruling, lies on the ineffectiveness of both the application of the per se rule, prior to *Davis*, and the clarification standard proposed by the concurrent minority opinion. Regarding the clarification approach, Yuncker (1995) argues that it "presented difficulties because it tended to put the power to invoke the right to counsel at the will of the interrogating police officer. Police officers were able to circumvent or manipulate the desires of the suspect by attempting to clarify the ambiguous statement" (p. 734). For Yuncker, the clarification standard is at best risky and at worst may lead a suspect to waive their rights and self-incriminate.

Yuncker (1995) argues that the application of the per se – automatic rule when a suspect invokes counsel would also require that interrogation cease at the mention of an attorney, irrespective of whether the suspect was invoking the Miranda right to counsel. For Yuncker, this presents a dilemma for police, since the per se rule may interfere with the suspect's true intentions or desires for representation. As he notes, police officers should not have to determine whether a suspect's equivocal invocation for counsel is an actual invocation. Hence, he argues that the *Davis* ruling does not undermine *Miranda*, but rather gives suspects some level of control over the pressures of custodial interrogation.

Other legal scholars, such as Chen (1996), propose that the limitations inherent in *Davis* may be overcome by implementing the clarification standard: the opposite perspective to Yuncker's (1995). In Chen's view, clarifications may assist police interrogators in making correct determinations about the suspect's actual intentions when invoking counsel. Chen notes that considering the political makeup of the Court, the *Davis* decision is not unexpected. The Court was generally conservative and some of the justices voted along ideological lines. Yet, Chen argues that it is somewhat surprising that the Court did not adopt the concurring minority opinion recommending the clarification standard. For Chen, the latter best meets efficient police practice, unlike the per se bar rule:

> Instead of promoting police efficiency, the per se bar rule would deter the investigative process simply because the police would have to stop the questioning even when a suspect wants to give a statement. Again, the clarification approach, which provides the police with clear guidelines during interrogations, best meets the needs of efficient police practice. Whenever confronted with an ambiguous request, police must stop and clarify, and if the suspect desires to continue, the police can be sure that their continued interrogation will not result in inadmissible statements. Therefore, this approach minimizes the amount of lost and inadmissible confessions and increases investigative efficiency. (Chen, 1996, p. 646)

Chen adds that the Court's *Davis* majority opinion does not achieve the goal of protecting individual rights. The clarification approach, on the other hand, balances the intent of *Miranda* with the police's ability to investigate crime. By requiring police to stop an interrogation and clarify a suspect's equivocal request for counsel, it protects both the suspect's rights and prevents possible acquittals due to judges' throwing out inadmissible confessions. Levenberg (1995) also supports the use of clarifications with equivocal invocations for counsel. He proposed a modified clarification approach where the interrogators' response to the ambiguity is neutral and focuses solely on establishing the status of the suspect's invocation. In this approach, the police should inform the suspect of the consequences of the ambiguous invocation and ask the suspect to state whether they are asserting the right to counsel.

More contemporary research on the role of requests for clarification with invocations for counsel deemed equivocal has focused on the delivery of these types of requests and the legal limitations created by *Davis* during the interrogation process. Bazelon (2007) notes that the right to counsel is at its best ambiguous, since it can apply before, during, or after interrogation, and at its worst misleading and ineffective: "The Miranda warnings are intended to protect a suspect's Fifth Amendment right against compelled self-incrimination; however, the vagueness of the 'right to the presence of an attorney' combined with the intensity of the interrogation often render the suspect's Fifth Amendment privilege illusory" (p. 1009). Bazelon (2007) adds that the effect of the *Davis* ruling on suspects' ability to invoke counsel may be difficult for a suspect to overcome. He notes that sociolinguistic factors, such as being a member of a racialized group, may increase a suspect's tendency to use indirect modes of speech more often to avoid conflict. Racialized groups are also "…arrested on a disproportionate basis, and therefore, the Davis rule creates a strong bias against them" (p. 1030).

Another reason for the *Davis* standard to potentially interfere with the suspect's invocation for counsel is the interrogator's strategic use of clarifications. As Bazelon (2007) notes, the police can use clarifying questions to manipulate and deceive a suspect into not invoking counsel. He proposes instead the use of clarifications that address the limitations inherent in *Davis*. What the author describes as a temporal element that alerts the suspect of their right to have counsel present during interrogation:

> As an initial matter, implementing the proposed bright-line rule would not be a burden on law enforcement officials because it requires adding only two words to the standard Miranda warnings "during interrogation . . . ."
>
> One could argue that this proposed rule is already the rule of the Court, and that this proposal will not change existing law. This rule, however, differs from existing precedent in that it requires strict compliance with one of the Miranda warnings: the right to have counsel present during interrogation. Moreover, this rule is necessary in light of the fact that several circuits have not required law enforcement officials to make suspects aware of their right to have counsel present during interrogation, a right that is guaranteed by the Fifth Amendment. The rule, therefore, augments the Miranda protections, or at least calls for the Court to reaffirm precedent that has not been followed. (2007, p. 1038)

This proposal to clarify the language of *Miranda* and specify its function may benefit custodial suspects who are unaware of the function of the rights. Its effectiveness, as the presumption that suspects' invocations should be taken literally and/or that clarifications can establish a custodial suspects' true intent when invoking counsel, is questionable in practice in light of the invocation game.

6.3.2 Moving Forward in Light of Case Law: A Look at Some Approaches

There are numerous perspectives on how to improve the investigative goal of interrogations and reduce the probability of false confessions. One approach, which has been discussed extensively, is the recording of all police interrogations. Leo et al. (2013) argue that electronic recording of an interrogation is essential to establishing a confession's reliability. Otherwise, prosecutors, judges, juries, and appellate courts will not be able to identify whether police interrogators have contaminated or formatted a suspect's confession. For the authors, through a motion by the defense, courts in criminal cases should evaluate the reliability of evidence obtained through a confession. The latter could be accomplished in the same pretrial hearing that assesses the voluntariness of a suspect's statements. Leo et al. (2013) note that the Federal Rule of Evidence 403 (or its state counterpart) gives trial courts the authority "to exclude confession evidence whose probative value is substantially outweighed by the danger of unfair prejudice to the defendant, confusion of the issues, or misleading the jury" (p. 802). The authors add that under Rule 403, at any point during a criminal case, the trial judge has the discretion to evaluate the probative nature of the evidence, including evidence obtained through a confession, weigh its prejudicial effect, and exclude it from evidence, if appropriate.

Leo et al. (2013) reiterate that pretrial assessments of the reliability of confession evidence would address the high value placed on confessions. This often results in police closing investigations after a confession is obtained and end the police's effort to pursue other leads or corroborate a confession, even if contradicted by other evidence. The authors propose a possible solution – a statute that makes unreliable defendant statements in criminal cases inadmissible at trial: "if it was made under circumstances raising an undue risk that it is false [or that it will result in conviction of a factually innocent person]" (p. 836). For the authors, this proposed measure would address the problem of unreliable confessions, given the pervasiveness of police crafting custodial suspect's statements through a process of discursive contamination and formatting.

To improve the reliability of confessions, Sangero (2007) puts forth a complimentary perspective: the requirement of "strong corroboration" of confession evidence. The author argues that the *Miranda* rules only address the possibility that a confession may be involuntary. The matter of false confessions, which the author notes may be voluntary, is not properly addressed in the law. For Sangero, this is inconsistent with the considerable research demonstrating innocent persons providing a false confession, resulting in their wrongful conviction. In most of these cases, without the advent of genetic,

DNA, testing, much of these false confessions and wrongful convictions would not have been revisited and reversed. Yet, genetic testing is not possible for every case. Moreover, custodial suspects subject to interrogation may provide false confessions voluntarily, without explicit pressure from police.

Sangero (2007) adds that the general assumption that the criminal justice system functions properly (see also Cassell, 1999) should also be revisited:

> If the system does indeed operate properly, then, on the one hand, why should it be assumed that, without a confession, a guilty person would be acquitted? For, even without a confession, it should be possible and necessary to obtain other evidence that would incriminate the guilty person. On the other hand – again, if the system is supposedly working properly – why should it be assumed that an innocent person would be convicted instead? Moreover, if the focus on extracting confessions from interrogees is ceased, then it may be inferred that fewer innocent persons would be convicted even if not enough confessions would be extracted from the guilty. (Sangero, 2007, p. 107)

Sangero notes that confessions should be taken with a degree of skepticism. A confession, obtained with or without external pressures, is "not the 'queen of evidence,' but rather, it is the 'empress of wrongful convictions'" (p. 110).

The requirement of corroborating evidence for a confession may reduce the likelihood of a false confession being used at trial (and as evidence) and raises the voluntariness standard to a reasonable doubt standard. Sangero notes that police investigators should not limit themselves to the interrogation of suspects and trying to get a confession, but rather employ investigative techniques that provide evidence extrinsic to the suspect. The implementation of a strong corroboration, however, will require a change in the current, traditional standard, which the author argues only requires "slight" corroborative evidence:

> Essentially, the police investigation following the apprehension of a suspect is mostly directed at obtaining a confession. Furthermore, once the confession is obtained, the investigation usually ends. My explanation for this is complicated and, briefly, as follows: first, the police operate under a misguided conception of the guilt of the suspect (in direct contrast to the presumption of innocence); second, the confession is still considered to be particularly strong, almost conclusive, evidence; third, the key measure of the success of the police (and, I am afraid, also of the success of the prosecution) and the major criterion for the promotion of investigators (and, I fear, also for the promotion of prosecutors) is still the high percentage of convictions; fourth, extracting a confession – especially when some use of pressure is acceptable – is an easy and inexpensive approach in comparison with alternative methods of investigation; fifth, the courts, which are usually not willing to exclude confessions provided that the formal Miranda rules are abided by, are essentially sending a message to investigators that it is possibly reasonable to focus on extracting confessions from suspects; sixth, judges, in fact, allow the police to use detention (in disgraceful conditions) or the threat of detention, as a means of exerting pressure on interrogees so that they will confess to crimes that they are suspected of having committed; seventh, the confession may still be

considered to possess extra-evidentiary value in addition to the excessive evidentiary value already attributed to it. (2007, pp. 125–126)

Sangero concludes that society should move away from a confession culture that in essence encourages and values self-incrimination. He recommends that lawmakers enact legislation that reduces innocent persons being wrongfully convicted on the basis of confessions alone and move to objective "strong corroboration" that is independent of the confession and links the suspect to the crime. Of note, there are practical considerations to this proposal, ranging from the viability of (all/most) cases going to trial to the possible societal concerns of those accused of a crime being released while awaiting trial.

Another perspective that works in tandem with those previously discussed, is the requirement of legal assistance during custodial interrogation. At present in the United States, there is no such legal requirement. On the contrary, the majority opinion in *Miranda* made it clear that the interrogation must cease if a suspect states a desire for counsel, but a "station house lawyer" is not required to secure a suspect's request for legal representation. This is in contrast with other jurisdictions outside the United States, such as European states, where legal assistance is more accessible at the police station.

In 2008, the European Court of Human Rights (ECtHR) signaled to states that are members of the European Convention on Human Rights (ECHR) that the right to legal assistance in the pretrial period of investigation is essential to ensuring the right to a fair trial (under Article 6, ECHR). In the seminal case of *Salduz* v. *Turkey* (2008), the ECtHR held that every suspect in police custody, except for compelling circumstances, must be provided with access to an attorney prior to their first interrogation. Although much has been written about the impact of *Salduz* on legal reforms, "there has been less scrutiny of the manner in which legal assistance for detained suspects is arranged and provided. The ECtHR has consistently stated that the protection afforded to ECHR rights must be practical and effective, not theoretical and illusory. Accordingly, the practical logistics of the operation of the right to legal assistance are critical" (Daly & Conway, 2021, p. 619).

The manner in which ECHR member states select lawyers for detained suspects varies, ranging from utilizing an intermediary clearinghouse to the detainees making the phone calls themselves. In Scotland, for example, police are required to pass all requests for in custody legal advice to the Solicitor Contact Line (SCL). The latter is provided by the Scottish Legal Aid Board. In England and Wales, there is a similar protocol in which the police call the Defence Solicitor Call Centre (DSCC) conveying a custodial suspect's request for legal assistance. Legal advice is provided without remuneration to any custodial suspect who has received the caution. The intermediary step, however, is not followed by all jurisdictions. In Austria, Bulgaria, and Greece, often local law associations produce a list of lawyers from which the custodial suspect may choose. On occasion, custodial suspects make the phone call for legal assistance themselves or the police does so on their behalf. In the Netherlands and France, a mixed approach with some centralized referral system is employed. In Northern Ireland, the Law Society operating in Belfast set up a rotation system for duty solicitors. Outside of Belfast no formal rotation system is employed. In Poland, if a custodial suspect cannot provide the name of a lawyer for police to contact, police inform family members that they should make arrangements to secure an attorney. As Daly and Conway (2021) note this can be challenging and causes both variance in the quality of representation as well as delays in the delivery of legal assistance. They add that across Europe there is no standard process to selecting legal counsel.

Ireland is one of the cases in which the selection of counsel raises some important legal questions that should be considered when implementing legal assistance services. In Ireland, until 2014, legal advice to custodial suspects was limited to consultations. The change to allow lawyers to attend custodial interviews came about a circular issued by the Director of Public Prosecutions (DPP) to An Garda Síochána in May 2014 "instructing that, where requested, the attendance of solicitors should be facilitated, and that all suspects should be advised of this entitlement" (Daly & Conway, 2021, p. 625). This circular does not constitute a legal or constitutional right. It was not until 2015 that An Garda Síochána issued a Code of Practice on Access to a Solicitor by Persons in Garda Custody and the Law Society of Ireland issued Guidance for Solicitors Providing Legal Services in Garda Stations. To provide access to legal services at Garda stations, The Criminal Law Committee of the Law Society of Ireland created an online list of attorneys:

> who have registered as willing to attend at a station, divided by relevant division, which displays in a random order each time it is renewed. The list is provided for in the guidance for solicitors issued by the Law Society of Ireland. This "Find a Garda Station Solicitor" system would allow gardaí to provide a randomized printed list to detained suspects from which they could select a solicitor to be contacted. This has not, however, been formally adopted in any way, although it was referenced by the state in evidence to the European Committee for the Prevention of Torture during its 2019 visit to the state. (Daly & Conway, 2021, p. 626)

The use of lists of attorneys raised concerns about the actual random choice of attorneys being selected to provide legal assistance at Garda Stations. Daly and Conway analyzed what they describe as semistructured interviews of forty-four criminal defense attorneys in Ireland between the periods of 2018 and 2019. The authors' research provides some interesting findings. They note that the interviewees expressed a high level of concern that the system of selecting registered attorneys was not consistently applied in practice. Other important concerns raised by the interviewees include the failure to use the list, alternative (nonrandom) criteria for selecting attorneys, the selection by gardí (police) of preferred attorneys, rather than the clients, and the role of factors such as speed/expediency and suggestibility in the selection process.

In the study, the attorneys interviewed appeared to be supportive of the use of a list. Yet, they expressed concern over the clarity and fairness of the selection process. An important point raised, and which could affect any system not using a third party legal contact, is the police contacting an attorney on behalf of a custodial suspect. Daly and Conway (2021) note that: "This power of the police is only reinforced by the fact that, unlike in many jurisdictions, it is the gardaí making the phone call rather than the client or an intermediary. Some participants believed that the choice of clients can be actively overridden by gardaí" (p. 632). Thus, participants in the study expressed concern that the gardaí are not using the sanctioned list in favor of what they describe as "favorites." The allegations for gardaí selecting off list include financial reasons, which could constitute corruption, and the impact on the investigation. The latter reason was the most commonly cited. Here gardaí may prefer attorneys who are less likely to advise their clients to remain silent and who may make it "easier" for the gardaí to conduct the police interview. Attorneys who were willing to consult in person and attend promptly to the call also seemed to be favored by the gardaí. This gardaí's preference for expediency may also influence the custodial suspects who may be encouraged to choose a quicker release from detention than to wait for the attorney to arrive. In the study, the attorneys mentioned custodial suspects foregoing all together the right to counsel, contacting counsel to request that they do not attend the station, or not making contact at the time of arrest, as is the custodial suspect's right. Furthermore, and as insightful, many of the participants felt that the quality of the defense they offer influences whether they receive requests to attend the police stations. They also noted that less active, rights-driven solicitors are often selected or suggested by gardaí, which raises questions about whether the rights of the accused are being respected.

The case study in Ireland suggests that even in countries where legislation has passed to further protect custodial suspects' right to counsel, it is difficult to overcome past legal and police culture patterns that place a premium on obtaining a statement expediently. Legislative reforms that are not formalized and implemented consistently, with an emphasis on transparency, and which have little or no oversight at the police station, may fail to protect custodial suspects' rights. These issues are not unique to one country and need to be considered if, and when, legislation and/or the Court revisits the question of the need for "station house lawyers" available at all times to advise custodial suspects in the United States.

6.4 Concluding Remarks

To achieve police interrogation reform in the United States, there needs to be an understanding about the effects of the *Miranda* and *Davis* rulings in protecting custodial suspects' rights and the relationship between the law and how police conduct interrogations. *Miranda* addressed the need for additional safeguards to protect custodial suspects' right to counsel during custodial interrogation. Yet, the ruling did not define what constitutes an invocation for counsel that would cease a police interrogation. The *Davis* ruling, although narrowed invocations for counsel as those a reasonable police officer would understand as unequivocal/unambiguous, did not define what constitutes this type of unequivocal invocation. On the contrary, the ruling added uncertainty to the definition of requests for counsel and, in the process, bestowed additional power to police investigators in making the determination. In essence, *Davis* perpetuated and institutionalized the invocation game, framed in manipulation/deception, that has been observed in police interrogations, past and present. Since 1994, there has been no attempt of the Court to revisit the *Davis* ruling or a move toward creating legislation that addresses not only police reform, but also how police interview custodial suspects. The latter is needed to move the invocation game of interrogation, grounded in legally accepted manipulation and deception, to an investigative interview that gathers information, not confessions. To accomplish these reforms, new legislation needs to address three key points: (1) how police question suspects, (2) how police question members of vulnerable populations, and (3) how the law, and the requirement of counsel (at the police station) during custodial interrogation better secures custodial suspects' rights.

The first point takes us back to the clear divide shown in the book's corpus between justices who argue in favor of removing unnecessary obstructions to police investigation and those who rule, primarily, for the protection of individual constitutional rights. The former is argued most often. This raises the following inquiry, what does this mean for police interrogation reform? One possibility that has been discussed is that police interrogation reform can occur organically and independently of the law. This approach would not include extensive legislative involvement and/or changes to the law and would depend largely on the police reforming itself.

Although police officers have been part of important reform policies in some jurisdictions outside of the United States, leading to major reforms (e.g., PACE), historically this has not been the most effective approach in the United States. Without broader legislative and legal reforms, it will be difficult to overcome police culture that may not fully embrace reform.[8] As Robinson

[8] It is important to note that some police reform measures have been initiated by members of the court, such as a federal judge-led initiative implementing police reform in Puerto Rico. The latter

(2020) notes, there are four main barriers to police reform in the United States: (1) the decentralized nature of policing, (2) the culture of policing and not being open to change, (3) a lack of training based on science, and (4) lack of government leadership and initiatives. There is also the current focus on tactical skills, rather than on social interaction: "American policing in the future will be shaped by the men and women now coming into the police academies, yet at a time when there are calls for advancing 'guardian' culture in policing, many training academies are still organized as military-style boot camps emphasizing a 'warrior' approach" (p. 235).

The manner in which police officers question suspects in the United States is mediated by both present and past views of the role of police questioning in solving crime. Present policing culture, for example, may be recalcitrant to changes in the interrogation room due to the high value placed on obtaining a custodial suspect's confession. As Bull and Baker (2020) caution adopting a new interviewing approach may cause some police departments to push back. This is also highlighted in an older 2007 survey (Zalman & Smith, 2007) that suggests that changes to police interviewing practices may face resistance from police officers who conduct interrogations. Hence, addressing the potential push back will necessitate legislative recommendations and changes to police officers' criminal code of conduct that include how police question suspects. This will also require police investigators who conduct police interviews to be trained in noncoercive, rapport-based, interviewing methods and be required to maintain their skills. Training needs to also emphasize not only how police interrogators formulate questions, but how they follow up suspects' responses, particularly during the probing stage of police questioning. Even an interrogator who is trained and motivated to use noncoercive questioning tactics (e.g., using TED questions) may shift the interview as framed and change the suspects' preferences and discursive choices. This is the potential pitfall of any interrogation/interview technique and, as such, needs to be part of any training method, even noncoercive ones. Furthermore, and as noted previously, even the best interviewing techniques may turn into a game of misperception if the law facilitates it. Hence, changes to the law, such as the Court revisiting *Davis*, will also be needed to adapt legislation to current law regarding the reading of rights, suspects' invocations for counsel, and the presence of counsel, if requested. This point will be discussed in more detail later in the section.

The second point relates to the questioning of vulnerable suspects, specifically juveniles and L2 speakers. To protect L2 custodial suspects' rights there

resulted in the appointment of a monitor (or technical compliance adviser (TCA)), as well as a team of subject-matter experts to oversee police conduct in the Puerto Rico Police Department (see www.fedbar.org/wp-content/uploads/2016/09/PoliceReform-pdf-1.pdf).

needs to be a presumption of the need for an interpreter. Police investigators should not be tasked with making determinations about whether a custodial suspect has sufficient proficiency in the L2 to comprehend their legal rights. Police, on average, are not trained to determine their own or others' proficiency in the L2. As recommended in this chapter, police should instead follow a number of steps aimed at protecting an L2 custodial suspect's rights, including the dual presentation of the warnings (oral and written), asking the custodial suspect to read each warning out loud, adopting the in-your-own-words requirement, simplifying the waiver, avoiding complex legal jargon, and the electronic recording of custodial interrogations and delivery of rights. All linguistically mediated police interrogations should be videorecorded. These measures should also be in place for L2 witnesses and victims of crime that are subject to police interviewing. Adopting these linguistic safeguards will help further the protection of L2 speakers' rights who are questioned by law enforcement. These measures may require additional government funding for professional interpreting services, such as providing access to in person and/or remote interpreting at the police station.

Juveniles also require special attention in custodial settings. One of the most effective measures that have been studied and proposed in, and outside, the United States is the required presence of a lawyer during police questioning. The latter is consistent with research completed in Europe that suggests that juveniles are at a higher risk of providing inaccurate statements or false confessions and are more prone to compliance and suggestibility than adults. Furthermore, the absence of age-appropriate interview models for juvenile suspects also puts them at a higher risk. In light of the risks associated with interviewing juveniles, adopting research-informed recommendations would be beneficial when considering police interrogation reforms. An attorney's mandatory presence during custodial interrogation also appears to be positive. In addition, research cited in this chapter, such as the Belgium case study, points to the benefits of interviews that are conducted using an appropriate information-gathering style. Attorneys that took a cooperative position and adopt an active role also appear to be able to prevent or proactively tackle police coercion or misconduct during a custodial interview. Yet, an attorney's presence "is insufficient alone and must be accompanied by additional supporting mechanisms such as training specific to assisting juvenile suspects at the police station" (Schoovaerts et al., 2021, 67).

For juveniles, meaningful access to a lawyer is very limited: "no state guarantees lawyers for every child during interrogation, and only one state requires it under limited circumstances" (see National Juvenile Defender Center, 2017, p. 7). Furthermore, according to the United States Department of Justice, Office of Justice Programs (see Jones, 2004), many juveniles waive their rights. This issue appears to affect juveniles across the board, but disproportionately juveniles from poor and single parent backgrounds, as well as members of racialized groups (see Leiber & Stairs, 1999). These outcomes could be mitigated by requiring the presence of criminal defense lawyers at all stages of custodial questioning. These measures may also reduce recidivism among juvenile suspects and being caught in the system.

The third point deals with changes to the law. Although, it is unlikely that the Legislative Branch of the federal government will enact a law protecting custodial suspects, even juveniles, the need to protect custodial suspects' right to counsel will require either the Court revising the *Davis* ruling, which seems unlikely, or new legislation that addresses comprehensive police reform, including police interrogation reform. Police reforms, such as PACE, can provide guidance to new police reform legislation in the United States, if this route were considered. If *Davis* is revisited, the Court could also undo the lack of clarity raised in the ruling. As mentioned previously, there have been numerous recommendations from legal scholars as to how to address the shortcomings of *Davis*. These range from requiring police investigators to clarify an invocation for counsel they deem equivocal or ambiguous to returning to the undefined sentiment of *Miranda* that once a suspect invokes counsel, per se, all questioning must cease.

Revisiting the clarification approach in *Davis* will likely be an ineffective remedy. In the corpus, what judges often refer to as a request for clarification is linguistically a follow-up move most often aimed at dissuading the suspect from invoking counsel. This action may make it more likely that the suspect will waive their rights. In essence, police interrogators can, and do, use follow-up turns strategically as a means to manipulate the custodial suspect into changing their preferences (or choice to invoke counsel). As Chapter 4 describes, custodial interrogation in the United States is a type of invocation game. One that is designed to (passive-aggressively) change the custodial suspect's preferences from requesting an attorney to waiving their rights. This invocation game is probably best executed following more guilt-presumptive interrogation techniques, such as Reid, but as noted it would likely be present also with information gathering, rapport-based interviewing techniques, such as PEACE, if the *Davis* ruling stands and there is no legislative reform. The law facilitates, and possibly incentivizes, police investigators to deem invocations for counsel as equivocal/ambiguous. If the law did not assign the police as gatekeepers of suspects' right to counsel, and defined invocations for counsel broadly, police interrogation reforms would have a much higher probability of being enacted in practice. This point takes us, once more, to revisiting the per se standard.

Under the per se rule any reference to counsel, regardless of its equivocalness or ambiguity, ceases a police interrogation: "Indeed, the Court described Miranda as a 'rigid rule that an accused's request for an attorney is per se an invocation of his Fifth Amendment rights, requiring that all interrogation cease'" and has recognized the "undisputed right" to remain silent and to be free from questioning "until he ha[s] consulted with a lawyer" (Levenberg, 1995, p. 964). This approach, as noted, was not supported by the *Davis* Court. The justices thought the per se approach would limit effective law enforcement. Hence, the clarification approach was suggested by some of the justices in *Davis* to balance police's ability to interrogate suspects and protect suspects' rights. In theory, and from a linguistics perspective, requests for clarification may improve a suspects' ability to invoke counsel, if the police perceive the invocation as equivocal. Yet, this is in theory, not necessarily in practice. A follow-up turn of talk, which would be the clarification of a suspect's request for counsel, cannot aim to resolve the first/previous turn if the police interrogator already strategically deemed the invocation equivocal/ambiguous and the law permits that strategic interpretation. This takes us back to the very rights *Miranda* aimed to protect.

Miranda recognized that the goals of the interrogator and the interests of the suspect are in conflict in the adversarial system. The Court also recognized that the custodial suspect who waives their right to counsel may be doing so foolishly: the defendant who does not request counsel is the one who needs it the most. "The defendant who does not ask for counsel is the very defendant who most needs counsel." If the goal of police questioning were to get information, rather than a confession, then the presence of an attorney to protect a custodial suspect's rights would not be perceived as a barrier. On the contrary, the presence of counsel at the interrogation may serve several added functions. If the accused decides to talk to interrogators, the assistance of counsel can mitigate the dangers of untrustworthiness. With a lawyer present the likelihood that the police will practice coercion is reduced, and if coercion is nevertheless exercised the lawyer can testify to it in court. The presence of a lawyer can also help to guarantee that the accused gives a fully accurate statement to the police and that the statement is accurately reported by the prosecution at trial. A return to a broad interpretation of an invocation for counsel would provide the best path to changing the invocation game of police interrogation into an investigative interview endeavor. Limiting the overreliance on confession evidence and requiring corroboration through the investigative process would also potentially improve the reliability of suspect statements and reduce the number of false confessions obtained.

In sum, police interrogation reform requires a change of perspective on how to effectively balance the role of police officers in investigating crime, a common theme in judicial rulings, and individual constitutional rights. It also requires broader justice reforms that challenge accepted law-and-order rhetoric and unethical (albeit often legally sanctioned) police questioning practices, including the legal use of trickery and deception. As Leo (2008) rightly argues: "Police interrogation should be an investigative function. It should therefore not be guilt presumptive, and its purpose should not be to incriminate the suspect in order to build a case against him" (p. 357). This is the antithesis of the invocation game of police interrogation and can most effectively be addressed by overhauling current legal frameworks that facilitate the imbalance between police investigating crime and suspects being able to secure their Miranda rights.

Appendix: Jurisdictions and Case Counts

Court	Total	%
SCOTUS	**10**	**3%**
Circuit Courts	**86**	**29%**
United States Court of Appeals, First Circuit	3	
United States Court of Appeals, Second Circuit	2	
United States Court of Appeals, Fourth Circuit	5	
United States Court of Appeals, Fifth Circuit	10	
United States Court of Appeals, Sixth Circuit	11	
United States Court of Appeals, Seventh Circuit	11	
United States Court of Appeals, Eighth Circuit	1	
United States Court of Appeals, Ninth Circuit	28	
United States Court of Appeals, Tenth Circuit	8	
United States Court of Appeals, Eleventh Circuit	7	
District Courts by State/Territory	**196**	**65%**
United States District Court, M.D. Alabama, Northern Division	1	
United States District Court, S.D. Alabama, Southern Division	1	
United States District Court, D. Alaska	1	
United States District Court, D. Arizona	9	
United States District Court, E.D. California	9	
United States District Court, C.D. California, Eastern Division	1	
United States District Court, E.D. California, Sacramento Division	1	
United States District Court, C.D. California, Western Division	2	
United States District Court, C.D. California	7	
United States District Court, N.D. California	10	
United States District Court, D. Colorado	1	
United States District Court, D. Connecticut	2	
United States District Court, D. Delaware	1	
United States District Court, District of Columbia	2	
United States District Court, M.D. Florida	1	
United States District Court, S.D. Florida	2	
United States District Court, N.D. Georgia, Atlanta Division	3	
United States District Court, N.D. Georgia, Gainesville Division	1	
United States District Court, N.D. Georgia, Newnan Division	1	
United States District Court, D. Hawaii	1	
United States District Court, D. Idaho	1	

(*cont.*)

Court	Total	%
District Courts by State/Territory	**196**	**65%**
United States District Court, C. D. Illinois	2	
United States District Court, N.D. Illinois, Western Division	1	
United States District Court N.D. Indiana	1	
United States District Court, S.D. Indiana, Terre Haute Division	1	
United States District Court, N.D. Iowa, Cedar Rapids Division	1	
United States District Court, W.D. Iowa, Western Division	1	
United States District Court, N.D. Iowa, Western Division	1	
United States District Court, D. Kansas	1	
United States District Court, W.D. Kentucky, Louisville	1	
United States District Court, W.D. Kentucky, Owensboro Division	1	
United States District Court, E.D. Louisiana	1	
United States District Court, W.D. Louisiana	1	
United States District Court, D. Maine	5	
United States District Court, D. Maryland, Southern Division	1	
United States District Court, D. Massachusetts	2	
United States District Court, E.D. Michigan, Northern Division	1	
United States District Court, E.D. Michigan, Southern Division	6	
United States District Court, W.D. Michigan, Southern Division	1	
United States District Court, D. Minnesota	12	
United States District Court, S.D. Mississippi, Northern Division	1	
United States District Court, E.D. Missouri	2	
United States District Court, E.D. Missouri, Eastern Division	1	
United States District Court, E.D. Missouri, South Eastern Division	1	
United States District Court, W.D. Missouri, Central Division	1	
United States District Court, W.D. Missouri, Western Division	1	
United States District Court, D. Montana, Great Falls Division	1	
United States District Court, D. Nebraska	4	
United States District Court, D. New Mexico	4	
United States District Court, E. D. New York	10	
United States District Court, N.D. New York	2	
United States District Court, S.D. New York	6	
United States District Court, W. D. New York	4	
United States District Court, D. Nevada	3	
United States District Court, E.D. North Carolina, Western Division	1	
United States District Court, W.D. North Carolina	1	
United States District Court, N.D. Ohio, Eastern Division	2	
United States District Court, S.D. Ohio, Eastern Division	1	
United States District Court, S.D. Ohio, Western Division	3	
United States District Court, S.D. Ohio, Western Division, at Cincinnati	2	
United States District Court, N.D. Oklahoma	2	
United States District Court, D. Oregon	1	
United States District Court, M.D. Pennsylvania	2	
United States District Court, E.D. Pennsylvania	2	
United States District Court, W.D. Pennsylvania	1	
United States District Court, D. Rhode Island	1	
United States District Court, D. South Dakota, Central Division	3	

(*cont.*)

Court	Total	%
District Courts by State/Territory	**196**	**65%**
United States District Court, E.D. Tennessee	1	
United States District Court, E.D. Tennessee, Knoxville	2	
U.S. District Court, E. D. Tennessee, Southern Division Chattanooga	1	
United States District Court, M.D. Tennessee, Nashville Division	1	
United States District Court, E.D. Texas	1	
United States District Court, N.D. Texas, Dallas Division	1	
United States District Court, S.D. Texas, Galveston Division	1	
United States District Court, S.D. Texas, Houston Division	5	
United States District Court, D. Utah, Central Division	2	
United States District Court, D. Utah	1	
United States District Court, D. Vermont	1	
United States District Court, E.D. Virginia, Alexandria Division	1	
United States District Court, E.D. Virginia, Norfolk Division	2	
United States District Court, E.D. Virginia, Richmond Division	1	
United States District Court, W.D. Virginia	1	
United States District Court, Virgin Islands, St. Thomas and St. John	2	
United States District Court, N.D. West Virginia	4	
United States District Court, E.D. Wisconsin	4	
United States District Court, W.D. Wisconsin	1	
United States District Court, D. Wyoming	1	
Military Courts	**9**	**3%**
United States Court of Military Appeals	2	
United States Army Court of Military Review	4	
United States Air Force Court of Military Review	1	
United States Air Force Court of Criminal Appeals	1	
United States Navy-Marine Corps Court of Criminal Appeals	1	

Glossary

Ambiguity language that has more than one meaning; often used interchangeably with equivocal

Appeal a challenge to a previous legal determination

Arrest the use of legal authority to deprive a person of their freedom of movement

Bright-line rule an objective rule that resolves legal questions in a straightforward manner and helps resolve ambiguous issues by setting a basic standard that clarifies the ambiguity and establishes a simple response

Broad interpretation the interpretation or liberal construction of a constitutional or statutory provision that applies the original intent, purpose, and spirit of the writing to circumstances that are not specifically addressed by the constitution or statute

Case law law that is based on judicial decisions rather than law based on constitutions, statutes, or regulations

Clarification standard in custodial interrogation, a means by which the intent of an equivocal/ambiguous invocation may be clarified

Concurring (opinion) an opinion that agrees with the majority opinion but does not agree with the rationale behind it and not binding law

Custodial interrogation the questioning of a detained person by the police in connection with a criminal investigation, where the detained person may or may not be under arrest, and whenever they are not free to leave for other reasons

Custody in criminal law, a person is in custody when/after being arrested or convicted of a crime

Defendant in a criminal case, the person accused of the crime

De novo a court deciding issues anew without reference to any legal conclusion or assumption made by the previous court

Detention in criminal law, to detain an individual is to hold them in custody

Dissenting (opinion) an opinion filed by a judge who disagrees with the majority decision of a case and not binding law

En banc a decision by the full court of all the appeals judges

Equivocal a general rule when an expression may be taken in two senses

Habeas corpus a writ of *habeas corpus* is used to bring a prisoner or person detained before the court to determine if the person's imprisonment or detention is lawful

Harmless error an error by a trial judge in the conduct of a trial that an appellate court finds was not damaging enough to the appealing party's right to a fair trial to justify reversing the judgment, or to warrant a new trial

Judicial panel a set of judges who hear a cause of action, most frequently an appeal from a ruling of a trial court judge

Majority (opinion) a judicial opinion that is joined by more than half the judges deciding a case

Motion a request to a judge for an order or judgment

Opinion the explanation of a court's judgment – these may be published/ unpublished depending on whether the opinion has precedential value

Per curiam an opinion issued by the Court rather than by specific justices

Per se generally used in the law to mean that without referring to anything else, it is self-evident or inherent

Petitioner the party who presents a petition to the court

Rights a power or privilege held by individuals as the result of a constitution, statute, regulation, judicial precedent, or other type of law

Ruling a court's decision or judgment

Suspect a person who is believed to have committed a crime, but has not yet been found guilty

Unequivocal free of ambiguity or vagueness

Verdict a judicial decision given by a judge or court

Voluntariness a choice made of free will, rather than as the result of coercion or duress

Waiver an act of voluntarily giving up a right

Writ a written order of a judge requiring specific action by the person or entity to whom the writ is directed

References

About the U.S. Courts of Appeals. Retrieved June 12, 2022 from www.uscourts.gov/about-federal-courts/court-role-and-structure/about-us-courts-appeals.

Ainsworth, J. (1993). In a different register: The pragmatics of powerlessness in police interrogation. *The Yale Law Journal*, *103*(2), 259–322.

Ainsworth, J. (2008). You have the right to remain silent . . . but only if you ask for it just so: The role of linguistic ideology in American police interrogation law. *International Journal of Speech, Language & The Law*, *15*(1), 1–21.

Ainsworth, J. (2012). The meaning of silence in the right to remain silent. In L. Solan & P. Tiersma (Eds.), *The Oxford handbook of language and law* (pp. 287–298). Oxford: Oxford University Press.

Ainsworth, J. (2020). Miranda rights: Curtailing coercion in police interrogation: The failed promise of Miranda v. Arizona. In M. Coulthard, A. May, & R. Sousa-Silva (Eds.), *The Routledge handbook of forensic linguistics* (pp. 95–111). London: Routledge.

Alison, L. J., Alison, E., Noone, G., Elntib, S., & Christiansen P. (2013). Why tough tactics fail and rapport gets results: Observing Rapport-Based Interpersonal Techniques (ORBIT) to generate useful information from terrorists. *Psychology, Public Policy and Law*, *19*, 411–431.

Alison, L. J., Alison, E., Shortland, N., & Surmon-Bohr, F. (2020). *ORBIT: The science of rapport-based interviewing for law enforcement, security, and military*. Oxford: Oxford University Press.

Antaki, C., Richardson, E., Stokoe, E., & Willott, S. (2015). Dealing with the distress of people with intellectual disabilities reporting sexual assault and rape. *Discourse Studies*, *17*(4), 415–432.

Asher, N., & Lascarides, A. (2013). Strategic conversation. *Semantics and Pragmatics*, *6*, 1–58.

Baldwin, J. (1993). Police interview techniques. *The British Journal of Criminology*, *33*, 325–352.

Basar, T., & Olsder, G. J. (1999). *Dynamic noncooperative game theory*. Philadelphia, PA: Society for Industrial and Applied Mathematics.

Bazelon, A. S. (2007). Adding (or reaffirming) temporal element to the Miranda warning "you have the right to an attorney." *Marquette Law Review*, *90*(4), 1009–1042.

Bennett, P. G. (1977). Toward a theory of hypergames. *Omega*, *5*, 749–751.

Bennett, P. G. (1980). Hypergames, the development of an approach to modeling conflicts. *Futures*, *12*, 489–507.

Berk-Seligson, S. (2009). *Coerced confessions: The discourse of bilingual police interrogations*. New York: Mouton de Gruyter.

Blakemore, D. (1994). Echo questions: A pragmatic account. *Lingua. International Review of General Linguistics. 94*(4), 197–211.

Blutner, R. (2000). Some aspects of optimality in natural language interpretation. *Journal of Semantics, 17*(3), 189–216.

Brimbal, L., Kleinman, S. M., Oleszkiewicz, S., & Meissner, C. A. (2019). Developing rapport and trust in the interrogative context: An empirically-supported and ethical alternative to customary interrogation practices. In S. J. Barela, M. J. Fallon, G. Gaggioli, & J. D. Ohlin (Eds.), *Interrogation and torture: Integrating efficacy with law and morality* (pp. 141–196). Oxford: Oxford University Press.

Brimbal, L., Meissner, C. A., Kleinman, S. M., et al. (2021). Evaluating the benefits of a rapport-based approach to investigative interviews: A training study with law enforcement investigators. *Law and Human Behavior, 45*(1), 55–67.

Brooks, P. (2000). *Troubling confessions*. Chicago: University of Chicago Press.

Broscheid, A. (2011). Comparing circuits: Are some US Courts of Appeals more liberal or conservative than others? *Law & Society Review, 45*(1), 171–194.

Brown, P., & Levinson, S. C. (1987). *Politeness: Some universals in language usage*. Cambridge: Cambridge University Press.

Buckley, J. P. (2012). The Reid technique of interviewing and interrogation. Presentation. https://static.secure.website/wscfus/869641/uploads/oneday_-_master_current_Reid.pdf

Bull, R., & Baker, L. (2020). Obtaining valid discourse from suspects PEACE-fully: What role for rapport and empathy. In M. Mason & F. Rock (Eds.), *The discourse of police interviews* (pp. 42–64). Chicago: University of Chicago Press.

Burnett, H. (2019). Signalling games, sociolinguistic variation and the construction of style. *Linguistics and Philosophy, 42*, 419–450.

Busse, U. (2002). Changing politeness strategies in English requests: A diachronic investigation. In J. Fisiak (Ed.), *Studies in English historical linguistics and philology* (pp. 17–35). Frankfurt: Peter Lang.

Calderon, S., Mac Giolla, E., Ask, K., & Granhag, P. A. (2018). Drawing what lies ahead: False intentions are more abstractly depicted than true intentions. *Applied Cognitive Psychology, 32*(4), 518–522.

Cason, T. N., & Plott, C. R. (2014). Misconceptions and game form recognition: Challenges to theories of revealed preference and framing. *Journal of Political Economy, 122*(6), 1235–1270.

Cassell, P. G. (1999). The guilty and the "innocent": An examination of alleged cases of wrongful conviction from false confessions. *Harvard Journal of Law and Public Policy, 22*(2), 523–580.

Chan, J., & Dixon, D. (2007). The politics of police reform: Ten years after the royal commission into the New South Wales Police Service. *Criminology & Criminal Justice, 7*(4), 443–468.

Chen, T. (1996). Davis v. United States: Maybe should talk to lawyer means maybe Miranda is unraveling. *Pepperdine Law Review, 23*(2), 607–650.

Cho, I. K., & Kreps, D. M. (1987). Signaling games and stable equilibria. *The Quarterly Journal of Economics, 102*(2), 179–221.

Clarke, C., Milne, B., & Bull, R. (2011). Interviewing suspects of crime: The impact of PEACE training, supervision and the presence of a legal advisor. *Journal of Investigative Psychology and Offender Profiling*, *8*, 149–162.

Cleary, H. (2014). Police interviewing and interrogation of juvenile suspects: A descriptive examination of actual cases. *Law and Human Behavior*, *38*(3), 271–282.

Cleary, H. M. D., & Warner, T. C. (2016). Police training in interviewing and interrogation methods: A comparison of techniques used with adult and juvenile suspects. *Law and Human Behavior*, *40*(3), 270–284.

Collins, R., Lincoln, R., & Frank, M. G. (2002). The effect of rapport in forensic interviewing. *Psychiatry, Psychology, and Law*, *9*, 69–78.

Crawford, V. P., & Sobel, J. (1982). Strategic information transmission. *Econometrica: Journal of the Econometric Society*, *50*(6), 1431–1451.

Daly, Y., & Conway, V. (2021). Selecting a lawyer: The practical arrangement of police station legal assistance. *Journal of Law and Society*, *48*(4), 618–644.

Davis, D., Leo, R. A., & Follette, W. C. (2010). Selling confession: Setting the stage with the "sympathetic detective with a time-limited offer." *Journal of Contemporary Criminal Justice*, *26*(4), 441–457.

Dekker, P., & Van Rooy, R. (2000). Bi-directional optimality theory: An application of game theory. *Journal of Semantics*, *17*(3), 217–242.

DePaulo, B. M., Lindsay, J. L., Malone, B. E., Muhlenbruck, L., Charlton, K., & Cooper, H. (2003). Cues to deception. *Psychological Bulletin*, *129*, 74–118.

Dixon, D. (2010). Questioning suspects: A comparative perspective. *Journal of Contemporary Criminal Justice*, *26*(4), 426–440.

Dixon, D., & Maher, L. (2004). Containment, quality of life and crime control: Policy transfers in the policing of a street heroin market. In T. Newburn & R. Sparks (Eds.), *Criminal justice and political cultures* (pp. 234–266). Cullompton: Willan.

Drizin, S. A., & Reich, M. J. (2004). Heeding the lessons of history: The need for mandatory recording of police interrogations to accurately assess the reliability and voluntariness of confessions. *Drake Law Review*, *52*(4), 619–646.

Dunlap, B. (2014). Anyone can think like lawyer: How the lawyers' monopoly on legal understanding undermines democracy and the rule of law in the United States. *Fordham Law Review*, *82*(6), 2817–2842.

Ensor, B., & White, M. (2022, April 6). Police: Top detective defends controversial CIPEM interviewing method. *Stuff*. www.stuff.co.nz/national/crime/128241902/police-top-detective-defends-controversial-cipem-interviewing-method

European Court of Human Rights: *Annual Report* (2008). www.echr.coe.int/Documents/Annual_report_2008_ENG.pdf

Fabian, J. M. (2005). Life, death, and IQ: It's much more than just a score: The dilemma of the mentally retarded on death row. *Journal of Forensic Psychology Practice*, *5*(4), 1–36.

Fahsing, I. A., & Rachlew, A. (2013). Investigative interviewing in the Nordic region. In T. Williamson, B. Milne, and S. Savage (Eds.), *International developments in investigative interviewing* (pp. 65–91). London: Routledge.

Farrell, J. (1993). Meaning and credibility in cheap-talk games. *Games and Economic Behavior*, 5(4), 514–531.

Farrell, J., & Gibbons, R. (1989). Cheap talk with two audiences. *The American Economic Review*, 79(5), 1214–1223.

Feld, B. C. (2006). Police interrogation of juveniles: An empirical study of policy and practice. *Journal of Criminal Law and Criminology, 97*(1), 219–317.

Fox, B. (2014). On the notion of pre-request. *Discourse Studies, 17*(1), 41–63.

Fraiser, N. M., & Hipel, K. W. (1984). *Conflict analysis moves and resolution.* New York: North-Holland.

Frank, M. C., & Goodman, N. D. (2012). Predicting pragmatic reasoning in language games. *Science, 336*(2084), 998.

Fudenberg D., & Tirole J. (1991). *Game theory.* Cambridge, MA: MIT Press.

Gaines, P. (2020). The discourse structure of blame mitigation in a police interrogation. In M. Mason & F. Rock (Eds.), *The discourse of police interviews* (pp. 85–112). Chicago: University of Chicago Press.

Garrett, B. L. (2015, October 8). Serving life for a lie? *HuffPost.* www.huffpost.com/entry/serving-life-for-a-lie_b_82660129

Gee, H. (2009). An ambiguous request for counsel before and not after a Miranda waiver: United States v. Rodriguez, United States v. Fry and State v. Blackburn. *American University Criminal Law Brief, 5*(1), 51–68.

Geiselman, R. E. (2012). The cognitive interview for suspects (CIS). *American Journal of Forensic Psychology, 30*(3), 5–20.

Geiselman, R. E., Fisher, R. P., Firstenberg, I., Hutton, L., Sullivan, S. J., Avetissian, I. V., & Prosk, A. L. (1984). Enhancement of eyewitness memory: An empirical evaluation of the cognitive interview. *Journal of Police and Science Administration, 12,* 74–80.

Gharesifard, B., & Cortés J. (2010). Evolution of the perception about the opponent in hypergames, *Proceedings of the 49th IEEE Conference on Decision and Control,* 1076–1081.

Gharesifard, B., & Cortes, J. (2012). Evolution of players' misperceptions in hypergames under perfect observations. *IEEE Transactions on Automatic Control, 57*(7), 1627–1640.

Gharesifard, B., & Cortes, J. (2014). Stealthy deception in hypergames under informational asymmetry. *IEEE Transactions on Systems, Man, and Cybernetics: Systems, 6*(44), 785–795.

Gibbons, R. (1997). An introduction to applicable game theory. *Journal of Economic Perspectives, 11*(1), 127–149.

Gibbs, R. W. (1983). Do people always process the literal meanings of indirect requests? *Journal of Experimental Psychology: Learning, Memory, and Cognition, 9,* 524–533.

Gibbs, R. W. (1999). *Intentions in the experience of meaning.* New York: Cambridge University Press.

Gibbs, R. W., Buchalter, D., Moise, J., & Farrar, W. (1993). Literal meaning and figurative language. *Discourse Processes, 16,* 387–403.

Goffman, E. (1959). *The presentation of self in everyday life.* New York: Doubleday.

Goffman, E. (1967). *Interaction ritual: Essays on face-to-face behavior.* New York: Random House.

Goffman, E. (1981). *Forms of talk.* Philadelphia, PA: University of Pennsylvania Press.

Granhag, P. A., Oleszkiewicz, S., Sakrisvold, M. L., & Kleinman, S. M. (2020). The Scharff technique: Training military intelligence officers to elicit information from small cells of sources. *Psychology, Crime & Law, 26*(5), 438–460.

Grice, H. P. (1975). Logic and conversation. In P. Cole and J. L. Morgan (Eds.), *Syntax and semantics III: Speech acts* (pp. 41–58). New York: Academic Press.

Griffiths, L., & Milne, B. (2006). Will it all end in tiers? Police interviews with suspects in Britain. In T. Williamson (Ed.), *Investigative interviewing: Rights, research, regulation* (pp. 167–189). Cullompton: Willan.

Griffiths, A., Milne, B., & Cherryman, J. (2011). A question of control? The formulation of suspect and witness interview question strategies by advanced interviewers. *International Journal of Police Science and Management, 13*, 255–267.

Griffiths, A., & Rachlew, A. (2018). From interrogation to investigative interviewing: The application of psychology. In A. Griffiths & R. Milne (Eds.), *The psychology of criminal investigation* (pp. 154–178). London: Routledge.

Grisso, T. (1998). *Instruments for assessing understanding & appreciation of Miranda rights*. Professional Resource Press/Professional Resource Exchange.

Gudjonsson, G., & Pearse, J. (2011). Suspect interviews and false confessions. *Current Directions in Psychological Science, 20*(1), 33–37.

Guidelines for Communicating Rights to Non-Native Speakers (2012). www.aaal.org /guidelines-for-communication-rights

Harsanyi, J. (1967). Games with incomplete information played by "Bayesian players": The basic model, *Management Science, 14*, 159–182.

Hartwig, M., Meissner, C. A., & Semel, M. D. (2014). Human intelligence interviewing and interrogation: Assessing the challenges of developing an ethical, evidence-based approach. In R. Bull (Ed.), *Investigative interviewing* (pp. 209–228). New York: Springer.

Herman, L. (1987). The Supreme Court, the attorney general, and the good old days of police interrogation. *Ohio State Law Journal, 48*(3), 733–756.

Heydon, G. (2005). *The language of police interviewing*. Hampshire: Palgrave Macmillan.

Heydon, G. (2008). The art of deception: Myths about lie detection in written confessions. In L. Smets & A. Vrij (Eds.), *Cahiers police studies: Special investigative interviewing techniques: The use of written and oral analyses* (pp. 173–186). Gent: Politeia.

Heydon, G. (2012). Helping the police with their enquiries: Enhancing the investigative interview with linguistic research. *The Police Journal, 85*, 101–122.

High-value detainee interrogation group: Interrogation a review of the science (2016, September). www.fbi.gov/file-repository/hig-report-interrogation-a-review-of-the-science-september-2016.pdf/view

Holtgraves, T. M. (1994). Communication in context: The effects of speaker status on the comprehension of indirect requests. *Journal of Experimental Psychology: Learning, Memory and Cognition, 20*, 1205–1218.

Holtgraves, T. M. (2002). *Language as social action: Social psychology and language use*. Mahwah, NJ: Erlbaum.

Holtgraves, T. M. (2005). Comprehending conversational indirectness in a social context. In A. Katz & H. Colston (Eds.), *Social and cultural factors involved in figurative language processing* (pp. 73–98). Mahwah, NJ: Erlbaum.

Holtgraves, T. M., & Ashley, A. (2001). Comprehending illocutionary force. *Memory & Cognition, 29*, 83–90.

Hulstijn, J. (2011). Language proficiency in native and nonnative speakers: An agenda for research and suggestions for second-language assessment. *Language Assessment Quarterly 8*(3), 229–249.

Hulstijn, J. (2015). *Language proficiency in native and non-native speakers: Theory and research*. Amsterdam: John Benjamins.

Inbau, F. E., Reid, J. E., Buckley, J. P., & Jayne, B. C. (2001). *Criminal interrogation and confessions* (4th ed.). Gaithersberg, MD: Aspen.

Inbau, F. E., Reid, J. E., Buckley, J. P., & Jayne, B. C. (2005). *Criminal interrogation and confessions: Essentials of the Reid technique* (1st ed.). Sudbury, MA: Jones & Bartlett.

Inbau, F. E., Reid, J. E., Buckley, J. P., & Jayne, B. C. (2013). *Criminal interrogation and confessions* (5th ed.). Burlington, MA: Jones & Bartlett Learning.

Jäger, G. (2008). The evolution of convex categories. *Linguistics and Philosophy*, *30*(5), 551–564.

Jaszczolt, K. M. (2019). Rethinking being Gricean: New challenges for metapragmatics. *Journal of Pragmatics*, *145*, 15–24.

Johnson, A. (2020). "Are you saying you were stabbed . . . ?": Multimodality, embodied action, and dramatized formulations in "fixing" the facts in police interviews with suspects. In M. Mason & F. Rock (Eds.), *The discourse of police interviews* (pp. 268–298). Chicago: University of Chicago Press.

Jones, J. B. (2004, June) Access to counsel. Office of Juvenile Justice and Delinquency Prevention. *Juvenile Justice Bulletin 1*, 34. www.ojp.gov/pdffiles1/ojjdp/204063.pdf

Kassin, S. M. (1997). The psychology of confession evidence. *American Psychologist*, *52*, 221–233.

Kassin, S. M., & Gudjonsson, G. H. (2004). The psychology of confessions: A review of the literature and issues. *Psychological science in the public interest*, *5*(2), 33–67.

Kassin, S. M., & Kiechel, K. L. (1996). The social psychology of false confessions: Compliance, internalization, and confabulation. *Psychological Science*, *7*, 125–128.

Kassin, S. M., & Norwick, R. J. (2004). Why people waive their Miranda rights: The power of innocence. *Law and Human Behavior*, *28*(2), 211–221.

Kassin, S., Drizin, S., Grisso, T., Gudjonsson, G., Leo, R., & Redlich, A. (2010). Police induced confessions: Risk factors and recommendations. *Law and Human Behavior*, *34*(1), 3–38.

Kassin, S. M., Leo, R. A., Meissner, C. A., Richman, K. D., Colwell, L. H., Leach, A. M., & LaFon, D., (2007). Police interviewing and interrogation: A self-report survey of police practices and beliefs. *Law and Human Behavior*, *31*(4), 381–400.

Keysar, B., Barr, D. J., Balin, J. A., & Brauner, J. S. (2000). Taking perspective in conversation: The role of mutual knowledge in comprehension. *Psychological Science*, *11*(1), 32–38.

Klopf, G., & Tooke, A. (2003). Statement analysis examination technique. *FBI Law Enforcement Bulletin*, *72*(4), 6–14.

Kostelnik, J. O., & Reppucci, N. D. (2009). Reid training and sensitivity to developmental maturity in interrogation: Results from a national survey of police. *Behavioral Sciences & the Law*, *27*, 361–379.

Kovach, N. S., Gibson, A. S., & Lamont, G. B. (2015). Hypergame theory: A model for conflict, misperception, and deception. *Game Theory*, 1–20.

Kozinski, W. (2017). The Reid interrogation technique and false confessions: A time for change. *Seattle Journal for Social Justice*, *16*(2), 301–345.

Lamer Commission of Inquiry: Pertaining to the cases of Ronald Dalton, Gregory Parsons, Randy Druken (2006, June). www.gov.nl.ca/jps/files/publications-lamerreport.pdf

Landers, P. (2000, October 6). A false confession jailed Mr. Yakushiji; then fate intervened. *The Wall Street Journal*, pp. A1, A7–A8.

Language Assistance for Law Enforcement (2006, March 31). https://najit.org/wp-content/uploads/2016/09/LanguageforLawEnforcement2006.pdf

Leiber, M. J., & Stairs, J. M. (1999). Race, contexts, and the use of intake diversion. *Journal of Research in Crime and Delinquency*, *36*(1), 56–86.

Leo, R. A. (1996). Miranda's revenge: Police interrogation as a confidence game. *Law & Society Review*, *30*(2), 259–288.

Leo, R. A. (2001). Questioning the relevance of Miranda in the Twentieth-Century. *Michigan Law Review*, *99*(5): 1000–1029.

Leo, R. A. (2008). *Police interrogation and American justice*. Cambridge, MA: Harvard University Press.

Leo, R. A., & Ofshe, R. J. (1998). Consequences of false confessions: Deprivations of liberty and miscarriages of justice in the age of psychological interrogation. *Journal of Criminal Law and Criminology*, *88*(2), 429–496.

Leo, R. A., & White, W. S. (1999). Adapting to Miranda: Modern interrogators' strategies for dealing with the obstacles posed by Miranda. *Minnesota Law Review*, *84*(2): 397–472.

Leo, R. A., Neufeld, P. J., Drizin, S. A., & Taslitz, A. E. (2013). Promoting accuracy in the use of confession evidence: An argument for pretrial reliability assessments to prevent wrongful convictions. *Temple Law Review*, *85*(4), 759–838.

Levenberg, T. O. (1995). Fifth Amendment: Responding to ambiguous requests for counsel during custodial interrogations. *Journal of Criminal Law & Criminology*, *85*(4), 962–988.

Levinson S. (1983). *Pragmatics*. Cambridge: Cambridge University Press.

Marcus, P. (1993). A return to the "bright line rule" of Miranda. *William & Mary Law Review*, *35*(4), 93–146.

Mason, M. (2013). Can I get a lawyer? A suspect's use of indirect requests in a custodial setting. *International Journal of Speech, Language & the Law*, *20*(2), 203–227.

Mason, M. (2016). The "preparatory" and "argumentation" stages of police interrogation: A linguistic analysis of a criminal investigation. *Language & Communication*, *48*, 79–87.

Mason, M. (2020). The guilt-presumptive nature of custodial interrogations in the United States: The use of confrontation, appeals to self-interest, and sympathy/minimization in the Reid technique. In M. Mason & F. Rock (Eds.), *The discourse of police interviews* (pp. 65–84). Chicago: University of Chicago Press.

Mason, R. D., & Mason, M. (2021, November 20–22). The game of police interrogations [Conference presentation]. *Southern Economics Association, 91st Annual Meeting*, Houston, TX.

Mason, R. D., & Mason, M. (2023). Reconsidering Miranda rights: Modeling strategic action during the invocation stage of a police interrogation. *Rationality and Society*.

McFeeley, N. D. (2016). The historical development of habeas corpus. *Southwestern Law Journal*, *30*(3), 585–600.

McGurk, B., Carr, J., & McGurk, D. (1993). Investigative interviewing courses for police officers: An evaluation. *Police Research Series Paper*, 4. London: Home Office.

Meissner, C. A., Surmon-Böhr, F., Oleszkiewicz, S., & Alison, L. J. (2017). Developing an evidence-based perspective on interrogation: A review of the US government's high-value detainee interrogation group research program. *Psychology, Public Policy, and Law*, *23*(4), 438.

Meissner, C. A., Redlich, A. D., Michael, S. W., Evans, J. R., Camilletti, C. R., Bhatt, S., & Brandon, S. (2014). Accusatorial and information-gathering interrogation methods and their effects on true and false confessions: A meta-analytic review. *Journal of Experimental Criminology*, *10*, 459–486.

Mendez, J. E., & Areh, I. (Eds.). (2021). *Principles on effective interviewing for investigations and information gathering*. APT, Association pour la prévention de la torture.

Meyer, J. R., & Reppucci, N. D. (2007). Police practices and perceptions regarding juvenile interrogation and interrogative suggestibility. *Behavioral Sciences & the Law*, *25*, 757–780.

Milne, R. J. (1997). *Analysis and application of the cognitive interview* (Unpublished doctoral dissertation). University of Portsmouth.

Mosteller, R. P. (2007). Police deception before Miranda warnings: The case for per se exclusion of an entirely unjustified practice at a particularly sensitive moment. *Texas Tech Law Review*, *39*(4), 1239–1273.

National Children's Advocacy Center. (2019, February). *National Children's Advocacy Center's Child Forensic Interview Structure*. www.nationalcac.org/wp-content/uploads/2019/02/NCAC_CFIS_Feb-2019.pdf

National Juvenile Defender Center, Access Denied: A National Snapshot of States' Failure to Protect Children's Right to Counsel. (2017, May). https://njdc.info/wp-content/uploads/2017/05/Snapshot-Final_single-4.pdf

Noh, E. (1998). Echo questions: Metarepresentation and pragmatic enrichment. *Linguistics and Philosophy*, *21*(6), 603–628.

Noh, E. (2001). *Metarepresentation: A relevance-theory approach*. Amsterdam: John Benjamins.

Ofshe, R. J. (2007). Defending the innocent: Interrogation and false confession. *The Champion*, 10–15.

Parikh, P. (1991). Communication and strategic inference. *Linguistics and Philosophy*, *14*(5), 473–514.

Parikh, P. (2000). Communication, meaning, and interpretation. *Linguistics and Philosophy*, *23*, 185–212.

Parikh, P. (2001). *The use of language*. Stanford, CA: CSLI Publications.

Paulo, R. M., Albuquerque, P. B., & Bull, R. (2013). The enhanced cognitive interview: Towards a better use and understanding of this procedure. *International Journal of Police Science & Management*, *15*(3), 190–199.

Pavlenko, A. (2008). "I'm very not about the law part": Nonnative speakers of English and the Miranda warnings. *Tesol Quarterly*, *42*(1), 1–30.

Pavlenko, A., Hepford, E., & Jarvis, S. (2019). An illusion of understanding: How native and non-native speakers of English understand (and misunderstand) their Miranda rights. *International Journal of Speech Language and the Law*, *26*(2), 181–207.

Pinker, S., Nowak, M.A., & Lee, J.J. (2008). The logic of indirect speech. *Proceedings of the National Academy of sciences 105*(3), 833–838.

Pöchhacker, F. (2012). Interpreting participation: Conceptual analysis and illustration of the interpreter's role in interaction. In C. Baraldi & L. Gavioli (Eds.), *Coordinating participation in dialogue interpreting* (pp. 45–69). Amsterdam: John Benjamins.

Prates, R. C. (2014). Power in game theory. *Contributions to Game Theory and Management*, *7*, 282–289.

Rabin M. (1990). Communication between rational agents. *Journal of Economic Theory*, *51*, 144–170.

Raevaara L., & Sorjonen, M. (2014). Requesting for a product as an embodied action: Grammatical form of requests at convenience stores. In P. Drew & E. Couper-Kuhlen (Eds.), *Requesting in social interaction* (pp. 243–268). Amsterdam: John Benjamins.

Reid. (2018, November 1). A description of the Reid technique. https://reid.com/resources/investigator-tips/a-description-of-the-reid-technique

Richardson, B. H., Taylor, P. J., Snook, B., Conchie, S. M., & Bennell, C. (2014). Language style matching and police interrogation outcomes. *Law and Human Behavior*, *38*(4), 1–10.

Robinson, L. O. (2020). Five years after Ferguson: Reflecting on police reform and what's ahead. *ANNALS, AAPSS*, *687*, 228–239.

Rogers, R., & Drogin, E. Y. (2015). Miranda rights and wrongs: Matters of justice. *Court Review: The Journal of the American Judges Association*, *51*, 150–156.

Rogers, R., Rogstad, J. E., Gillard, N. D., Drogin, E. Y., Blackwood, H. L., & Shuman, D. W. (2010). "Everyone knows their Miranda rights": Implicit assumptions and countervailing evidence. *Psychology, Public Policy, and Law*, *16*(3), 300–318.

Salduz Act, *Belgian Law Gazette*, September 5, 2011.

Sangero, B. (2007). Miranda is not enough: A new justification for demanding strong corroboration to a confession. *Cardozo Law Review*, *28*(6), 101–139.

Savage, S., and Milne, R. (2007). Miscarriages of justice: The role of the investigative process. In T. Newburn, T. Williamson, & A. Wright (Eds.), *Handbook of Criminal Investigation* (pp. 610–627). Cullompton: Willan.

Schegloff, E. (2007). *Sequence organization in interaction*. Cambridge: Cambridge University Press.

Schlangen, D. (2004). Causes and strategies for requesting clarification in dialogue. *Proceedings of the 5th SIG dial Workshop on Discourse and Dialogue at HLT-NAACL*, 136–143.

Schollum, M. (2017). Bringing PEACE to the United States: A framework for investigative interviews. *International Association of Chiefs of Police Journal*, *10*, 30–37.

Schoovaerts, H., Vanderhallen, M., & McIntyre, S. J. (2021). Lawyers and children: Is there a need for mandatory legal assistance in suspect interviews? *International Journal of Police Science & Management*, *23*(1), 55–72.

Seidmann, D. J., & Stein, A. (2000). The right to silence helps the innocent: A game-theoretic analysis of the Fifth Amendment privilege. *Harvard Law Review*, *114*, 430–510.

Shuy, R. W. (1998). *The language of confession, interrogation, and deception*. Thousand Oaks, CA: Sage.

Simon, D. (2012). *In doubt: The psychology of the criminal justice process*. Cambridge, MA: Harvard University Press.

Skelton, M. S., & Connell III, J. G. (2004). The routine booking question exception to Miranda. *University of Baltimore Law Review, 34*(1), 55–91.

Snook, B., Eastwood, J., Stinson, M., Tedeschini, J., & House, J. C. (2010). Reforming investigative interviewing in Canada. *Canadian Journal of Criminology and Criminal Justice, 52*(2), 215–229.

Stevens, J., Benz, A., Reuße, S., & Klabunde, R. (2015). A strategic reasoning model for generating alternative answers. In *Proceedings of the 53rd Annual Meeting of the Association for Computational Linguistics and the 7th International Joint Conference on Natural Language Processing, 1*, 534–542.

Stevens, J. S. (2016). When do we think strategically? *Zeitschrift für Sprachwissenschaft, 35*(1), 97–108.

St-Yves, Michel. (2009). Police interrogation in Canada: From the quest for confession to the search for the truth. In T. Williamson, B. Milne, & S. P. Savage (Eds.), *International developments in investigative interviewing* (pp. 92–110). Portland, OR: Willan Publishing.

Sundby, S. E. (2020). The Court and the suspect: Human frailty, the calculating criminal, and the penitent in the interrogation room. *Washington University Law Review, 98*, 123–187.

Taylor, H. (2002, March 20). Nationwide love affair with NYPD has not changed nationwide attitudes toward the police. *The Harris Poll #13*.

Tkacukova, T., & Oxburgh, G. E. (2020). Patterns of cooperation between police interviewers with suspected sex offenders. In M. Mason & F. Rock (Eds.), *The discourse of police interviews* (pp. 136–155). Chicago: University of Chicago Press.

Tedeschini, D. J. (2008). "But we've always done it this way!" A progressive approach to police interview and interrogation training. *The Wisconsin Defender, 16*(1), 1–11.

Terkourafi, M. (2011). The puzzle of indirect speech. *Journal of Pragmatics, 43*, 2861–2865.

Tomasi, T., & Velona, J. (1987). All the Presidents Men? A study of Ronald Reagan's appointments to the US Courts Of Appeals. *Columbia Law Review, 87*(4), 766–793.

Tversky, A., & Kahneman, D. (1986). Rational choice and the framing of decisions. *The Journal of Business, 59*(4), 251–278.

Urbanik, P., & Pavlenko, A. (2021). Securing understanding in a second language: Communication of rights in investigative interviews in the US and Norway. In R. Blackwood, & U. Røyneland (Eds.), *Spaces of multilingualism* (pp. 92–112). London: Routledge.

van Rooij R. (2004). Signaling games select Horn strategies. *Linguistics and Philosophy, 27*(4), 493–527.

van Rooij R. (2008). Games and quantity implicatures. *Journal of Economic Methodology, 15*(3), 261–274.

Varsos, C., Flouris, G., Bitsaki, M., & Fasoulakis, M. (2021). A study of misinformation games. *Pacific Rim International Conference on Artificial Intelligence*, 76–87.

Vrij, A. (2015). Verbal lie detection tools: Statement Validity Analysis, Reality Monitoring and Scientific Content Analysis. In P. A. Granhag, A. Vrij, & B. Verschuere (Eds.), *Detecting deception: Current challenges and cognitive approaches* (pp. 3–36). Chichester: Wiley Blackwell.

Vrij, A. (2018). Deception and truth detection when analyzing nonverbal and verbal cues. *Applied Cognitive Psychology, 33*(2), 160–167.

Walsh, D. W., & Milne, R. (2008). Keeping the PEACE? A study of investigative interviewing practices in the public sector. *Legal and Criminological Psychology, 13*, 39–57.

Walton, D. (2003). The interrogation as a type of dialogue. *Journal of Pragmatics, 35*, 1771–1802.

Wang, M., Hipel, K. W., & Fraser, N. M. (1989). Solution concepts in hypergames. *Applied Mathematics and Computation, 34*(3), 147–171.

Weisselberg, C. D. (2008). Mourning *Miranda*. *California Law Review, 96*(6), 1521–1601.

Williamson, T. (2006). Towards greater professionalism: Minimizing miscarriages of justice. In T. Williamson (Ed.), *Investigative interviewing. Rights, research, regulation* (pp. 147–166). Portland, OR: Willan Publishing.

Working group on the prevention of miscarriages of justice of the federal–provincial–territorial heads of prosecutions committee (2004). *Report on the Prevention of Miscarriages of Justice*. Ottawa: Department of Justice (FPT Report).

Yuncker, T. J. (1995). Davis v. United States: The unambiguous decline of ambiguous requests for counsel during custodial interrogation. *Widener Journal of Public Law, 4*(2), 711–754.

Zalman, M., & Smith, B. (2007). The attitudes of police executives toward Miranda and interrogation policies. *Journal of Criminal Law and Criminology, 97*, 873–942.

Legal Cases

Atkins v. *Virginia*, 536 U.S. 304 (2002).

Alvarez v. *Gomez*, 185 F.3d 995 (9th Cir. 1999).

Ball v. *State*, 347 Md. 156, 172, 699 A.2d 1170 (1997).

Berghuis v. *Thompkins*, 560 U.S. 370 (2010).

Brecht v. *Abrahamson*, 507 U.S. 619 (1993).

Cannady v. *Dugger*, 931 F.2d 752 (11th Cir. 1991).

Cape v. *Francis*, 741 F.2d 1287 (1984).

Clanton v. *Cooper*, 129 F.3d 1147 (10th Cir. 1997).

Clark v. *Murphy*, 317 F.3d 1038 (9th Cir. 2003).

Connecticut v. *Barrett*, 479 U.S. 523 (1987).

Davis v. *United States*, 512 U.S. 452 (1994).

Devenpeck v. *Alford*, 543 U.S. 146 (2004).

Dickerson v. *United States*, 530 U.S. 428 (2000).

Edwards v. *Arizona*, 451 U.S. 477 (1981).

Fare v. *Michael C.*, 442 U.S. 707 (1979).

Flores v. *Muniz*, 1:16-cv-01475-LJO-MJS (HC), E.D. Cal. (2018).

Frazier v. *Cupp*, 394 U.S. 731 (1969).

Fry v. *Pliler*, 551 U.S. 112 (2007).

Harris v. *New York*, 401 U.S. 222 (1971).

Illinois v. *Perkins*, 496 U.S. 292 (1990).

Johnson v. *Booker*, 2:09-CV-10108, E.D. Mich. (2014).

Kyger v. *Carlton*, 146 F.3d 374 (6th Cir. 1998).

Lopez v. *Janda*, EDCV 13–1196-DOC (MAN), C.D. Cal. (2015).
Lord v. *Duckworth*, 29 F.3d 1216 (7th Cir. 1994).
Maryland v. *Shatzer*, 559 U.S. 98 (2010).
McNeil v. *Wisconsin*, 501 U.S. 171 (1991).
Michigan v. *Mosley*, 423 U.S. 96 (1975).
Michigan v. *Tucker*, 417 U.S. 433 (1974).
Miranda v. *Arizona*, 384 U.S. 436 (1966).
Missouri v. *Seibert*, 542 U.S. 600 (2004).
Moran v. *Burbine*, 475 U.S. 412 (1986).
Nash v. *Estelle*, 597 F.2d 513 (5th Cir. 1979).
Newell v. *Ryan*, CV-12–02038-PHX-JJT, D. Ariz. (2019).
New York v. *Quarles*, 467 U.S. 649 (1984).
Oregon v. *Elstad*, 470 U.S. 298 (1985).
Owen v. *Alabama*, 849 F.2d 536 (11th Cir. 1988).
People v. *Burton*, 6 Cal. 3d 375, 491 P.2d 793 (1971).
People v. *Portelli*, 15 N.Y.2d 235 (1965).
Poyner v. *Murray*, 964 F.2d 1404 (4th Cir. 1992).
Renteria v. *Foulk*, NO. CV 14–2104-AB (KLS), C.D. Cal. (2016).
Rhode Island v. *Innis*, 446 U.S. 291 (1980).
Robinson v. *Borg*, 918 F.2d 1387 (9th Cir. 1990).
Rodriguez v. *McDonald*, No. 12–56594 (9th Cir. 2017).
Salduz v. *Turkey*, ECHR 36391/02, Grand Chamber, (2008).
Sessoms v. *Runnels*, 691 F.3d 1054 (9th Cir. 2012).
Smith v. *Endell*, 860 F.2d 1528 (9th Cir. 1988).
Smith v. *Illinois*, 469 U.S. 91 (1984).
Soffar v. *Cockrell*, 300 F.3d 588 (5th Cir. 2002).
Stansbury v. *California*, 511 U.S. 318 (1994).
State v. *Blackburn*, 766 N.W.2d 177, 182 (S.D. 2009).
State v. *Carrillo*, 156 Ariz. 125 (Ariz. 1988).
State v. *Harris*, 305 S.W.3d 482 (Mo. Ct. App. 2010).
State v. *Melton*, 239 Neb. 506 (Neb. 1991).
State v. *Rettenberger*, 1999 UT 80 (Utah 1999).
Taylor v. *Jackson*, No. 17–1762 (6th Cir. 2017). (Ga. 2017).
United States v. *Alamilla-Hernandez*, 8:08CR451, D. Neb. (2009).
United States v. *Al-Saimari*, 982 F. Supp. 2d 1285 (D. Utah 2013).
United States v. *Boyce*, 594 F.2d 1246 (9th Cir. 1979).
United States v. *Brown,* 01-6072. (10th Cir. 2002).
United States v. *Brown*, CR05-73-S-EJL, D. Idaho (2005).
United States v. *Cheely*, 36 F.3d 1439 (9th Cir. 1994).
United States v. *Crawford*, 372 F.3d 1048 (9th Cir. 2004).
United States v. *Davis*, No. GJH-17-493 (D. Md 2018).
United States v. *De La Jara*, 973 F.2d 746 (9th Cir. 1992).
United States v. *Feyler*, 55 F. Supp. 2d 55 (D. Me. 1999).
United States v. *Fouche*, 833 F.2d 1284 (9th Cir. 1987).
United States v. *Fry*, CR-09–44-N-JLQ, 2009 WL 1687958, D. Idaho (2009).
United States v. *Garibay*, 143 F.3d 534 (9th Cir. 1998).
United States v. *Gray*, R-15–08076-PCT-DGC (D. Arizona 2015).

United States v. *Hunter*, 708 F.3d 938 (7th Cir. 2013).
United States v. *Jacques*, 744 F.3d 804 (1st Cir. 2014).
United States v. *Jardina*, 747 F.2d 945 (5th Cir. 1984).
United States v. *Lux*, 905 F.2d 1379 (10th Cir. 1990).
United States v. *March*, 999 F.2d 456 (10th Cir. 1993).
United States v. *Monroe*, 264 F. Supp. 3d 376 (D.R.I. 2017).
United States v. *Ogbuehi*, 18 F.3d 807 (9th Cir. 1994).
United States v. *Posada–Rios*, 158 F.3d 832 (5th Cir. 1998).
United States v. *Prestigiacomo*, 504 F. Supp. 681 (E.D.N.Y. 1981).
United States v. *Priest* (1969), 409 F.2d 491 (5th Cir. 1969).
United States v. *Rodriguez*, 07–10217 2008 (9th Cir. 2008).
United States v. *Rutledge*, 900 F.2d 1127 (7th Cir. 1990).
United States v. *Salazar Orellana*, 1:09-CR-475-WSD-CCH-3 (N.D. Georgia 2010).
United States v. *Santistevan*, 701 F.3d 1289 (10th Cir. 2012).
United States v. *Smith*, CR. 07–30097, 2008 DSD 5 (D.S.D. 2008).
United States v. *Thompson*, 866 F.2d 268, 272 (8th Cir . 1989).
United States v. Williams, 2:15-cr-00069-JDL-1 (D. Me. 2015).
Vega v. *Tekoh*, 597 U.S. ___ (2022).
Wolf v. *Hennessy*, CV 06–0084-PHX-JAT. (D. Arizona 2008).
Wood v. *Ercole*, 644 F.3d 83 (2d Cir. 2011).
Woosley v. *McEwen*, DCV 09–2335–PA (SH) (C.D. California 2014).

Index

This index is organized in word-by-word order. All case names are in *italics*. Tables are indicated by the word "(table)" in parentheses.

For EU product safety concerns, contact us at Calle de José Abascal, 56–1°,
28003 Madrid, Spain or eugpsr@cambridge.org.

www.ingramcontent.com/pod-product-compliance
Lightning Source LLC
LaVergne TN
LVHW022214200926
848481LV00006B/1965
9781009055017